# JAWAHARLAL
# NEHRU

# JAWAHARLAL NEHRU

## Rebel and Statesman

### B. R. NANDA

DELHI
OXFORD UNIVERSITY PRESS
OXFORD   NEW YORK
1995

Oxford University Press, Walton Street, Oxford OX2 6DP

Oxford New York Toronto
Delhi Bombay Calcutta Madras Karachi
Kuala Lumpur Singapore Hong Kong Tokyo
Nairobi Dar es Salaam Cape Town
Melbourne Auckland Madrid

and associates in
Berlin Ibadan

ISBN 0 19 563684 8

Typeset by Guru Typograph Technology, New Delhi 110045
printed at Pauls Press, New Delhi 110020
and published by Neil O'Brien, Oxford University Press
YMCA Library Building, Jai Singh Road, New Delhi 110001

TO BABA

# Preface

My book *The Nehrus* was published in 1962. Originally conceived as a biography of Motilal Nehru, it developed inevitably into a book about both father and son, covering Motilal's entire career and the first forty years of Jawaharlal's life.

This volume is a sequel to *The Nehrus*—but of a different kind. Rather than write in a biographical mode, I have chosen to deal in the form of essays with various aspects of Jawaharlal Nehru's life, ideas and work. These seek to deal in depth with issues not only for an academic audience, but also for the general reader. I trust these essays will help to place Nehru's role in historical perspective both during the years of struggle for India's independence and his years as Prime Minister. Most of these essays have been written recently; a few are earlier pieces which seem to have stood the test of time and continue to be relevant to the understanding of Nehru and his work.

In the preparation of this volume, as of my previous books, I have received constant support from my wife, not only in creating conditions enabling me to pursue my research and writing, but in letting me think aloud while my ideas on various themes were being formed. My son Naren has read these essays and his comments have been of great value to me. I am also indebted to Professor T.N. Madan for reading the manuscript and offering me his considered views. Needless to say, I alone am responsible for the views expressed in the book.

*New Delhi*                                                B.R. NANDA
*15 May 1995*

# Principal Abbreviations

| | |
|---|---|
| *CWMG* | Collected Works of Mahatma Gandhi |
| *CWN* | Collected Works of Netaji |
| NAI | National Archives of India |
| NMML | Nehru Memorial Museum and Library |
| NP | Nehru Papers |
| *SWJN* | Selected Works of Jawaharlal Nehru |

# Contents

# List of Plates

# 1

## The Young Nationalist

### I

Jawaharlal was barely sixteen years old when he arrived at Harrow in 1905. Soon after his arrival he asked his father to send him an Indian newspaper, 'not the *Pioneer*'.[1] In December 1905, he was pleasantly surprised to read in *The Times* that the *Swadeshi* movement had spread to Kashmir, where the people were reported to have bought up, by public subscription, all the English sugar and burnt it. 'The movement must be very strong indeed,' he wrote to his father, 'if it reached even the Kashmiris'.

Jawaharlal read the proceedings of the Indian National Congress with particular interest. When his father wrote from Calcutta that the Moderates and the Extremists had been at loggerheads in the 1906 Congress, he was disappointed. 'I am sorry to hear,' he wrote, 'that the Congress was not a success. I am impatiently waiting for your next letter to know the result of the proceedings. I do hope the different parties worked smoothly together, and there were no dissensions among the delegates. A most foolish thing this seems to me; for not only do they do no good to themselves but they do harm to their country they both pretend to serve. There couldn't have been any great difference or disagreement among the delegates, as our friends the Anglo-Indians would hardly have failed to wire the fact over here.'

Such passionate nationalism may seem surprising in an Indian boy of seventeen studying in an English public school, whose home in Allahabad was one of the most anglicized, whose father was an admirer of British ways and British institutions, and counted high British dignitaries among his friends. However, we must remember the great gulf which, at the turn of the century, divided the British and the Indian, the rulers and the ruled. Educated Indians had not forgotten the hysteria of the European community during the agitation over the Ilbert Bill, when Lord Ripon was ridiculed as a 'White Baboo',[2] and a correspondent of the *Englishman* could seriously assert that 'the only people who have any right to India are the British; the so-called Indians have no right whatsoever'. Not only were Indians excluded from responsible posts in the administration of their own country; they received frequent and galling reminders of their inferior status. Compartments in railway trains and benches in public parks were reserved for 'Europeans only'. Long before the word was coined, 'apartheid' was practised by the most fashionable clubs in the principal towns of India. Many of them did not admit 'natives' even as guests; in Bombay and Calcutta it was not uncommon for an Indian gentleman to wait in the carriage, while his European wife went into the club. Nevinson, the noted British journalist, wrote after his visit to India in 1907–8 that there were in every part of the country Englishmen who 'still retained the courtesy and sensitiveness of ordinary good manners. But one's delight in finding them proved their rarity.'[3] It was a significant commentary on racial prejudice that, right through the First World War, the Baden-Powell organization refused to admit Indian children as scouts. All this deeply hurt proud and sensitive members of the intelligentsia. Intellectually, they might feel equal, or even superior, to individual Europeans, but socially they were branded as an inferior race. No wonder the western-educated middle class passionately longed for what an Australian writer[4] has called 'freedom from the white man's contempt'.

Some of the flagrant examples of racial arrogance were seen on the railways. In 1907, Keir Hardie, the Labour M.P., boarded a train at Madras and found two Indians in a first class compartment. As Hardie entered, one of the Indians got up and said, 'Shall we move to another compartment, sir?' Hardie stared at the man, and enquired if he had paid his fare. 'Oh, yes,' he replied, 'but English gentlemen do not as a rule like to travel with natives.'[5] Not all Indian gentlemen were equally obliging. Some of them refused to give in to the white man's bullying, and then there were 'incidents'.

One of Jawaharlal's cousins, the 'strong man' of the Nehru family, was often involved in these 'incidents', and when they were related at home, young Jawaharlal's blood boiled. He was (he wrote later) 'filled with resentment against the alien rulers of my country who misbehaved in this manner, and when an Indian hit back, I was glad'.[6] He 'dreamt of brave deeds, of how sword in hand I would fight for India and help in freeing her'.[7]

## II

On the day the Nehrus arrived in London, the newspapers carried the news of the crushing defeat inflicted on the Russian fleet by the Japanese navy off Taushima. The victory of an Asian country over a great European power thrilled Jawaharlal. The transition from Allahabad to Harrow seemed to stimulate rather than suppress his interest in politics. 'The great question of the hour,' he wrote to his father on 12 January 1906, 'is of course the General Election. Everybody is excited about it, and even in the streets you see some people talking about it. . . . Today is the first day of the polling.' When Campbell-Bannerman formed his ministry, Jawaharlal was the only boy in his class who, much to the surprise of his teacher, reeled off the names of the entire cabinet. A few days later when the Headmaster's House at Harrow, of which Jawaharlal was a member, held a 'mock election' young Nehru's political instincts vibrated to the excitement:

Great preparations were made for two days for it and all the House was busy with placards for the respective candidates. The only difficulty in the beginning was to find a Liberal candidate. Almost everybody in this House is a strong Conservative, and the remaining few are half and half. Out of the latter the Liberal was chosen, although he himself was a better Unionist. On a half-holiday afternoon the lectures took place in a room which had been provisionally turned into a Committee Room, and the same evening the polling took place. The Conservative of course won.

Not long after his arrival at Harrow, Jawaharlal's political proclivities almost got him into trouble with the authorities. A letter addressed to 'Master Joe, Harrow' was opened by the Headmaster, Joseph Wood, who shared the nickname of 'Joe' with Jawaharlal. Wood was shocked at its seditious tone. 'I think you will agree with me,' he wrote to Motilal, 'that it is not the sort of letter for a boy to receive at an English school.' When Motilal explained that the writer was Rameshwari Nehru, the wife of Jawaharlal's cousin Brijlal, Dr Wood hastened to make amends: 'I am intensely amused to hear, that it was a charming young lady who defied the British *Raj*. Give her my kind regards, and say I hope, some day, when she knows us better, she will like us more.'

There was no one at Harrow to whom Jawaharlal could confide his inmost thoughts, but he scoured *The Times* for Indian news, and avidly devoured the pages of the *Indian People* and other journals mailed to him from Allahabad. Motilal's own letters contained a good deal of information about political developments in India, although he himself during these years hovered uncertainly on the periphery of national politics. He was present at the Benaras (1905) and Calcutta (1906) sessions of the Indian National Congress, but more as a spectator than as an active participant. The reasons for this are not far to seek. For one thing, Motilal's work at the High Court continued to make heavy demands on his time. 'My immediate surroundings remain unchanged,' he wrote to Jawaharlal on 23 November 1905: 'Clients! Clients!! Clients!!! One small brain to cope with half of the work of the High Court. The other half goes to Sunderlal.' For another, he was not at all happy at the course Indian politics had taken after the partition of Bengal. 'The anti-partition movement,' he told his son, was 'the most stupid and, I may add, the most dishonest thing I have ever seen. . . .' Preoccupied as he was with his heavy—and lucrative—legal practice, and out of harmony with the prevailing current of public opinion, Motilal had neither the time nor the inclination to give up the comfortable position of a critical looker-on at the political drama.

### III

Early in 1907 events conspired to push Motilal to the centre of the stage . An open rupture between the Moderates and the Extremists had been averted at the Calcutta Congress (December 1906), but the tension between the two wings of the Congress had not abated. The year opened with a propaganda offensive by the Moderates. In February Gokhale visited Allahabad. Motilal was present, along with other prominent citizens, at the railway station to welcome him. As the distinguished visitor came out, a large and enthusiastic crowd of students, which had been held back outside the station limits, shouted: *Gokhale ki Jai*, and surrounded Motilal's carriage, in which Gokhale was to drive to the house of his host, Tej Bahadur Sapru. The students unhorsed the carriage and insisted on drawing it. Gokhale pleaded with them; he threatened to return to Calcutta. But the students were adamant: amidst deafening cries of *Bande Mataram*, they pulled the carriage through the streets of Allahabad. Next day Gokhale delivered a lecture on 'The Work Before Us'; Motilal, who presided at the meeting, told his son that the lecture was 'a masterpiece of close reasoning and sound commonsense expressed in the best and purest English'. There were two more lectures by Gokhale on 'Swadeshi' and 'A Few Words to Students'. Motilal gave a garden party at Anand Bhawan and invited 'all the leading Indian and European ladies and gentlemen' of Allahabad to meet the distinguished leader of the Congress.

The enthusiasm which the students of Allahabad had displayed during Gokhale's visit was inspired less by his politics than by his personality. Only a few days earlier they had given Tilak a thunderous welcome. It was obvious that Allahabad and the United Provinces were beginning to be convulsed with the Moderate–Extremist conflict, and Motilal would, willy nilly, be drawn into it. In January 1907, there was a meeting of Moderate politicians at Anand Bhawan, at which the possibilities of a provincial conference were discussed; it was suggested that Motilal should preside over it. He was not at all keen to plunge into politics and asked for time to consider the proposal. The news, however, leaked to the press and it became awkward for him to withdraw. 'I have been compelled to accept it [the presidency of provincial conference],' he wrote to his son.

It is entirely a new line for me and I have very grave doubts of being able to justify the expectations of my friends. What I am particularly afraid of is the student class. They of late have developed a remarkable aptitude for rowdyism, and no sober and serious thinker can expect to secure an uninterrupted hearing from an audience composed of this element. Tilak was here the other day specially to address the students. . . . He succeeded to such an extent that the students of the Muir College (specially those of the Hindu Boarding House) have assumed an attitude of open defiance to the more moderate leaders of these provinces. Sunderlal and Malaviya are openly abused. I have so far escaped, but cannot be safe much longer as my views are even more moderate than those of the so-called Moderates. At present the boys declare that they will all be happy to follow my lead, as they think I have given enough proof of my independent and fearless adherence to my own views in matters social, etc. Whether they will think so when they hear my political views is a totally different question. I have, however, courted the storm and must brave it to the best of my ability.

Jawaharlal did not share these misgivings. He was delighted at the prospect of his father's entry into active politics. 'I am sure,' he wrote (19 February 1907), 'you will be as successful in the new line as you have been in other fields. You have already kept away from it far too long, but that, I hope, will add a new zest to it.' He urged his father to agree to preside over the conference. 'However you disagree with the details of the Congress programme,' he argued, 'you cannot but agree with its general aim . . . your [presidential] address is certain to be a brilliant one; only I hope it will not be too moderate. Indians are as a rule too much so, and require a little stirring up.' 'You may not agree with the ways of the new Extremist party,' young Nehru continued, 'but I do not think that you are such a slow and steady sort of person as you make yourself out to be.' This was an extraordinarily shrewd judgement of his father's political make-up; but many years were to pass, and much was to happen to father and son and to India, before the truth of this judgement was vindicated.

Motilal's presidential address received the qualified approval of his son:

You are still very Moderate, but I hardly expected you to become an Extremist. I personally like to see the Government blamed and censured as much as possible. . . . As regards John Bull's good faith I have not so much confidence in him as you have. . . .[8]

On 31 July 1907, Jawaharlal left Harrow for Trinity College, Cambridge. From the strait-jacket of a public school, the transition to university could not but be exhilarating. Young Nehru's nationalist ardour was immediately fanned by the freer climate of the university, the intellectual stimulus of fresh reading, discussions with fellow Indian students and, above all, by the strong breeze of discontent from the Indian subcontinent.

## IV

For India 1907 was a critical year. The tensions which had been accumulating since Curzon's viceroyalty had reached bursting point. The Minto–Morley partnership had not been able to assuage Indian feeling. 'You cannot enter at this date, and with public opinion, mind you, watching you, upon an era of pure repression,' Morley had publicly warned a gathering of British members of the I.C.S., 'Gentlemen, we have seen attempts in the lifetime of some of us here tonight, attempts in Continental Europe to govern by pure repression. Has any one of them really succeeded?'[9] Privately, the Secretary of State exhorted the Viceroy to curb the over-zealous bureaucracy and to keep the political temperature low.

Morley was to discover, as other Secretaries of State discovered before and after him, that India could not be governed from London. Sir Bampfylde Fuller, the Lieutenant-Governor of the newly-created province of East Bengal, had endeavoured to suppress sedition by banning public meetings, tightening espionage, prosecuting schoolboys for preaching Swadeshi, and even by playing upon the vested interests and the hotheadedness of his 'favourite wife'—the Muslim community. It was, however, in Punjab that the political cauldron boiled over in the summer of 1907. Early in May, the Government of India received a minute[10] from Sir Denzil Ibbetson, the Lieutenant-Governor of Punjab, on the political situation in the province, which he described 'as exceedingly serious and exceedingly dangerous'. The prosecution of the editor of the *Punjabi*, a nationalist paper, had stirred up feeling in Lahore; tension was mounting in Rawalpindi, Ambala, Ferozepore, Multan, and other towns. The most disconcerting feature of the unrest was that it had spread to the countryside; strikes of minor revenue officials and cases of withholding land revenue had been reported; carriages and other conveniences had been denied to officers on tour, policemen were being pilloried and adjured to quit the service of an alien Government. 'Everywhere people are sensible of a change, of a new air, a *nai hawa*, which is blowing through men's minds,' wrote Sir Denzil,

the well-disposed classes stand aghast at our inaction and wonder whether the gods, wishing to destroy us, have made us mad. And their astonishment will, before long, inevitably turn into contempt for a Government, which can (as they regard the matter) so abrogate its functions, as to permit sedition to flourish unrebuked, and for a ruling race who tamely submit to open and organized insult. It is difficult to say what their [agitators'] precise object is, and probably a good many of them hardly know themselves. . . . Some of them no doubt, look to driving us out of the country, at any rate from power, either by force, or by the passive resistance of the people as a whole. But the immediate object of all seems to be to make our government of the country impossible; and probably the idea of the greater number is that we shall, then, in order to escape from an *impasse*, be compelled to give them a larger share of power and of appointments, and to introduce the changes which they desire.

Sir Denzil was convinced that the brain behind the agitation was Lajpat Rai, a leader of the Arya Samaj, a religious body which in his opinion had a strong political slant in the Punjab. He did not favour the prosecution of Lajpat Rai nor of his chief lieutenant Ajit Singh: if it succeeded it would make martyrs of them; if it failed it would be a disastrous blunder. He demanded their immediate deportation, and asked for special powers for 'strong executive action' to suppress political meetings and newspapers.

Sir Denzil's minute was received in Simla on 3 May 1907. Within ten days, Regulation III of 1818 had been resurrected from the dusty state archives and applied to the 'dangerous revolutionary Lajpat Rai', who was taken in a special train (bypassing Calcutta) to Diamond Harbour, where the steamer *Guide* was waiting to carry him to his ultimate destination—Mandalay gaol in Burma.

'I was astounded to read the news from India,' Jawaharlal wrote on 17 May. The same day Motilal included in his weekly letter from Allahabad a trenchant resume of the political situation in which neither the Government nor the Extremists were spared:

The whole position can be summed up in a very few words. A set of moral cowards has been placed at the head of an administration which is to govern a people who are both moral and physical cowards. The latter kicked up a row in the hope of impressing the former with their power and importance. The former got frightened, and, not knowing exactly what to do, laid their hands on the most prominent man in the Punjab simply with the object of overawing the people. This has had the desired effect. . . . The arrest and deportation of Lajpat Rai, unjustifiable and inexcusable as it is, has shown what stuff our countrymen are made of. It is nothing but a storm in a tea-cup, and it is all over now—only we are put back half a century. The forces which were slowly and silently working for the good of the country have received a sudden check.

He cautioned his son not to be unduly alarmed by the news from India: 'It is in the interest of both Government and the people to exaggerate. Each has to justify its action. . . .'

Perhaps these strictures on the Extremists were made for the benefit of his son, whose political consciousness was sharpening fast. 'Do not go near the *Majlis* or the *Native* club or whatever it is called,' Motilal warned Jawaharlal when he went up to Cambridge. The warning was not heeded. 'I went the other day to a meeting of the *Majlis* here,' came the answer, 'just to see if they were as bad as they were painted. I failed to discover anything reprehensible in it.' As regards the *Native Club*, Jawaharlal reported that there was one in Cambridge, 'but it was for eating natives'.

A few weeks earlier, Motilal had a twinge of anxiety on reading in the newspapers that there had been disturbances in Ireland where his son was holidaying. 'In your last letter,' Jawaharlal wrote from Dublin on 12 September 1907,

you asked me not to go near Belfast on account of the riots, but I would have dearly liked to have been there for them. About a fortnight ago, there was a chance of our having similar scenes here, but to my mortification the whole thing ended in a fiasco. The tramway employees were on the point of striking, and if they had done so, there would have been a little fighting in the streets of Dublin.

The visit to Ireland had put new ideas into the head of the young nationalist. 'Have you heard of the Sinn Fein in Ireland?,' he asked his father,

it is a most interesting movement and resembles very closely the so-called Extremist movement in India. Their policy is not to beg for favours but to wrest them. They do not want to fight England by arms, but to ignore her, boycott her, and quietly assume the administration of Irish affairs. . . . Among people, who ought to know, this movement is causing . . . consternation. They say that if its policy is adopted by the bulk of the country, English rule will be a thing of the past.

V

The militant nationalism of his eighteen year-old son did not please his father who, in his forty-seventh year, was making a cautious, almost tentative entry into active politics on the side of a party wedded to slow and ordered progress. As the tension between the two wings of the Congress mounted, Motilal became, along with Malaviya and Sunderlal, the target of the Extremist press in his own province. He retaliated with a hard-hitting article in the *Pioneer* and sent a copy to his son. Jawaharlal's reactions were sharply critical:

I had till now an idea that you were not so very moderate as you would have me believe. The article almost makes me think that you are 'immoderately Moderate'. I would have said that the article had been written by a person with strong loyalist tendencies if I had not known you better. . . .

Having overshot his mark, Jawaharlal received an immediate reproof. Motilal in his reply (10 January 1908) retorted:

You know me and my views well enough to understand that I do not approve of opinions expressed by you, but boys must be boys. . . . We are living in very critical times and events are crowding so fast that the present situation cannot last very long. . . . It is unnecessary to enter into any discussion on this subject. Within a year or two, there will be no doubt left in the mind of anyone as to the correctness and otherwise of the attitude of the various so-called political parties in India.

Events had indeed already moved to a dramatic climax at Surat, where the Indian National Congress met for its twenty-third session in December 1907. Motilal had been reluctant to attend the session; he was not well and feared that the long train journey would aggravate his asthma. But his Moderate friends in Allahabad were insistent and Gokhale telegraphed him to come without fail.

It is hardly necessary to recapitulate the oft-told story of the Surat Congress: the bitter controversies surrounding the choice of the president and the place for the session; the manoeuvres of the Moderates for the election of Dr Rash Behari Ghose; the fears of the Extremists that they were being elbowed out of the Congress and that the programme of Swadeshi and boycott adopted by the

Calcutta Congress was being jettisoned; the abortive efforts at mediation behind the scenes; the ominous adjournment of the session on the opening day; the stormy scenes on the following day with Tilak on the platform; the flying missile—the fateful shoe—which touched off the unseemly scuffle; the brandishing of sticks, the unrolling of turbans, the broken chairs and the bruised heads; and finally the crowning humiliation when the police arrived to clear the hall. Motilal was one of the prominent Moderate delegates and had been called upon to second the proposal for the election of Dr Rash Behari Ghose as president just before the last tumultuous scenes; he returned from Surat with redoubled dislike of Extremist policies and tactics. The reactions of his son (who had not yet received the freezing dose his father had administered in the letter dated 10 January), were the very opposite.

*Jawaharlal to Motilal, 2 January 1908*: We expected lively things at Surat and our expectations were more than fulfilled. It is of course a great pity that such a split should have occurred. But it was sure to come and the sooner we have it, the better. You will most probably throw all the blame on Tilak and the Extremists. They may have been to blame for it, but the Moderates had certainly a lot to do with it. I do not at all object to Rash Behari Ghose being president, but the manner in which he was declared president in the face of opposition can hardly be defended from any point of view. The Moderates may represent part of the country, but they seem to think, or at any rate try to make others believe, that they are the 'natural leaders' and representatives of the whole country. The manner in which some of them try to ignore and belittle all those who differ from them would be annoying, if it was not ridiculous.

'I firmly believe', Jawaharlal concluded,

that there will hardly be any so-called Moderates left in a very few years' time. By the methods they are following at present, they are simply hastening the doom of their party.

Though he had only the reports in the British press and his own Extremist sympathies to guide him, young Nehru's analysis of the Surat fiasco was remarkably near the truth, and his forecast of the future of the Moderate party was almost prophetic. But if he expected his father to swallow these pronouncements, he had seriously miscalculated. There was a touch of irony in Motilal's reply (24 January): 'I am favoured with your views as to the conduct of the Moderates and Extremists at Surat in December last, and feel flattered by the compliment you have paid to the Moderates, knowing of course that your father is one.' 'I am sorry,' Jawaharlal replied, 'you don't approve of my opinions, but I really can't help holding them in the present state of affairs . . . anyhow I have not the presumption of imagining that my opinions are infallible.' After this half-hearted apology, he was tempted into a thoughtless witticism: 'The Government must be feeling very pleased with you at your attitude. I wonder if the insulting offer of a *Rai Bahadurship*, or something equivalent, would make you less of a Moderate than you are.'

Motilal was furious, but refrained from referring to this subject in his weekly letters. From a number of sources, however, Jawaharlal was left in no doubt of his father's reaction. He even talked of fetching the young hothead home. It was not until April 1908, that the storm blew over, when Jawaharlal begged to be pardoned for an offence, which 'I did not intend to commit', and Motilal closed the controversy with a confession:

I do not of course approve of your politics and have on certain occasions expressed myself very strongly, as you know, I can, when I wish to. This is, however, neither here nor there. My love for you knows no bounds, and unless there is some very remarkable change in me, I do not see how it can be affected.

One wonders whether Motilal realized his own responsibility for the political precocity of his son. His letters to Harrow covered the political scene almost as fully as the domestic. He could, if he had wished, have avoided the subject altogether. Perhaps he thought it was safer to allow the boy to let off steam and channel his interest along prudent lines. Jawaharlal, for his part, had shrewdly discerned in his father a deep vein of defiance beneath the placid surface of Moderate politics. Cautious as he was in advocating political changes, Motilal exhibited a prickly intolerance of bureaucratic or racial arrogance. 'Our Chief Justice is developing a temper,' he wrote in one of his letters. 'I was surprised to see Sunderlal and Chaudhuri submitting to it. Encouraged by their example, he tried to be nasty to me. I paid him back in his own coin, and he is now milk and honey with me.' And when the Prince of Wales laid the foundation-stone of the Medical College at Lucknow in December 1905, Motilal was almost apologetic about his presence at the ceremony: 'As I have subscribed Rs 1000, I am on the Central Committee and as such have to be present. Otherwise there is no charm for me in such gatherings.'

The father's avowed displeasure did not moderate the son's radicalism. Jawaharlal's political consciousness—academic as it was at this time—was to be further sharpened on the intellectual grindstone of Cambridge. There are signs that from 1908 onwards, Motilal himself began to drift from his Moderate moorings. How far he was influenced by the views of his son it is difficult to say, as his own pride and the compulsion of events were also contributory factors.

This was the first political clash between father and son, but already it is possible to faintly trace the pattern of the future. Towards the ever-growing radicalism of his son, Motilal's attitude was successively to be one of indignation, opposition, conflict, conversion and, finally, championship.

## NOTE AND REFERENCES

1. British owned and edited, the *Pioneer* was the organ of European opinion and was then published from Allahabad.
2. S. Gopal, *The Viceroyalty of Lord Ripon* (London, 1953), p. 146.
3. H.W. Nevinson, *The New Spirit in India* (London, 1958), p. 117.
4. MacMahon Ball, *Nationalism and Communism in East Asia* (Melbourne, 1956), p. 15.
5. E. Hughes, *Keir Hardie* (London, 1956), p. 155.
6. J. Nehru, *Autobiography* (London, 1958 rpt), p. 6.
7. Ibid., p. 16.
8. B.R. Nanda, *The Nehrus, Motilal and Jawaharlal* (London, 1962), pp. 59–61.
9. Viscount Morley, *Indian Speeches* (London, 1909), p. 67.
10. Minute dated 3 May 1907, National Archives of India (henceforth, NAI).

# 2

## The Triumvirate: Gandhi, Motilal, and Jawaharlal

### I

The relationship between Gandhi and the two Nehrus offers a fascinating study in the interplay of personalities and politics during a crucial decade, the 1920s, in the history of Indian nationalism. Considering the sharp differences in their world-views and temperaments it seems miraculous that these three men of exceptional intelligence, integrity, and determination should have found it at all possible to work together. And it is a curious paradox that the latent tensions, the overt conflicts, and the eleventh-hour compromises which punctuated their political partnership enhanced rather than diminished their contribution to the cause of Indian freedom.

Jawaharlal Nehru tells us in his autobiography that no two men could have been more different than Gandhi and Motilal: Gandhi was the 'saint, the stoic, the man of religion, one who went through life rejecting what it offers in the way of sensation and physical pleasure', while Motilal was 'a bit of an epicure who accepted life and welcomed its many sensations and cared little for what may come in the hereafter'. It is not, therefore, surprising that Motilal's conversion to Gandhian politics was neither quick nor easy. Even though he had broken with his Moderate friends in the Indian National Congress in 1918 over the Montagu–Chelmsford reforms, Motilal's immediate reactions to Gandhi's call for a satyagraha campaign in February 1919 against the Rowlatt Bills were extremely hostile. The elder Nehru's entire career as a lawyer, legislator, and Congressman predisposed him against civil disobedience, which struck him not only foolish but futile: it could land a few hundred people in jail, but was hardly likely to affect the apparatus of the British administration in India. So when his son announced his intention to join the satyagraha struggle, Motilal was astounded. It was all very well for Jawaharlal to say that he was going to jail, but did he realize the repercussions of this step on the professional fortunes of his old father nearing his sixtieth year, the health of his ailing mother, and the happiness of his nineteen year old wife? Jawaharlal was torn between his political convictions and family affections, but decided to follow Gandhi. Motilal then sought the intervention of the Mahatma, who came to Allahabad in the second week of March 1919, and advised Jawaharlal to be patient awhile and not to do anything which would upset his father.

The domestic crisis in Anand Bhawan was postponed rather than resolved; it was soon overshadowed by a catastrophe—the Jallianwala Bagh massacre and the martial law in Punjab—which shook the Indian subcontinent, and incidentally brought father and son into political alignment. They hastened to provide such succour and relief as they could to the victims of martial law. Motilal was a member of the committee appointed by the Congress to enquire into the Punjab tragedy. The Committee included, besides Gandhi, eminent lawyers such as C.R. Das, M.R. Jayakar, and Abbas Tyabji. For Motilal, as for other members of the committee, this close association with Gandhi was an instructive experience. The Mahatma's incisive intellect, moral sensitivity, passion for justice, rock-like will, conscious humility, and flair for polemics and publicity were a strange but effective combination. Jawaharlal had already fallen under his spell; by the end of the year his father had developed a wholesome respect for Gandhi which was to survive basic temperamental differences as well as the vicissitudes of politics.

'The most revered Indian of today', was Motilal's description of Gandhi in his presidential address to the Amritsar Congress in December 1919. He also described satyagraha as 'a new force with tremendous potentialities'. This did not mean, however, that he either fully understood or identified himself with Gandhi's methods. Indeed, like most other Congress leaders, he was bewildered by the political philosophy of the Mahatma, and the abrupt changes which characterized his attitude to the Raj in the first half of 1920. The fact is that while Gandhi had by then captured the imagination of the Indian masses, he had also awakened much doubt and heart-searching amongst the intelligentsia. At the special session of the Indian National Congress at Calcutta in September 1920, his programme of non-cooperation was opposed by a phalanx of nationalist leaders, including C.R. Das, B.C. Pal, Madan Mohan Malaviya, Annie Besant, G.S. Khaparde, N.C. Kelkar, and M.A. Jinnah. Even Lajpat Rai, the president of the session, was non-committal on non-cooperation. Pattabhi Sitaramayya, the official historian of the Congress, recorded many years later that Motilal was the only notable Congress leader to support Gandhi at Calcutta. It can safely be surmised that Motilal's conversion to non-cooperation was as much due to Gandhi's persuasive advocacy, as to the invisible pressure from his son. Motilal prided himself on his objectivity, but in this, the greatest decision of his life, he was guided as much by his heart as by his head. It was love of his son that enabled him to take the last fateful step over the precipice.

Immediately after the Calcutta Congress, Motilal resigned his membership of the UP Legislative Council, wound up his legal practice, withdrew his thirteen-year-old daughter, Krishna, from the local school, disposed of his horses, carriages, dogs, treasured crystal and china. Life at Anand Bhawan underwent a metamorphosis. The number of servants was drastically curtailed, foreign finery was discarded and cartloads of it consigned to public bonfires. From the select club of the élite of Allahabad, Anand Bhawan was turned into a caravanserai, frequented by party members sojourning in or passing through Allahabad—humble looking folk, clad in homespun khadi.

The annexation of Anand Bhawan was an important landmark in Gandhi's conquest of the Congress and emergence as the unquestioned leader of Indian nationalism. Motilal became a legendary figure, whose sacrifices for the national cause, like those of his friend C.R. Das in Bengal, cast a spell over his generation. He became not only the outstanding Congress leader in the United Provinces, but figured in the highest echelons of the Congress. He was appointed one of its three general secretaries, and since the office of the All India Congress Committee was located in his house at Allahabad, the brunt of the work was borne by him. He brought to his political work the same singleness of purpose, eye for detail, and strong common-sense which had enabled him to dominate the Allahabad Bar.

Motilal was not a man to be swept off his feet even by a Mahatma; he was no blind follower, and had occasional differences with Gandhi in the conduct of the non-cooperation movement. He could not see the wisdom of Gandhi's parleys with the new Viceroy, Lord Reading in May 1921. Nor did he appreciate the Mahatma's insistence on hand-spinning as a qualification for civil resisters. But Motilal's most serious differences with Gandhi came in February 1922 when, after the Chauri Chaura tragedy, the Mahatma revoked plans for civil disobedience in Bardoli on the grounds that the atmosphere in the country was not conducive to non-violence. When the news reached Motilal in Lucknow jail, where he was serving a six-month term along with his son, he was beside himself with anger. Was the Congress, he asked, a political body or a testing ground for the experiments of a Mahatma?

The programme which Gandhi commended to the country just before his arrest—hand-spinning and weaving, Hindu–Muslim unity, and removal of untouchability—did not impress those who were burning to mount a final assault on British imperialism. Demoralization and confusion characterized the Congress ranks after Gandhi's imprisonment. In the summer of 1922, the Civil Disobedience Enquiry Committee, appointed by the All India Congress Committee, after touring the country reported that the country was not ready for civil disobedience. There was one issue, the boycott of legislative councils, on which the committee was sharply—and evenly—divided. Among those who were in favour of revoking the boycott were Motilal Nehru and C.R. Das. They argued that council entry was not a negation, but an extension of the principle of non-cooperation to a new field: the 'sham legislatures' set up by the British. They were opposed by a strong section in the Congress led by C. Rajagopalachari and Vallabhbhai Patel, who came to be known as 'No-Changers', to whom it was almost an act of sacrilege to tone down the non-cooperation programme while its author was in jail. When the issue came up before the Gaya Congress in December 1922, with C.R. Das in the chair, the No-Changers won a victory over their opponents, the 'Pro-Changers'.

Motilal and C.R. Das picked up the gauntlet and defied the

verdict of the Gaya Congress by forming a new party within the Congress, the Swaraj Party. They had a tough time at the hands of their opponents for the greater part of 1923, but luckily a compromise was worked out between the two factions just in time to enable the Swaraj Party to fight the general elections in November 1923. The party won, what Lord Reading, the Viceroy, privately described as a 'notable victory'. It was returned in strength to the Central Legislative Assembly and won an absolute majority in the C.P. Council. In the Bengal Council, the Swarajists had only 47 members in a House of 114 members, but C.R. Das, with his remarkable vigour, skill, and tenacity, fought the British Governor and the bureaucracy to a standstill, and forced them to suspend the constitution. The major confrontation between the Swarajists and the government, however, took place in the Central Legislative Assembly at Delhi and Simla, where Motilal, with the support of some of the Moderate and Muslim members, threw out the budget and inflicted a series of defeats on the government.

At this juncture a new strand was added to the political situation by the premature release of Gandhi from jail on grounds of health after a serious operation. His return to politics in early 1924 revived the controversy which had rocked the Indian National Congress during the preceding two years. Motilal and C.R. Das came down to Bombay where Gandhi was convalescing, for talks with him, but could not convince him of the wisdom of the Swarajist strategy. They considered the Mahatma's approach to the political situation unrealistic; they did not think his 'constructive work' added up to a serious political programme, they did not like his reduction of all political issues to a moral algebra; they were certain that the council programme was in the best interests of the Congress and the country. Gandhi doubted the possibility of achieving much through legislatures with limited powers set up by the British Government; he considered the policy of obstruction from within the councils neither feasible nor advisable; he was certain that more could be achieved through work among the people than through verbal fireworks in the councils.

The differences between the Swarajist leaders and the Mahatma were so sharp that a split in the Congress in the summer of 1924 appeared a distinct possibility. Gandhi could have outvoted the Swarajists, but a scramble for power was utterly repugnant to him.

Motilal Nehru, perhaps primed by his son, was equally anxious for a *modus vivendi.* The result was the 'Calcutta Agreement' in November 1924, signed by Gandhi, C.R. Das, and Motilal, which virtually made the Swaraj Party the agent of the Congress for the conduct of its political activities. The 'No-Changers', Gandhi's faithful followers, were bewildered by, what seemed to them, his total surrender to the Swarajists. A year later, Gandhi explained his reasons for this act of self-abnegation in a letter to Dr M.A. Ansari: 'I could not convince the Swarajists of the error of council entry, and knowing also that my best friends and co-workers had become Swarajists, I took it that I could not do less than throw my weight with them as against other parties.' Time was to prove the sagacity of Gandhi's approach.

The spectacular victories of the Swaraj Party in the Central Legislative Assembly in 1924 had been made possible by a pact with the 'independents' led by Jinnah. Motilal's feeling of victory over the No-Changers did not last long. The pact with Jinnah broke down in 1925, when he withdrew his support. As if this was not enough, Motilal was faced with a revolt by a section of his own party in the Central Provinces, who called themselves 'Responsivists', advocated acceptance of the office, and secured the support of some of the senior Swarajist leaders of Maharashtra. Further, the atmosphere in the legislatures and the country came to be vitiated by religious discord. The general election of 1926, fought on petty and communal issues, left the Swaraj Party badly mauled. Finding the task of party management increasingly burdensome, Motilal became increasingly dependent on Gandhi's advice and assistance which were invariably and unreservedly given.

The occasion on which Motilal needed Gandhi's assistance most came in 1928 when the Nehru Report, outlining a constitution for free India, framed by an All-Parties Committee headed by the elder Nehru himself, was being assailed by young radicals in the Indian National Congress led by his own son. Although father and son had been comrades-in-arms in the non-cooperation movement, and were together in Lucknow jail in 1921–2, there was a wide divergence in their political outlook. Jawaharlal did not join the Swaraj Party in the twenties, and was completely out of tune with communal and factional politics; he devoted himself to the organizational work of the Congress as secretary of the UP Congress

Committee or as general secretary of the All India Congress
Committee. His visit to Europe in 1926–7, in the course of which
he attended the 'Congress of Oppressed Nationalities' at Brussels,
and paid a brief visit to the USSR, gave a sharp edge to his politics.
On his return to India, he carried a resolution through the Madras
Congress demanding complete independence. His activities in the
youth and trade union movements disconcerted his father. But the
real clash came in the autumn of 1928 on the question of dominion status, which Motilal had accepted as a common denominator
acceptable to the Congress as well as to other parties, for the Nehru
Report. As the time for the Calcutta Congress approached, Motilal
began to wonder whether, like his friend C.R. Das at Gaya six years
earlier, he would suffer the humiliation of seeing his own policies
repudiated by the very session over which he presided. Motilal
summoned Gandhi to his rescue. The Mahatma had been a silent
spectator at Guwahati Congress in 1926 and the Madras Congress in 1927. It is doubtful if he would have gone to Calcutta in
December 1928, or taken much interest in the proceedings of the
Congress, but for the elder Nehru's importunities.

As Motilal had anticipated, the Nehru Report came under fire at
the Calcutta Congress. Behind closed doors Congress leaders discussed the contentious issue of Dominion Status versus complete
independence, which threatened to split the party. In the Subjects
Committee, which screened the resolutions for the plenary session,
the discussions were long, heated, and bitter. On 27 December,
Gandhi suggested a *via media*; the Congress should adopt the
Nehru Report in entirety, including the dominion status formula,
but if it were not accepted by the government within two years, the
Congress should opt for complete independence and fight for it, if
necessary, by invoking the weapon of civil disobedience. Jawaharlal
wanted to reduce the notice to the government to one year. That
evening there were further discussions, as a result of which Gandhi
moved on the following day (28 December) an amended resolution
giving London only one year to accept the dominion status formula. The amended resolution was carried in the Subjects Committee by 118 votes to 45, but Jawaharlal was absent, and Subhas
Bose did not take part in the debate. Three days later, when
Gandhi's resolution came up before the plenary session, Bose
opposed it and was supported rather inconsistently and half-

heartedly by Jawaharlal. Gandhi was infuriated by this backsliding. 'When we have no sense of honour,' he said, 'when we cannot allow our words to remain unaltered for twenty-four hours, do not talk of independence.' The voting—1350 for and 973 against—gave Gandhi's resolution a clear majority, but the issue hung in the balance till almost the last moment.

Jawaharlal's vacillation at Calcutta, the conflict between his convictions and his loyalty to his father, Gandhi, and the Congress, was then and later a subject of much adverse comment. But vacillation, like silence, is sometimes useful in politics. It was a sound instinct which kept Jawaharlal from breaking with the Congress old guard in December 1928. As events were to show, it was he, not they, who had won at Calcutta. 'Complete independence,' instead of being the catchword of a few young radicals, bade fair to become the battle-cry of the Indian National Congress. And most important of all, the way had been opened for Gandhi's return to active politics. The master-stroke of the Mahatma, the election of Jawaharlal Nehru to the presidency of the Lahore Congress, was yet to come.

A few months later, Motilal needed Gandhi's intervention to wean away his followers in the Swaraj Party from their infatuation with the councils; many of them were reluctant to recognize that the boycott of the legislatures was inevitable if the Lahore Congress opted for independence and approved of a civil disobedience campaign to attain it.

It was customary in the mid-twenties to dismiss Gandhi as a 'spent bullet', and label his politics as visionary. It would seem in retrospect that, behind his seeming obscurities and contradictions, there was a remarkable clarity of perception and consistency of method. The total perspective in which he saw the policies of the British Government, the role of the Swaraj Party, and his own work in that critical decade may be glimpsed in his reaction to a hectoring speech by Birkenhead, the Secretary of State for India, in July 1925:

He [Birkenhead] thinks that non-cooperation was a dreadful mistake. The vast majority of us think that it alone has awakened this sleeping nation from its torpor, it alone has given the nation a force, a strength beyond measure. The Swaraj Party is a result of that force.

While Motilalji will be fighting in the Assembly and leading the Swaraj Party in the place of Deshbandhu [C.R. Das] I shall be leaving no stone unturned to prepare the atmosphere needed for civil disobedience, a vocation for which I seem to be more fitted than for any other.

A chastened Motilal told the Lahore Congress in December 1929 that the purpose for which the Swaraj Party was founded had not been realized, that the councils had distracted Congressmen from the real goal, that some of their ablest men had been entrapped by the government in one committee or another. Five years earlier, at the height of the crisis in the Congress, Gandhi had confided to Mahadev Desai that deep down he had the faith that, 'tired like a broken soldier come for rest,' the Swarajists would be disillusioned one day and return to his camp. Gandhi's faith was vindicated in December 1929. The resumption of the Congress leadership by Gandhi and the imminence of another mass movement after the Lahore Congress, led to the liquidation of the Swaraj Party, the historic function of which had been to fill the political vacuum between two Gandhian struggles.

# 3

## Gandhi and Jawaharlal

### I

'Are we rivals?' Gandhi asked in the *Harijan* of 25 July 1936, and himself answered: 'I cannot think of myself as a rival to Jawaharlal or him to me. Or, if we are, we are rivals in making love to each other in the pursuit of the common goal.' It is doubtful if Gandhi's explanation carried conviction to the young socialists, who looked up to Nehru as the leader of the militant Left, or even to the British officials, who pinned their hopes on a split in the nationalist ranks.

The crisis in the Congress leadership in 1936 was a grave one—graver than the public knew—but this was not the first occasion when Gandhi and Nehru had differed. They had had serious differences in 1922 on the aftermath of Chauri Chaura tragedy, in 1928 on complete independence versus Dominion Status, in 1929 on the Viceroy's declaration, in 1931 on the Gandhi–Irwin Pact, in 1932 on the fast against separate electorates for untouchables, and in 1934 on the withdrawal of the civil disobedience movement.

The width of the intellectual gulf that divided them was revealed by Nehru himself in his autobiography which he wrote in 1934–5 in gaol. Among Nehru's colleagues were several who expected and even incited him to revolt against the Mahatma's dominance in the Congress. On 4 March 1936, just as he was leaving for India, Subhas Bose begged him not to consider his 'position to be weaker than it really is. Gandhi will never take a stand which will alienate you.'[1] Four years later, J.P. Narayan pleaded with Nehru to leave the Congress and form a new party 'to fulfil the remaining part of the political task and the main part of the social task of the Indian revolution'.[2]

Nehru did not heed these siren voices. He did not carry his differences with Gandhi to breaking point: the clash of ideas between himself and Gandhi did not turn into a clash of wills. Nor did he encourage his followers to organize an opposition to Gandhi's leadership, or to plan a split in the Congress party. Despite differences of thought, temperament, and style, Gandhi and Nehru stood together for more than a quarter of a century. It was one of the longest, most intriguing, and fruitful partnerships in the history of nationalism.

How two men, divided not only by twenty years of age, but by deep intellectual and temperamental differences, could work together for so long is an enigma to anyone who seriously studies their lives and the history of this period. The young aristocrat from Allahabad seemed to have little in common with the strange charismatic figure that burst upon the Indian political stage in 1919 with almost elemental force. The primary school in Porbandar, where young Gandhi wrote the alphabet in dust with his fingers, or the Bhavnagar college where he painfully struggled with lectures in English, belonged altogether to a different world from that of European governesses and resident tutors in Allahabad, Harrow, Cambridge, the Inns of Court in England in which young Nehru grew up. True, Gandhi also went to England to study for the bar in the late 1880s. But young Gandhi poring over the Bible and the *Gita*, and desperately fighting back the recurring temptation of 'wine, women and meat' was cast in an altogether different mould from that of the handsome, Savile Row-clad Kashmiri youth who prided himself on his agnosticism and Cyrenaicism, frequented the theatre, admired Oscar Wilde and Walter Pater, and dabbled in Irish politics and Fabian economics. In the course of his twenty-odd years' stay in South Africa, Gandhi fashioned for himself a peculiar, almost unique philosophy of life which, though baffling to many of his contemporaries, was firmly grounded on deeply held convictions.

How could Jawaharlal Nehru with his enthusiasm for science and humanism take to a saint with prayers and fasts, inner voices and the spinning wheel? This is a question to which biographers, historians, and political commentators will continue to seek answers. It has been suggested that Jawaharlal had a compulsive need to depend on someone: that at first the mentor was his father Motilal, and then Gandhi.[3] M.N. Roy suspected that Jawaharlal's mind was a slave to his heart; that he deliberately suppressed his own personality 'to purchase popularity' and become 'a hero of Indian nationalism . . . as the spiritual son of Gandhi'.[4] Hiren Mukerjee has hazarded the theory that Gandhi won over and astutely kept Jawaharlal on his side to exploit his charisma and influence with India's youth in the interest of the Congress party, which was really controlled by vested interests.[5] These interpretations have the merit of simplicity, but they do not fit the facts of a partnership which extended over nearly three decades. The story of this partnership, the strains to which it was subjected, and the factors which enabled it to survive show that it was not simply a case of domination of one by the other; that Jawaharlal needed Gandhi as much as Gandhi needed him; that political calculation no less than emotional affinity kept them together through all these years.

## II

When Gandhi returned to India at the age of forty-five early in 1915, his personality had already been formed. To his Western-educated contemporaries he seemed a quaint figure in politics. His South African record had endowed him with a halo, but in the shadow of the Great War, public opinion was worried less about the Indian minority in South Africa than about India's political future. Gandhi's view that unconditional support to the British war effort would earn its reward from a grateful Empire in the hour of victory, seemed to most of his contemporaries extraordinarily naïve. And, as if this was not enough, Gandhi was also harping on the superiority of the Indian over Western civilization, denouncing industrialism, and advocating village handicrafts. All this must have sounded strangely unpolitical and anachronistic to Jawaharlal Nehru, who had returned to India in 1912 after seven years in England. Though he had seen Gandhi at the Bombay Congress in 1915, and again at Lucknow a year later, Jawaharlal was not really attracted to him until after the Champaran and Kaira campaigns and the anti-Rowlatt Bill agitation. There were good reasons why Gandhi's satyagraha campaigns should have made an impact on Jawaharlal. Seven years at the Allahabad High Court, as his father's junior, had left Jawaharlal bored with the 'trivialities and technicalities' of the legal profession. The game of making money did not really excite him. He was groping for a new Weltanschauung. Political terrorism had little attraction for him. The annual sessions of the Indian National Congress, and the armchair politics with which the élite of Allahabad amused itself seemed to him much too tame. He was drawn to Gokhale's Servants of India Society with its band of political sannyasins, but he was repelled by its association with 'moderate politics'. When Gandhi published the satyagraha pledge and announced direct action to protest against the Rowlatt Bills, Jawaharlal was excited by the prospect of effective political action.

Motilal Nehru did not find it easy to reconcile himself to an extra-constitutional agitation, but Gandhi counselled patience to his son, and prevented him from taking an irrevocable step. Soon afterwards, in the wake of the tragedy of the martial law in Punjab, Motilal came into closer contact with Gandhi, and was surprised to find in him not a starry-eyed saint but a politician with a keen practical sense.[6] Before long the entire Nehru family fell under the Mahatma's spell, and learnt to seek solace and support from the saint of Sabarmati. This was an emotional bond independent of, but not without its influence upon politics: differences of ideology and tactics become a little less intractable if there is a reserve of mutual respect and affection.

## III

Gandhi's first impact on young Nehru was strong indeed. Jawaharlal was, in his own words, 'simply bowled over by Gandhi straight off'.[7] The call to non-violent battle against the British Raj in 1919–20 struck a chord. 'I jumped at it. I did not care for the consequences.' His life underwent a metamorphosis. He turned his back on the legal profession, simplified his life, gave up smoking, turned vegetarian, and began to read the Gita regularly, 'not from a philosophical or theological point of view', but because 'it had numerous parts which had a powerful effect upon me'.[8] He was fired by the missionary fervour of a new convert. 'Non-cooperation is to me', he wrote to the Chief Secretary to the UP Government, 'a sacred thing and its very basis is truth and non-violence.'[9] He was filled with excitement, optimism, and buoyant enthusiasm. He experienced 'the happiness of a person crusading for a cause'.[10]

From this state of ecstasy, there was a rude awakening in February 1922. After a riot at Chauri Chaura in the United Provinces Gandhi called off civil disobedience. Jawaharlal, who was in prison at the time, received the news with 'amazement and consternation'.[11] He did not see how the violence of a stray mob of excited peasants in a remote village could justify the reversal of a national struggle for freedom. If perfect non-violence was to be regarded as a *sine qua non* for all the three-hundred-odd million Indians, would it not reduce Gandhi's movement to a pious futility? A letter from Gandhi somewhat mollified Jawaharlal, but it was only much later, with the perspective that time gives, that he realized that Gandhi's decision was right, that 'he had to stop the rot and build anew'.[12]

The Chauri Chaura tragedy brought Jawaharlal down to earth. The exaltation of the non-cooperation days faded away. He had no stomach for the factional and communal politics of the mid-twenties. He served as Allahabad's Mayor and as General Secretary of the All India Congress Committee. These activities provided useful outlets for his boundless energy, but he did not recover his zest for politics, and indeed for life, until he visited Europe during 1926–7 for the treatment of his ailing wife. Under the stimulus of fresh reading and contacts with revolutionaries and radicals of three continents, the realization dawned that Indian politics had been much too vague, narrow and parochial. He learnt to trace links not only between British imperialism in India and colonialism in other countries of Asia and Africa, but also between foreign domination and vested interests in his own country. The Brussels Congress of Oppressed Nationalities and the brief visit to the Soviet Union gave a tremendous impetus to these ideas. When he returned home in December 1927, he persuaded the Madras Congress to pass resolutions in favour of 'complete independence'. He denounced feudalism, capitalism, and imperialism, and talked of organizing workers, peasants, and students.

Jawaharlal's performance at the Madras Congress deeply disturbed Gandhi. He wrote to Jawaharlal:

You are going too fast, you should have taken time to think and become acclimatized. Most of the resolutions you prepared and got carried could have been delayed for one year. Your plunging into the 'republican army' was a hasty step. But I do not mind these acts of yours so much as I mind your encouraging mischief-mongers and hooligans . . . If . . . careful observation of the country in the light of your European experiences convinces you of the errors of the current ways and means, by all means enforce your own views, but do please form a disciplined party.[13]

Gandhi's objection was not so much to the radical views of the younger man, as to the light-hearted way in which brave declarations were made without any serious effort to implement them. It was all very well to talk of 'complete independence', but did the Indian people have the will to enforce such a demand? 'We have almost sunk to the level of a school boys' debating society', the Mahatma told Jawaharlal. A few months later, he told Motilal Nehru, who headed the committee which was to draft an All-Parties Constitution (the Nehru Report) that 'unless we have created some force ourselves, we shall not advance beyond the position of beggars. . . . We are not ready for drawing up a constitution till we have developed a sanction for ourselves.'[14] The only sanction that Gandhi could forge was that provided by a non-violent struggle.

In December 1928, when the advocates of independence and Dominion Status clashed at the Calcutta Congress, Jawaharlal is reported to have told Gandhi: 'Bapu, the difference between you and me is this: You believe in gradualism; I stand for revolution.' 'My dear young man', Gandhi retorted, 'I have made revolutions while others have only shouted revolutions. When your lungs are exhausted and you really are serious about it you will come to me and I shall then show you how a revolution is made.'[15] After a long, heated argument, much vacillation and 'mental distress', Jawaharlal eventually fell into line with Gandhi's compromise formula. Dominion Status was accepted as the basis of the new constitution, provided the British Government conceded it before the end of 1929.

To many of his young admirers Jawaharlal's attitude at the Calcutta Congress smacked of political cowardice; to Subhas Bose and members of the Independence for India League it seemed an abject betrayal. But it was a sound instinct which kept Jawaharlal from breaking with the Congress Old Guard and the Mahatma. He seems to have sensed that if there were any conservatives at the Calcutta Congress, Gandhi was not one of them. As events were to prove, it was Jawaharlal, not the Old Guard who won at Calcutta.

There were some apparent disappointments and setbacks, such as Congress leaders' reaction to Lord Irwin's declaration on Dominion Status in November 1929 and the peace parleys in Delhi just before the Lahore Congress. Nevertheless, the fact remained that within a year 'complete independence', instead of being the catchword of a few young radicals, became the battle-cry of the Congress party, and Gandhi was back at its helm to direct, to Jawaharlal's delight, another satyagraha struggle against the British Raj.

<h1 style="text-align:center">IV</h1>

After the Calcutta Congress the political atmosphere became electric. Gandhi abandoned a trip to Europe which he had been planning and called for a boycott of foreign cloth. There were rumours of Jawaharlal's imminent arrest as he threw himself into the organizational work of the Congress with redoubled vigour. Politics again acquired for him a sense of purpose, urgency, and adventure. All the signs pointed to Gandhi's return to the active leadership of the party. A majority of the provincial Congress committees voted for him to preside over the Lahore session in December 1929. Gandhi declined the honour, but persuaded the All India Congress Committee to confer it on Jawaharlal. The thought that he had come to the highest office in the Congress 'not by the main entrance or even a side entrance', but by a 'trap door' which had bewildered the audience into acceptance[16] Nehru found humiliating. Nevertheless, the fact that he was to preside over the momentous session at Lahore and to unfurl the flag of independence on the bank of the Ravi at midnight on 31 December 1929 rocketed his prestige overnight. The Lahore Congress gave a tremendous boost to Jawaharlal's popularity with the masses; it raised his stock with the intelligentsia and made him a hero of India's youth.

As the new year dawned, events moved swiftly. With the observance of the Independence Day and the launching of the Salt Satyagraha, the political scene began to be transformed under the magic touch of the Mahatma. And once again, in the midst of a struggle against the British Raj, Jawaharlal felt that sense of complete identification with Gandhi he had experienced ten years earlier. His mood found eloquent expression in the tribute he paid to Gandhi as the Mahatma marched to Dandi on the western coast for breach of the Salt Laws:

Today the pilgrim marches onward on his long trek, the fire of a great resolve is in him, and surpassing love of his miserable countrymen. And love of truth that scorches and love of freedom that inspires. And none that passes him can escape the spell, and men of common clay feel the spark of life.[17]

The Salt Satyagraha sucked the entire Nehru family into its vortex. Jawaharlal was the first to be arrested; he was followed by his father, his sisters, and his wife. But once again history repeated itself, and Gandhi called off the movement when it seemed to be on the crest of a rising wave. Nehru was in Delhi in February and March 1931, and in touch with the Mahatma during his talks with the Viceroy. Nevertheless, the contents of the Gandhi–Irwin Pact on 4 March, and particularly its second clause concerning the safeguards in the new constitution, came as a great shock to Jawaharlal:[18]

So I lay and pondered on that March night and in my heart there was a great emptiness as of something precious gone, almost beyond recall. . . . The thing had been done, our leader had committed himself; and even if we disagreed with him, what could we do? Throw him over? Break from him? Announce our disagreement? That might bring some personal satisfaction to an individual, but it made no difference to the final decision.[19]

Gandhi observed Jawaharlal's distress, took him out for a walk, and tried to allay his fears. Jawaharlal was not convinced, but at the Karachi Congress, a few days later, he swallowed his dissent, and even sponsored the resolution supporting the Gandhi–Irwin Pact. His motive in doing so was to prevent an open rift in the party, and to strengthen the hands of Gandhi who was to represent the Congress at the Round Table Conference in London.

## V

In December 1931, when Gandhi returned from his abortive trip to London, Jawaharlal was already in gaol. The Gandhi–Irwin Pact went to pieces, civil disobedience was resumed, the Congress was

outlawed, and more than sixty thousand people were convicted for
civil disobedience. Jawaharlal had one of his longest spells in gaol—
a total of 1,170 days—between December 1931 and September
1935. It was towards the close of this period that he wrote his
autobiography. The author's preface referred to the 'mood of self-
questioning', and the 'particularly distressful period' of his life in
which the book was written. The distress stemmed not only from
the anxiety about his wife, who was hovering between life and death
in Indian and Swiss sanatoria, but also from the decline of the
struggle against the British Raj. As he recalled the story of his life
and the course of the movement to which he had given his all,
Jawaharlal noted the conflicting pulls which Gandhi exerted on
him:

For it was clear that this little man of poor physique had something
of steel in him, something rocklike which did not yield to physical
powers, however great they might be. And inspite of his unimpressive
features, his loin-cloth and bare body, there was a royalty and kingliness
in him which compelled a willing obeisance from others. . . . His calm,
deep eyes would hold one and gently probe into the depths, his voice,
clear and limpid would purr its way into the heart and evoke an
emotional response. It was the utter sincerity of the man and his
personality that gripped. He grave the impression of tremendous reserves of power.[20]

Despite his admiration for the Mahatma, Nehru found much in
Gandhi that puzzled and even infuriated him. When he learned
about Gandhi's fast against separate electorates for the depressed
classes he felt angry with the Mahatma,

at his religious and sentimental approach to a political question and
his frequent references to God in connection with it. He even seemed
to suggest that God had indicated the very day of the fast. What a
terrible example to set.

As he thought of the tragic possibilities of the fast he was seized
with despair.

If Bapu died! What would India be like then? And how would her
politics run? There seemed to be a dreary and dismal future ahead. So
I thought and thought and confusion reigned in my head and anger
and hopelessness and love for him who was the cause of this upheaval.[21]

The untouchability fast was not the only occasion when Gandhi's religious idiom jarred on Nehru. In 1934, the Mahatma suggested that the terrible earthquake which Bihar had just suffered was a divine punishment for the sin of untouchability. It struck Nehru as a 'staggering remark . . . anything more opposed to scientific outlook it would be more difficult to imagine'.[22] A few months later Gandhi's statement, calling off civil disobedience because of the failure of a 'valued companion to perform his full prison task', left Jawaharlal gasping with its emotional irrelevance. Jawaharlal had

. . . a sudden and intense feeling that something broke inside me, a bond that I had valued very greatly had snapped. I felt terribly lonely in this wide world . . . Again I felt that sensation of spiritual isolation, of being a perfect stranger out of harmony, not only with the crowds that passed me, but also with those whom I had valued as dear and close colleagues.[23]

On occasion Gandhi struck Jawaharlal as 'a medieval Catholic saint'.[24] Gandhi's philosophy of 'one step enough for me' seemed much too empirical, his political style too abrupt and unpredictable, his doctrine of non-violence too lofty for the common run of mankind. The autobiography reflects Nehru's doubts and self-questioning and mental conflict.[25] Was not non-violence already hardening into 'an inflexible dogma' and 'taking its place in the pigeonholes of faith and religion . . . [and] becoming a sheet anchor for vested interests'?[26] Was it not an illusion to imagine that a dominant imperialist power would give up its domination over a country, or a class would give up its superior position and privileges, unless effective pressure amounting to coercion was exercised?[27] Was it not romantic to hope for the conversion of princes, landlords, and capitalists into trustees of their properties for the commonweal, or to expect khadi and village industries to solve the long-term problems of India's poverty? Was not Gandhi's emphasis on the spinning-wheel overdone and foredoomed to failure in an industrialized world?[28]

These doubts assailed Jawaharlal as he wrote his autobiography. Some of them had found expression in his talks with Gandhi in 1933 when he was briefly out of gaol. There was a public exchange of letters, in the course of which the Mahatma had acknowledged with typical understatement that while they agreed in 'the enunciation of ideals, there are temperamental differences between us'.[29]

While Nehru was in gaol during the next two years, these differences grew sharper. His ideas were taken up by a band of young Congressmen who were disillusioned by the failure of civil disobedience and attracted to socialist doctrines. In the 1920s, the Congress leadership had been challenged by young radicals on political issues, such as dominion status versus independence. In the 1930s, the challenge was to be on economic as well as on political issues; the contest was to be more serious not only for the coherence of the Congress party, but for the relations between Nehru and Gandhi. It is impossible to understand their relations at this time without noting their diverse social philosophies.

## VI

Though Jawaharlal had sampled Fabian literature and attended Bernard Shaw's lectures as a student in Cambridge and London, his enthusiasm for Marxism and the Russian Revolution was derived from reading and reflection in gaol, and the visit to Europe in 1926–7, which had included a four-day trip to Moscow. It is significant that one of the aims of the Independence for India League, which he and Subhas Bose had founded in 1928, was the revision of the economic structure of society on a socialist basis. In his presidential address at the Lahore Congress, Jawaharlal avowed himself a socialist and asserted that 'socialism had permeated the entire structure of society and the only point in dispute is the pace and methods of advance to this realization'. A little earlier, he had presided over the All India Trade Union Congress and argued that, despite the bourgeois character of the Congress, it represented the only effective force in the country. In March 1931, due largely to Gandhi's support, he was able to push through the Karachi Congress a resolution[30] on fundamental rights and economic policy, which envisaged, among other things, the state ownership of key industries and services, mineral resources, railways, waterways, shipping, and other means of transport. It is true that this resolution was only mildly socialist, but socialist ideas had not yet gained much currency in the Congress party. What Acharya Narendra Deva told Nehru in 1929 about the UP Independence League was true of most protagonists of socialism in the Congress in 1931: 'We may all generally believe in the necessity of reconstructing our society on a new basis, but the ideas of most of us are vague and indefinite and most of us do not know how to proceed about the business.'[31]

Not until 1934 was the initiative for the formation of a socialist group in the Congress taken by a number of young Congressmen who happened to be in Nasik gaol and shared the disenchantment with Gandhi's leadership in the wake of his withdrawal of civil disobedience. Among them were Jayaprakash Narayan, Asoka Mehta, Achyut Patwardhan, Yusuf Meherally, and S.M. Joshi. They were later joined by Narendra Deva, Sri Prakasa, Sampurnananda, N.G. Ranga, and others. They swore by Marxism, talked of the inevitability of class war, called for planned economic development on the Soviet model, discounted Gandhi's leadership, and doubted the efficacy of non-violence in solving Indian political and social problems. Gandhi was their chosen target. Jayaprakash Narayan described him as 'autochthonism'.[32] He considered Gandhi was played out and could not carry the people further.[33] It was only by drawing in the masses, the peasants, and the workers, that the Congress could broaden its base, rid itself of its defeatist mentality, 'socialize' the nationalist struggle, and forge a massive imperialist front.[34]

Gandhi was not impressed by the political wisdom of these young men, whom he described as a body of 'men in a hurry'. The talk of class war, expropriation, and violence was repugnant to him. Nevertheless—and this was characteristic of Gandhi—he refused to be a party to the muzzling of Congress Socialists. Indeed, he helped them to secure a larger representation in the All India Congress Committee by the introduction of a single transferable vote.[35] He also announced his own formal retirement from the Congress organization to enable his critics, including the young socialists, to express their views without being inhibited by his presence.

Nehru was in gaol when the Congress Socialist party was founded. He never became an office-bearer, or even a member of this party. But there is no doubt that he was its hero, and that from him it derived its inspiration. Some of the most prominent members of the party, such as Narendra Deva, Jayaprakash Narayan, and Achyut Patwardhan were close to Nehru and shared his outlook on national and international issues. Nehru's socialism was, however, not doctrinaire. Nor did he plan 'to inoculate the masses with the virus of Communism', as the Government of India suspected.[36] 'I am certainly a socialist', he wrote in March 1938, 'I believe in the socialist theory and method of approach. I am not a Communist chiefly because I resist the Communist tendency to treat Communism as holy doctrine, and I do not like being told what to think and what to do.' He made no secret of his faith in scientific socialism. He believed in curbing the profit motive, in promoting public ownership of key industries, and in using the machinery of the state to regulate economic activity. Gandhi's approach was different.

When not yet forty, Gandhi had developed a social philosophy of his own, based on a faith in non-violence and a distrust of industrialism and the modern state. The India of Gandhi's dreams was 'a federation of small village republics', providing only for the essential needs of the community. Based on the principle of thoroughgoing decentralization of economic and political structures, its aim was to reduce the temptation for exploitation from within and aggression from without. It was to imitate neither British not Soviet models, but was to be tailored to Indian conditions. It was to be, in Gandhi's words, *Ram Rajya*, 'the sovereignty of the people based on pure moral authority'.[37] 'I tell my socialist friends', he said at Faizpur in December 1936, 'you are not talking anything new. Our ancestors always said, "this is God's earth. It is neither of the capitalists nor of *zamindars* nor of anybody. It belongs to God." '[38]

Congress Socialists did not take the Mahatma's claim to be a socialist seriously. To them, as to Nehru, the Mahatma's socialism was a kind of 'muddled humanitarianism'.[39]

## VII

Imprisonment and his wife's ill health had kept Jawaharlal out of Indian politics for nearly four and a half years. Curiously, while he was behind prison bars, his political stock had risen; his was a name to conjure with among the masses as well as the intelligentsia; his autobiography was soon to give him a worldwide reputation as a writer. Gandhi was aware of Nehru's popularity as well as his differences with the Congress leadership. Nevertheless, he secured his election to the Presidency of the 1936 Congress, which met at

Lucknow a few days after Jawaharlal's return from Europe. Conscious of the fact that the socialists were a tiny minority in the party, Nehru included only three of them, Jayaprakash Narayan, Achyut Patwardhan and Narendra Deva, in the Congress Working Committee, and gave the remaining eleven seats to the Old Guard—the 'Gandhiites'. The Committee found it hard to settle down as a happy family. The political temperature had risen before Nehru's return. His militant address at the Lucknow Congress raised it further. The Congress Socialists seemed anxious to drive their advantage home; the older leaders were suspicious and nervous; Nehru himself was on edge. 'Today I feel', he wrote to a friend on 3 May 1936, 'that there will be a tug-of-war in India between rival ideologies. . . . I feel myself very much on the side of one ideology and I am distressed at some of my colleagues going the other way.'[40] Two days later he wrote about his sense of intellectual isolation in the Congress Working Committee. 'The last dozen years have been years of hard and continuous work for me, of self-education and study and thought. . . . But others . . . have not taken the trouble to think or study and have remained vaguely where they were. But the world changes.'[41] By the end of June, the crisis, unknown to the public, came to a head when seven members of the Congress Working Committee sent their resignations to Nehru. A split in the party appeared to be in the offing.

It is tempting to dramatize the 1936 crisis as a tug-of-war between the Right and the Left in the Congress with Gandhi backing the Right. But could Gandhi, who had roused the Indian peasantry to a consciousness of its strength in Champaran, Kaira, and Bardoli be fairly labelled a reactionary? Was it not Gandhi who had made the nationalist movement really conscious of its responsibility to the underdog and made poverty a live issue. The dispute, really, was not only on the adoption or rejection of the socialist creed; the political issue still predominated. The members of the so-called Right wing in the Congress executive—Rajendra Prasad, Vallabhbhai Patel, and others—looked askance at the Socialist group largely because of the threat it seemed to them to pose to the unity of the party. The party was still illegal in the whole of the North-West Frontier Province and parts of Bengal. Anti-Congress forces, encouraged by the Government, were raising their heads. A general election was due at the end of the year. And just when the party needed a united front, the Congress Socialists were embarrassing the leadership, talking of class war, frightening off potential supporters, and making new enemies. The slogans of class struggle against moneylenders and landlords by Kisan Sabhas and socialist conferences all over the country could prove costly to the Congress at a general election in which barely 10 per cent of the population was entitled to vote. A peasants' conference in Andhra had gone so far as to demand for Congress legislators freedom to vote on issues concerning the peasants.[42] This was a demand which cut at the very root of party discipline; Nehru, who was the Congress President, rejected it out of hand. Nevertheless, it revealed a dangerous drift towards disintegration, which had to be checked, if the Congress was to survive as a strong and effective instrument to fight British imperialism.

It was thus not only ideological differences, but conflicting readings of the political situation which brought on the crisis in the Congress executive. Perhaps, even more important was the mistrust between the Old Guard and the Congress Socialists. Each feared being edged out of the party. Nehru suspected that there was a conspiracy to destroy him politically. 'When I reached Bombay', he wrote to Gandhi on 5 July 1936, 'many people stared hard at me, hardly believing that I was still politically alive.' Gandhi was not, of course, a party to such a plot. He resolved the crisis with admirable speed, skill, and firmness. He insisted on the withdrawal of the resignations, and vetoed the reference of the dispute to the All India Congress Committee on the grounds that a public discussion would only aggravate and distort the differences among the leaders, confuse and demoralize the rank and file, and ruin the party's prospects at the election. 'I am firmly of opinion', the Mahatma wrote, 'that during the remainder of the year all wrangling should cease and no resignations should take place.' He played down the crisis, described it as a tragi-comedy,[43] and pulled up Nehru for his edginess: 'If they [members of the Congress Working Committee] are guilty of intolerance, you have more than your share of it. The country should not be made to suffer for your mutual intolerance.'[44] Though as late as November 1936 Edward Thompson was predicting that the Congress would split and 'Nehru will lead a group into the wilderness',[45] the crisis was really over.

Nehru was prudent enough not to heed the advice of the

hotheads among his admirers, who were urging him to extreme courses. If he had broken with Gandhi and the Congress in 1936, he would have dealt a blow not only to the Congress, but to his own political future. It was obvious that so long as Gandhi remained at the helm of the Congress, it was unlikely that any rival nationalist party could emerge or compete with it. Nehru could sway crowds, inspire intellectuals, reel off press statements and articles, run the AICC office, and travel from one end of the country to the other, but he was unsuited for the role of party manager. He did not have Gandhi's gift for discovering, training, and harnessing to the national cause men and women of varying abilities and temperaments. 'I function individually', he told Subhas Bose, 'without any group or any person to support me.'[46] This detachment, admirable in its own way, limited his room for manoeuvre within the party. When Bose reproached him for not backing him up against Gandhi, Nehru frankly said that a head-on collision with the Mahatma was likely to be suicidal. 'The Left', he warned Bose, 'was not strong enough to shoulder the burden by itself, and when a real contest came in the Congress, it would lose and then there would be a reaction against it.' Bose could win the election and become Congress President against Pattabhi Sitaramayya, but Nehru doubted whether Bose could carry the Congress in a clear contest with what was called Gandhism. Even if he won a majority within the Congress, it would not ensure Bose sufficient backing in the country. And in any case a mass struggle against the Government without Gandhi was inconceivable. Finally, Nehru warned Bose that there were many 'disruptive tendencies' already in the country, and it was not right to add to them and weaken the national movement.[47]

What Nehru came to realize in 1938, Gandhi had seen two years earlier. An open rift in the Congress in 1936 would have crippled the Congress organization at a critical juncture, and would have been a godsend to the British Government. It was not by seceding from the Congress, but by influencing it from within, that Nehru was to push it in the direction in which he desired it to go.

It was during this crisis that Gandhi, with remarkable candour, revealed his reasons for supporting Nehru's candidacy for the Congress Presidency in 1936, even though his ideas were in conflict with those of a majority of his colleagues in the party leadership.

'You are in office', wrote Gandhi to Jawaharlal on 15 July 1936, 'by their unanimous choice, but you are not in power yet. . . . To put you in office was an attempt to put you in power quicker than you would otherwise have been. Anyway that was at the back of my mind when I suggested your name for the crown of thorns.'[48] Thus it transpires that Nehru's elevation to the Congress Presidency in 1936 was not, as Hiren Mukerjee suggests, 'to imprison the socialist wave in a strong little reservoir of Gandhi's own making',[49] but to launch Nehru with a favourable wind on the wide and stormy ocean of Indian politics.

It is true that in 1936–7 Nehru could not have his way on two crucial issues: elections to the new legislature and the formation of Congress ministries. But, given Nehru's influence, the decisions on these issues did not dampen Indian nationalism. And the election campaign, largely because of the prominent part he took in it, had the effect of awakening the masses. Finally, when the Congress accepted office, it was on its own terms and not those of the British Government. The continual criticisms from Nehru and his social-ist friends had the salutary effect of preventing the Congress ministries from sliding into a bureaucratic rut. Nehru's Presidency thus decidedly gave a radical twist to Congress politics in 1936–7. Even E.M.S. Namboodiripad acknowledges that the presence of a left-wing leader at the head of the Congress 'enormously strength-ened the forces of the left; the ideas of socialism, of militant and uncompromising anti-imperialism, of anti-landlord and anti-capi-talist struggles . . . began to grip the people on a scale never before thought possible'.[50]

In 1936, as in 1928, Nehru had stooped to Gandhi, but he had stooped to conquer. It is true that he was not able to get his views and programmes accepted immediately, or in their entirety, but he was able to influence the final decisions much more from within the party than he would have been able to do if—like Subhas Bose—he had left it to plough his own lonely furrow.

## VIII

Gandhi's intervention had the effect of tiding over the crisis in the Congress in 1936. Jawaharlal continued as President and was in fact re-elected for another year. He was not, however, in step with his colleagues in the Working Committee. Gandhi sensed Nehru's unhappiness and irascibility. 'Somehow or other, everything I say and even perhaps do', he wrote to Nehru, 'jars on you . . . you must bear with me till my understanding becomes clear or your fears are dispelled.'[51] 'I can't tell you', he wrote on another occasion, 'how positively lonely I feel to know that nowadays I can't carry you with me.'[52] Often the Mahatma would seek Nehru's approbation for whatever he was doing. When sending a copy of one of his articles in the *Harijan*, he told him on 15 July 1937 'When you see it you will please tell me if I may continue to write so. I do not want to interfere with your handling of the whole situation. For I want the maximum from you for the country. I would be doing distinct harm, if my writing disturbed you.' A note on Gandhi's talks with Jinnah was accompanied by the exhortation to Nehru, 'not to hesitate to summarily reject it, if it does not commend itself to you'.[53]

The differences between the two men during these years were often on current issues, representing a difference of approach or emphasis. Nehru, for instance, was not entirely happy about Gandhi's interview with the Governor of Bengal on the release of the detenus, or about the embargo on Congress participation in popular agitation in the princely states. The slow implementation of the reforms by the Congress ministries vexed him, while most of his colleagues felt that he did not make a sufficient allowance for the limitations under which they worked. The activities of the Congress Socialists provided another cause for misunderstanding.[54] Some of them, who were close to Nehru, made no secret of their conviction that Gandhi was 'finished', that he was incapable of giving any further lead against the British Raj, that his technique of non-violence could not take the country to the final goal. After reading a book on the Russian Revolution, Rafi Ahmed Kidwai confided to Nehru: 'If we want to make further progress, we will have to make an attempt to destroy the mentality created by the CD (civil disobedience). . . . We will have to give up the present standards of scrupulousness, personal integrity, honesty and political amiability.'[55] Truth and non-violence, Narendra Deva told Nehru, were 'noble ideas. . . . But they are so much being misused today in India that the day is not far distant when they will stink in our nostrils.'[56] J.P. Narayan saw a real danger of the Congress being converted,

. . . from a democratic organization of the millions of the downtrodden people into a hand-maid of Indian vested interests. A vulgarization of Gandhism makes this transition easy, and gives this new Congress the requisite demagogic armour. . . . We are faced today with the real danger of Indian industry being made a synonym for Indian nationalism.[57]

It is not unlikely that what his friends were saying reflected Nehru's own inner misgivings at this time. The intellectual hiatus between him and Gandhi tended to blow up even small tactical differences into minor crises. But there were also basic divergences between their reading of the political situation. During the two years preceding the war, Nehru was disconcerted by, what seemed to him, the tendency of the Congress ministries to compromise with the existing order. He was dismayed by the lack of intelligent interest on the part of his colleagues in the developments which were hastening the zero hour in Europe. And he was almost driven to despair by their inability to grasp the significance of the National Planning Committee and its many sub-committees, which had under his guidance held as many as seventy-two meetings in twenty months. 'I have never been able to understand or appreciate the labours of the Committee', Gandhi blandly told Jawaharlal on 11 August 1939, 'I have not understood the purpose of the numerous sub-committees. It has appeared to me that much labour and money are being wasted on an effort which will bring forth little or no fruit.'[58]

Because of all these differences with Gandhi and most of the Congress leaders, Nehru felt 'out of place and a misfit', and welcomed an opportunity in 1938 to visit Europe for a few months 'to freshen up' his tired and puzzled mind.[59]

## IX

The outbreak of war in September 1939 added yet another strand to a complex situation. It set into motion forces which were to transform not only party alignments in India, but the structure of power in the world. It was also to reveal a fundamental cleavage between Gandhi and Nehru in their attitudes towards the war. 'Perhaps this is the most critical period in our history', Gandhi wrote to Nehru on 26 October 1939, 'I hold very strong views on the most important questions which occupy our attention. I know you too hold strong views on them, but different from mine. Your mode of expression is different from mine.'[60]

Nehru had been publicly hailed by Gandhi as his 'guide' on international affairs. It was at Nehru's instance that the Indian National Congress had denounced every act of aggression by the fascist powers in Manchuria, Abyssinia, Spain, and Czechoslovakia, and taken the Western powers to task for their policy of 'appeasement' towards the dictators. Nevertheless, Nehru had a lurking feeling that Gandhi had often accepted his viewpoint on international affairs 'without wholly agreeing with it'.[61] The Mahatma was second to none in his hatred of the tyrannies set up by the Fascist and Nazi regimes. He defined Hitlerism as 'naked ruthless force reduced to an exact science worked with scientific precision'. Gandhi regarded Nazism and Fascism as symptoms of a deep-seated disease—the cult of violence. He did not, however, believe that violence could be neutralized with counter-violence. Through the pages of his weekly paper, the *Harijan*, he exhorted the victims of aggression, the Abyssinians, the Czechs, and the Poles, to defend themselves with non-violent resistance. 'There is no bravery', he argued, 'greater than a resolute refusal to bend the knee to an earthly power.' Even after Hitler had swiftly overrun Poland in 1939, and Europe was gripped by fear and foreboding, the Mahatma continued to affirm that non-violence could serve as an effective shield against aggression.

Neither Nehru, nor the majority of the members of the Congress Working Committee, nor indeed the rank and file of the party shared Gandhi's boundless faith in the efficacy of non-violence. Clearly, Nehru did not view the war as an occasion for its assertion: the really important point was how the monstrous war-machine built by Hitler was to be stopped and destroyed before it could enslave mankind. Nehru had never accepted non-violence as a method for all situations or all times:

The Congress had long ago accepted the principle and practice of non-violence in its application to our struggle for freedom and in building up unity in the nation. At no time had it gone beyond that position or applied the principle to defence from external aggression or internal disorder.[62]

It soon became obvious that behind the façade of unity, the

Congress leaders had serious differences in their approach to the war. The primary motivation of radicals like Jayaprakash Narayan was anti-British, of Nehru anti-Fascist, and of Gandhi anti-war. These differences would have come sharply into focus, had the British Government under the influence of Churchill and Linlithgow not shortsightedly tried to 'freeze' the constitutional position for the duration of the war. So long as there was no question of effective Congress participation in the Central Government, the question of whether India's support of the Allies was to be moral (as Gandhi advocated), or military (as Nehru proposed), remained purely academic. There were two occasions, however, when the vicissitudes of war seemed to bring a *rapprochement* between the Congress and the Government within the realm of practical politics: in 1940 after the French collapse and in 1941–2 after the Japanese triumph in South-East Asia. On both these occasions Gandhi found that the majority of his colleagues were ready to switch from a pacifist stand to wholehearted participation in the Allied war effort in return for a reciprocal gesture by the British Government. The Congress parleys with Sir Stafford Cripps finally broke down not on the issue of violence versus non-violence, but on constitutional and administrative details of a provisional government for the effective prosecution of the war.

The period immediately preceding and following the Cripps Mission in 1942 was a testing time for Jawaharlal. He had little love for the British Government, but he was dismayed by its obstinate refusal to read the writing on the wall. Meanwhile, Indian public opinion was reaching the height of frustration. Between British folly and Indian frustration, the Allied cause, and particularly the future of the hard-pressed Chinese and the Russians, was trembling in the balance. In the aftermath of the Cripps Mission, Gandhi's decision to launch a mass struggle created a further painful dilemma for Nehru. The idea of launching mass civil disobedience when the war was on India's doorstep seemed at first fantastic. His mind was full of thoughts of citizen armies, home guards, and guerilla warfare to beat off the Japanese invaders. Deep heart-searching and anguish led him even to think of deviating from the Congress policy towards the war. It was with some difficulty that he was persuaded not to strike out his own line on cooperation with the Allies.[63] During the months of May and June, he had long talks with Gandhi, who wrote later to the Viceroy: 'I argued with him [Jawaharlal] for days together. He fought against my position with a passion which I have no words to describe.'[64] Eventually, Nehru fell into line with the 'Quit India' stand, even though he was conscious that it 'gave second place to logic and reason' and 'was not a politician's approach but of a people grown desperate and reckless of consequences'.[65] Nehru agreed to support the 'Quit India' policy, but before he did so he had persuaded Gandhi to agree that Allied troops would remain on Indian soil during the war, and the 'provisional' government of free India would throw all its resources into the struggle against Fascism. For Gandhi, with his passionate commitment to non-violence, this was, as Nehru noted, 'a bitter pill'.[66] Nehru's decision to support the Mahatma on the 'Quit India' movement was thus not really the one-sided compromise it was made out to be by some of his critics. M.N. Roy wrote:

Godly power of the Mahatma has overpowered the human wish of the romantic politician [Nehru]. . . . In vain has he dilated upon his differences and final agreement on fundamentals with Mr Gandhi, for throughout his whole career, he has blindly followed Mr Gandhi. In fact he has no independence of thought or action.[67]

What M.N. Roy failed to see was that in reaching a compromise Nehru did not make all the concessions. If the internationalist had given in to the nationalist in Nehru, the pacifist had given in to the patriot in Gandhi.

## X

After spending nearly three years in gaol, Nehru was released in June 1945 just before the Simla Conference convened by the Viceroy, Lord Wavell. This was the starting point for a series of triangular negotiations between the British Government, the Congress, and the Muslim League which culminated in the transfer of power and partition of India two years later. In these negotiations, the leading part was played by Nehru, Vallabhbhai Patel, and Abul Kalam Azad, but they remained in touch with Gandhi and took his advice. Only in the last phase of the negotiations, towards the end of 1946 and the beginning of 1947, when Gandhi was busy touring the riot-torn countryside of East Bengal and Bihar, did his influence on events become minimal. This may have been due partly to his absence from Delhi—the hub of political activity—and partly to the swiftness with which the political landscape changed during this period, catalyzed by the eagerness of the Muslim League to cash in on the British decision to quit India and the anxiety of the Congress for swift and smooth transfer of power. In the aftermath of the Muslim League's 'Direct Action Day' at Calcutta in August 1946, communal violence spread like a prairie fire, and threatened to engulf the whole country. At the centre the conflict between the Congress and Muslim League, members paralysed the Interim Government. As the danger of a civil war loomed on the horizon, Nehru, Vallabhbhai Patel, and most of the Congress leaders came to the painful conclusion that the partition of the country was a lesser evil than a forced and fragile union; that it was a worthwhile attempt to salvage three-quarters of India from the chaos that threatened the whole. Against this background the Congress Working-ing Committee mooted the partition of the provinces of the Punjab and Bengal in March, and accepted the Mountbatten Plan for the transfer of power (and the partition of the country as its corollary) in June. The final decision was taken against Gandhi's advice.

Michael Brecher has suggested that Nehru and Patel opted for the partition of the country because they were 'tempted by the prize of power'.[68] Human motives are rarely unmixed, but in the summer of 1947 partition seemed the lesser evil not only to Nehru and Patel, but to the entire Congress leadership, with a few exceptions such as those of Abdul Ghaffar Khan and Jayaprakash Narayan. Gandhi's eleventh hour proposal that the Viceroy call upon Jinnah to form an exclusively Muslim League Government was a bold gesture, but the Congress leaders, after their experience of association with Muslim League ministers in the Interim Government, were in no mood to endorse it. Nor did Gandhi's alternative of a mass struggle appeal to them. Struggle against whom? The British were in any case going, and the Muslim League with its calculated mixture of bluster and bullying was hardly susceptible to the moral nuances of satyagraha. J.B. Kripalani explained the predicament of even those who prided themselves on being Gandhi's blind followers. 'Today also I feel that he [Gandhi] by his supreme fearlessness is correct and my stand is defective. Why then am I not with him? It is because I feel that he has as yet found no way of tackling the [Hindu–Muslim] problem on a mass basis.'[69]

To Nehru and Patel it seemed in the spring and summer of 1947 that the Mahatma's idealism had outrun the needs of a critical and developing crisis, that the intransigence of the Muslim League and the mounting chaos in the country really left no alternative to partition, that to insist on unity under such circumstances was to court an even greater disaster.

Gandhi's rocklike faith in non-violence was admirable, but to most of his colleagues he seemed at the time an uncompromising prophet rather than a practical statesman. It was not for the first time that Gandhi found himself isolated. In 1940, the Congress had declined to accept non-violence as a shield against external danger; seven years later, it refused to embrace it as a shield against internal disorder.

Gandhi seems to have had a lingering regret that in the final stages of the negotiations with the British Government, he had been bypassed by Nehru and Patel.[70] Nevertheless, he lent them his powerful support at the crucial meetings of the Working Committee and the All India Congress Committee.[71] During the five and a half months which remained to him, he wore himself out in an effort to heal the wounds inflicted by the partition, and became in the words of Mountbatten, a 'one-man boundary force for keeping the peace in disturbed areas'. Gandhi was not the man to nurse a grievance, and there is no evidence to show that the events leading to partition created any permanent estrangement between him and Nehru.

As Prime Minister, Nehru continued to lean on Gandhi for advice and moral support during the latter half of 1947. A tragic reminder of this dependence came to Nehru within a few hours of the tragedy on 30 January 1948: 'I was sitting in my chair . . . worried about Bapu's funeral. The colossal problem that it presented baffled me. Suddenly, I said, let me go and consult Bapu.'[72]

Gandhi's death sublimated Nehru's relationship with him. The heroic fight of the Mahatma against fanaticism and violence in his last months, and finally his martyrdom burnt themselves into Nehru's soul. The memory of 'the Master'—as Nehru loved to recall him—was suffused with a fresh glow, and nourished by mingled feelings of love, gratitude, and guilt remained with him till the last. He told a correspondent in 1957 that he could not write at length on Gandhi as 'I get emotionally worked up and that is no mood to write. If I was a poet, which I am not, perhaps that mood might help.'[73] The awesome responsibility of running the party and the government perhaps gave him a fresh retrospective insight into the methods of the Mahatma, who had borne the burden of conducting the movement for nearly thirty years. The process of intellectual reconciliation had indeed begun in Gandhi's lifetime; this can be seen by comparing the *Autobiography* with the *Discovery of India,* in which the criticism of Gandhi's ideas has been considerably toned down. In the intervening decade, Nehru had gone a long way towards rediscovering not only India, but Gandhi.

## XI

The political equation between Gandhi and Nehru, extending as it did over a quarter of a century, was not static. It was continually evolving, and seeking a new equilibrium in response not only to the inner drives of two men of exceptional energy and integrity, but to the realities of the changing political scene in India. During the first ten years, the partnership was really between Gandhi and Motilal, young Nehru's role being that of a favourite and earnest disciple of the Mahatma. The Lahore Congress brought Jawaharlal to the forefront of national politics, but it was not until the late thirties that he really became a factor to reckon with in the higher echelons of the Congress. It is an indication of his rising political stature that while in the twenties his dissent was merely an inconvenience to the Congress establishment, in 1936 it brought the party to the verge of a split. He owed his position in the party and the country in a great measure to his own qualities: his high idealism and dynamism, tireless energy and robust optimism, infectious faith in the destiny of his party and his country, his glamour for youth and charisma for the masses. Nevertheless, it is doubtful if he could have reached the apex of party leadership so early and decisively, if Gandhi had not catapulted him into it at critical junctures in 1929 and 1936.

Gandhi knew that Jawaharlal was not a 'blind follower' and had a mind of his own. Their philosophies of life diverged widely, but they were at one in their desire to rid the country of foreign rule and its gross poverty and social and economic inequalities. Gandhi wanted to harness Nehru's great talents and energies and was confident of containing his impetuous and rebellious spirit. 'He is undoubtedly an extremist', Gandhi wrote soon after Nehru's election to the Congress Presidency in 1929, 'thinking far ahead of his surroundings. But he is humble enough and practical enough not to force the pace to the breaking point.'[74] Seven years later, on the eve of a serious crisis in the party, the Mahatma assured an English correspondent: 'But though Jawaharlal is extreme in his presentation of his methods, he is sober in action. So far as I know him, he will not precipitate a conflict. . . . My own feeling is that Jawaharlal will accept the decision of the majority of his colleagues.'[75]

To the question why two men with such diverse backgrounds, and temperament remained together, the simple answer is that they needed each other. In 1919, young Nehru needed Gandhi to provide an outlet to his passionate but pent-up nationalism, and Gandhi, about to enter the Indian political arena, was on the lookout for able lieutenants. He had already enlisted Mahadev Desai, Vallabhbhai Patel, and Rajendra Prasad. It is not surprising that young Jawaharlal should have caught the Mahatma's perceptive eye and evoked from the outset special consideration. Jawaharlal was to become Gandhi's link with the younger generation and his window on the world. Informed by study and travel, he became Gandhi's mentor on international affairs. His passion for clarity and logic often clashed with the Mahatma's intuitive and pragmatic approach, but he discovered before long that the Mahatma had an uncanny sense of the mood of the Indian masses, their potential and their limitations, and that his political decisions were in fact sounder than the explanations with which he clothed them. Nehru realized the indispensability of Gandhi's leadership and, therefore, never pressed his differences to an open breach with him. Whatever his inner doubts about the possibilities of non-violence for changing the hearts of those who wielded political and economic power, Jawaharlal felt certain that Gandhi was leading the country in the right direction. Indeed, realizing Gandhi's receptivity, flexibility, and unpredictability, Nehru continued to hope that eventually the Mahatma's weight would be thrown in favour of radicalizing India's politics and economy.

Whatever their political differences, it is important to remember that Gandhi's link with Jawaharlal Nehru transcended the political nexus. The Mahatma's extraordinary capacity to love and be loved was experienced by many of his colleagues and their families, but for the Nehru family he seems to have had a special corner in his heart. With Motilal his equation was that of a colleague rather than that of a mentor. Jawaharlal was doubtless a disciple, but a favourite one: the Mahatma's face shone with pleasure and pride in the company of young Nehru, whom he hailed as his son long before he described him as his 'heir'. Intellectual and political differences did not diminish Gandhi's affection, which was deeply reciprocated by Jawaharlal. There was hardly a major domestic decision—whether it was the treatment of his ailing wife, the education of his daughter, or the marriage of his sister—on which Jawaharlal did not seek the Mahatma's advice and blessing. It was to 'Bapu' that the family instinctively turned for solace in moments of grief. When Kamala Nehru was dying in Switzerland, Jawaharlal was cabling her condition daily not only to her mother in India but to Gandhi as well.

Gandhi had much less difficulty in understanding Nehru than Nehru had in understanding him. The Mahatma seems to have sensed almost immediately the deep loneliness, idealism, and restless energy of young Nehru even better than Motilal had done. Indeed, in the earlier years, Gandhi acted as a bridge between father and son. For Gandhi, the crucial test came when, after his visit to Europe in 1927, Jawaharlal suddenly seemed to have outgrown the political and economic framework of the party. Gandhi's reaction to young Nehru's rebellion was characteristic. He did not attempt to muzzle him. On the contrary, he encouraged him to be candid about the differences: 'I suggest a dignified way of unfurling your banner. Write to me a letter for publication showing your differences. I will print it in *Young India* and write a brief reply.'[76] Subsequently, when Jawaharlal was straining at the leash after signing the Delhi Manifesto welcoming Lord Irwin's declaration on Dominion Status for India, Gandhi told him: 'Let this incident be a lesson. Resist me always when my suggestion does not appeal to your head or heart. I shall not love you the less for that resistance.'[77]

Gandhi's refusal to impose his ideas on Nehru could not but have a moderating influence on Jawaharlal. The lack of resistance from the Mahatma reduced the incentive for an open revolt. Repeatedly Gandhi offered to retire altogether, and to leave the field to Nehru and others. Since Gandhi did not owe his influence in the party to any office, it made him the less vulnerable: it was pointless to seek to throw out a leader who was always willing to retire voluntarily.

It was not without much inner conflict and anguish that Nehru was able to reconcile the conflict between his mind and heart, between his own convictions and loyalty to Gandhi and the party. Yet nobody knew more than Nehru how much he owed to Gandhi. It was from the Mahatma that he imbibed an ethical outlook, a concern for the 'naked hungry mass' of India, and faith in peaceful and patient methods, and in good means as a lever for good ends, in argument and persuasion rather than in coercion.

The working partnership between Nehru and Gandhi lasted till the end, but their philosophies of life never really converged. In October 1945, a few months before the negotiations for the final demission of British power began, Gandhi wrote to Nehru: 'I am now an old man . . . I have, therefore, named you as my heir. I must, however, understand my heir and my heir should understand me. Then alone shall I be content.' The Mahatma went on to express his conviction that truth and non-violence could only be realized in the simplicity of village life and to envisage independent India, as was his wont, as a federation of self-reliant village republics. Nehru replied,

The question before us is not one of truth versus untruth and non-violence versus violence. One assumes as one must, that true cooperation and peaceful methods must be aimed at, and a society which encourages these must be our objective. The whole question is how to achieve this society and what its content should be. I do not understand why a village should necessarily embody truth and non-violence. A village, normally speaking, is backward intellectually and culturally and no progress can be made from a backward environment. Narrowminded people are much more likely to be untruthful and violent. . . .[78]

This scepticism about the feasibility of the rural Utopia, as outlined in the *Hind Swaraj*, was not confined to Nehru; it was shared by almost the entire Congress leadership, and the intelligentsia, who never learned to appreciate Gandhi's philosophic anarchism, unqualified commitment to non-violence, and criticism of science and technology, industrialism, and institutions of the West.

The argument between Gandhi and Nehru in 1945 on what

constituted the good society remained inconclusive, but Nehru adhered to the line he had always taken in public and private. 'We cannot stop the river of change', he had written in his autobiography, 'or cut ourselves adrift from it, and psychologically, we who have eaten the apple of Eden cannot forget the taste and go back to primitiveness.'[79] Hardly anyone affected surprise when, in Gandhi's lifetime, the Constituent Assembly set itself the task of framing a constitution for a strong nation–state, based on parliamentary democracy, with all the paraphernalia of a civil service, army, navy, and air-force, along with an infrastructure of modern industry. For Nehru and his colleagues the question in 1947, as a shrewd critic recently pointed out, was not that of 'personal loyalty' to Gandhi, but 'a matter of social perspective and principles . . . a choice between a strong industrial (and military) state versus a commonwealth of barely self-sufficient agricultural communities'.[80] Nehru chose the first, as indeed he had even said during the Mahatma's lifetime that he would.

Nehru would have been the last person to profess that he was following Gandhi's blueprint for an independent India during his years in power. Even if it had been possible to recognize such a blueprint, it could hardly have been adapted to the mechanism of the modern state. *Sarvodaya*, unlike socialism, cannot be legislated into existence. The changes it postulates in the minds and hearts of men can be better attempted through voluntary efforts and the example of devoted men, rather than through the authority of parliaments, cabinets, civil services, courts, and the police. In fairness to Nehru, it must, however, he acknowledged that he applied Gandhi's ideas as far as he could to the needs of a modern nation–state. In that process 'something of Gandhi was knocked out, everything could not be absorbed. But nobody absorbed so much of Gandhi as Nehru did or incorporated so much of him in the inexorable working of statehood.'[81] The spirit of Gandhi may be seen in Nehru's consistent respect for individual liberty and secularism, his rejection of violence and regimentation, and his determination to find a national consensus within the parliamentary system. Like Gandhi, Nehru had a deep concern for the small peasant, the landless labourer, and the industrial worker. The concept of Five Year Plans, though far removed from Gandhian economics, stressed the uplift of rural India and included programmes for community development, village self-government, and cottage industries. Indeed, the point has recently been made that the Planning Commission in India gave away hundreds of crores to subsidize village handicrafts, 'as a form of rural unemployment relief and as a tribute to Gandhi's sacred memory'.[82]

In foreign policy Nehru was not Gandhian enough to advocate unilateral disarmament of India, nor did he turn the other cheek to Pakistan and China. Nevertheless, throughout his years of office, he threw his weight in favour of non-alignment with military blocs, conciliation, peaceful negotiation of differences between nations, and the widening of the area of peace. The deep conviction with which, despite difficulties and rebuffs, he pursued these aims doubtless stemmed from his long association with Gandhi. During his twilight years, in a world darkened by growing cynicism, violence, and ruthlessness, Nehru was speaking more and more in Gandhian accents, pleading for the linking of the 'scientific approach' with the 'spiritualistic approach',[83] and warning the Planning Commission against the dangers of 'giganticism'.[84] And almost the last thing he wrote pointed out that while progress in science, technology, and production was desirable, 'we must not forget that the essential objective to be aimed at is the quality of the individual and the concept of *Dharma* underlying it'.[85]

## NOTES AND REFERENCES

1. Subhas Bose to Nehru, 4 March 1936, Nehru Papers (henceforth, NP), in Nehru Memorial Museum and Library, New Delhi (henceforth, NMML).
2. J.P. Narayan to Nehru, 20 July 1940 (NP).
3. Percival Spear, 'Nehru', in *Modern Asian Studies*, vol. I (Jan. 1967), p. 18.
4. M.N. Roy, 'Jawaharlal Nehru: An Enigma or a Tragedy', in A.B. Shah (ed.), *Jawaharlal Nehru: A Critical Tribute* (Bombay, 1965), p. 39.
5. Hiren Mukerjee, *The Gentle Colossus: A Study of Jawaharlal Nehru* (Calcutta, 1964), pp. 71–5.
6. B.R. Nanda, *The Nehrus: Motilal and Jawaharlal* (London, 1962), p. 23.
7. Tibor Mende, *Conversations with Mr Nehru* (London, 1956), p. 23.
8. Ibid., pp. 24–31.
9. J. Nehru to G.A. Lambert, Chief Secy, Govt of UP, 4 July 1921 (NP).

10. J. Nehru, *An Autobiography* (London, 1958 rpt), p. 77.
11. Ibid., p. 81.
12. Ibid., p. 86.
13. Gandhi to J. Nehru, 4 Jan. 1928 (NP).
14. Gandhi to Motilal, 3 March 1928 (NP).
15. Pyarelal 'Gandhi–Nehru: A Unique Relationship', in *Link*, New Delhi, 30 May 1965.
16. J. Nehru, *An Autobiography*, p. 194.
17. Quoted in D.G. Tendulkar, *The Mahatma* (Bombay, 1952), vol. 3, p. 31.
18. Gandhi told Lord Irwin (Halifax) that Jawaharlal had wept on his shoulder 'over this tragedy of the betrayal of India'. *See* Francis Watson (ed.), *Talking of Gandhi* (Bombay, 1957), p. 63.
19. J. Nehru, *An Autobiography*, pp. 257–9.
20. Ibid., pp. 129–30.
21. Ibid., pp. 370–1.
22. Ibid., p. 490.
23. J. Nehru to Gandhi, 13 Aug. 1934 (NP).
24. J. Nehru, *An Autobiography*, p. 403.
25. J. Nehru to Colonel J.C. Wedgewood, 23 April 1941 (NP).
26. Nehru, *An Autobiography*, p. 547.
27. Ibid., p. 544.
28. Ibid., p. 525.
29. Quoted in *Indian Annual Register*, 1933, vol. 2, p. 358.
30. According to J.B. Kripalani, but for the powerful backing of Gandhi, the resolution had at that time little chance of being accepted by the Congress leadership. J.B. Kripalani, *Indian National Congress* (Bombay, 1946), p. 12.
31. Narendra Deva to J. Nehru, 9 Feb. 1929 (NP).
32. J.P. Narayan, *Why Socialism?* (Benares, 1936), p. 84.
33. Hari Kishore Singh, *A History of Praja Socialist Party* (Lucknow, 1959), p. 42.
34. Narendra Deva, *Socialism and the National Revolution* (Bombay, 1946), p. 28.
35. Sampurnanand, *Memories and Reflections* (Bombay, 1962), p. 77.
36. Telegram, Govt of India to the Secy of State for India, 24 Oct. 1933, Home Pol. Confdl F. 31 of 1933 (NAI).
37. Quoted in Shanti S. Gupta, *The Economic Philosophy of Mahatma Gandhi* (Delhi, n.d.), p. 136.
38. *Indian Annual Register*, 1936, vol. 2, p. 238.
39. J. Nehru, *An Autobiography*, p. 515.
40. J. Nehru to Sri Prakasa, 3 May 1936 (NP).
41. J. Nehru to Syed Mahmud, 5 May 1936 (NP).
42. *Indian Annual Register*, 1936, vol. 2, p. 285.

43. Gandhi to J. Nehru, 15 July 1936 (NP).
44. Ibid., 8 July 1936.
45. *News Chronicle,* 12 Nov. 1936.
46. J. Nehru to Subhas Bose, 4 Feb. 1939 (NP).
47. Ibid., 3 April 1939.
48. Gandhi to J. Nehru, 15 July 1936 (NP).
49. Mukerjee, *The Gentle Colossus,* p. 71.
50. E.M.S. Namboodiripad, *The Mahatma and the Ism* (New Delhi, 1958), p. 74.
51. Gandhi to J. Nehru, 5 April 1937 (NP).
52. Ibid., 25 April 1938.
53. Ibid., 30 April 1938.
54. On 30 July 1937, Gandhi sent Jawaharlal extracts from a speech of Yusuf Meherally with the remark, '[it] is an eye-opener for me. I wonder how far it represents the general socialist view. . . . I call it a bad speech of which you should take note. This is going contrary to Congress Policy'. (NP).
55. Rafi Ahmed Kidwai to J. Nehru (undated) (NP).
56. Narendra Deva to J. Nehru, 10 Dec. 1937 (NP).
57. J.P. Narayan to J. Nehru, 23 Nov. 1938 (NP).
58. Gandhi to J. Nehru, 11 Aug. 1939 (NP).
59. J. Nehru to Gandhi, 28 April 1938 (NP).
60. Gandhi to J. Nehru, 26 Oct. 1939 (NP).
61. J. Nehru to Subhas Bose, 4 Feb. 1939 (NP).
62. J. Nehru, *The Discovery of India* (Calcutta, 1946), p. 536.
63. Abul Kalam Azad, *India Wins Freedom* (Bombay, 1959), p. 65.
64. Quoted in Michael Brecher, *Nehru: A Political Biography* (London, 1959), p. 286.
65. J. Nehru, *The Discovery of India,* pp. 576–7.
66. Ibid., p. 576.
67. *Dawn,* 28 June 1942.
68. Brecher, *Nehru: A Political Biography,* p. 379.
69. *Congress Bulletin,* no. 4, 10 July 1947, p. 9.
70. Ram Manohar Lohia gives an account of the Working Committee meeting in his *Guilty Men of the Partition* (Allahabad, 1960), p. 9.
71. Pyarelal, *The Last Phase* (Ahmedabad, 1958), vol. 2, p. 251.
72. Quoted in Pyarelal, 'Gandhi–Nehru: A Unique Relationship', p. 32.
73. Mukerjee, *The Gentle Colossus,* p. 31.
74. *Young India,* 3 Oct. 1929.
75. Gandhi to Agatha Harrison, 30 April 1936 (NP).
76. Gandhi to J. Nehru, 17 Jan. 1928 (NP).
77. Ibid., 4 Nov. 1929.
78. Quoted in Pyarelal, *Towards New Horizons* (Ahmedabad, 1959), p. 5.
79. J. Nehru, *An Autobiography,* p. 511.

80. N.K. Bose and P.H. Patwardhan, *Gandhi in Indian Politics* (Bombay, 1967), p. 85.
81. M. Chalapathi Rau, *Gandhi and Nehru* (Bombay, 1967), p. 102.
82. Bose and Patwardhan, *Gandhi in Indian Politics*, p. 85.
83. *The Statesman*, 1 Dec. 1958.
84. Quoted in Shriman Narayan, *Letters from Gandhi, Nehru, Vinoba* (Bombay, 1968), p. 10.
85. Foreword by Nehru to Shriman Narayan, *Socialism in Indian Planning* (Bombay, 1964).

# 4

## *Playing for High Stakes*

### I

'I was always, like my father, a bit of a gambler,' Jawaharlal wrote in his *Autobiography*, 'at first with money, and then for higher stakes, with the bigger issues of life.' Ten years later, in another moment of self-revelation, Jawaharlal wrote in *The Discovery of India* that 'the call of action stirs strange depths within me, and after a brief tussle with thought I want to experience again "that lovely impulse of delight" which turns to risk and danger and faces and mocks at death.' Motilal Nehru seems to have noticed this trait in his son's character very early, and had a twinge of anxiety in 1907 on reading in the newspapers about disturbances in Ireland just when seventeen-year-old Jawaharlal was on a visit to that country.

Jawaharlal wrote to his father from Dublin on 12 September 1907:

In your last letter you asked me not to go near Belfast on account of the riots, but I would have dearly liked to have been there for them. About a fortnight ago there was a chance of our having similar scenes there, but to my mortification, the whole thing ended in a fiasco. The tramway employees were on the point of striking, and if they had done so, there would have been a little fighting in the streets of Dublin.

Jawaharlal's love of adventure occasionally resulted in perilous escapades. In the summer of 1910 he had the narrowest escape in the course of a holiday cruise to Norway. One day the party left the boat for an overland excursion; Jawaharlal and an Englishman, more energetic than the rest, were the first to reach a small hotel where the party was to spend the night. Tired and hot after the stiff climb—the hotel was nearly five thousand feet above sea-level—they expressed a wish for a bath. Somewhat bewildered by this unusual request, the hotel staff directed them to a stream nearby—a shallow but wild mountain torrent fed by a glacier. As they plunged into the ice-cold water, their limbs were nearly numbed; but worse was to follow. Jawaharlal's foot slipped, he lost control, and began to drift helplessly with the current. Fortunately his English companion managed to get out on to the bank, run along it, catch hold of his legs and pull him out. 'The exciting part of it,' Jawaharlal informed his father, 'lies in the fact that there was a mighty waterfall of about 400 feet quite near.' To Motilal there was nothing exciting in the incident; it is difficult to say whether he was more indignant at his son's recklessness or relieved at his miraculous escape. Jawaharlal was unrepentant; though the accident had not been of his seeking, he was highly pleased with the 'adventure and would not have missed it for a lot'.

Six years later, soon after his marriage, Jawaharlal had another miraculous escape from death while he was on holiday in Kashmir. After spending a few days in the valley, he went off with a cousin on a mountain expedition beyond Zoji-la pass. The two young men had neither the experience nor the equipment necessary for climbing high peaks. Stepping on to fresh snow, Jawaharlal slipped down a steep gorge and, for a critical moment his life trembled in the balance, as it had done in that mountain torrent in Norway. Once again, fate in the person of his companion pulled him back from the brink of death.

It may seem odd that Jawaharlal should have left his sixteen-year-old wife and gone off on a hazardous mountain expedition at such a time. But his spirit was too restless to be satisfied with the pleasant but pointless routine of many of his contemporaries. He needed a cause to live for, and die for. If he had been born thirty years earlier, he might have been one of Vivekananda's faithful apostles of reawakened Hinduism; thirty years later, he might have led an expedition to Mount Everest. In his forties, while in gaol, he wistfully recalled Walter de la Mare's lines:

Yea, in my mind these mountains rise,
Their perils dyed with evening's rose;
And still my ghost sits at my eyes
And thirsts for their untroubled snows.

For an Indian youth, in the stirring years of the First World War, the path of adventure led not to the solitudes of a monastery, nor to the slopes of unconquered peaks, but to the struggle against foreign rule.

## II

As a child Jawaharlal had 'dreamt of brave deeds, of how, sword in hand, I would fight for India and help in freeing her'. His letters from Harrow and Cambridge reveal a precocious but intense interest in politics and a pronounced bias in favour of the Extremist party in the Indian National Congress headed by Tilak. He conceived a great admiration for the Sinn Fein movement in Ireland. 'Their policy,' he wrote to his father, 'is not to beg for favours, but to wrest them. They do not want to fight England by arms, but to ignore her, boycott her and quickly assume the administration of Irish affairs.'

After his return from England Jawaharlal started taking an interest in the Congress politics of Allahabad, but found them uninspiring. He toyed with the idea of joining the Servants of India Society founded by Gokhale, in which members, subsisting on a pittance, dedicated themselves to the service of the country. But while he was attracted by Gokhale's personality, he was repelled by the politics of the Moderate party. In 1917, when the internment of Annie Besant stirred the stagnant pools of Indian politics, Jawaharlal was delighted. 'The atmosphere,' he recalled later, 'became electric and most of us young men expected big things in the near future.' However, Annie Besant's release, coupled with Edwin Montagu's declaration of August 1917, defused the political situation.

Gandhi's advent on the political scene in February–March 1919 focused young Nehru's pent-up nationalism, and opened up to him the visions of 'risk and adventure' for which his soul hungered. He was somewhat bewildered by Gandhi's political idiom, but captivated by his personality, which struck him as

humble and clear-cut and hard as a diamond, pleasant and soft-spoken. His eyes were mild and deep, yet out of them blazed out a fierce fire. . . . This little man of poor physique had something of steel in him, something rock-like, which did not yield to physical powers, however great they might be.

The Champaran agitation had revealed that the quaint little

man, seemingly so unworldly, possessed keen political acumen and a formidable political weapon. Gandhi's announcement of satyagraha against the Rowlatt Bills early in 1919 evoked an immediate response from young Nehru.

It is easy to forget that in the spring of 1919, Gandhi was an unknown quantity in Indian politics. His plan for satyagraha against the Rowlatt Bills instantly provoked a statement signed by a galaxy of senior Indian politicians charging him with undermining the stability of the society and the state. Jawaharlal's own father—who had been active in nationalist politics for more than a decade—was sceptical of the wisdom as well as the efficacy of Gandhi's method. 'The heart is a fool,' Motilal had once remarked, 'the only safe guide is the head.' Motilal did not like the idea of his son being imprisoned, and in March 1919 sought Gandhi's help in restraining Jawaharlal from extreme courses.

A year later, when an order was served by the United Provinces government on Jawaharlal, externing him from Mussoorie, his father exhorted him not to precipitate a crisis. 'The consequences,' he wrote,

are so obvious both from the public and private points of view that it is hardly necessary to discuss them. It will mean the final break-up of the family, and the upsetting of all public, private and professional work. One thing will lead to another, and something is sure to turn up which will compel me to follow you to the jail or something similar.

In the event, Motilal found that Jawaharlal was determined to go the Gandhi way. Having failed to pull him back, he decided that it was better for father and son to march together—even if it was to prison. At the Calcutta Congress in September 1920, the elder Nehru was the only front-rank Congress leader who supported Gandhi's non-cooperation programme. On returning from Calcutta, both father and son renounced their legal practice and made drastic changes in their way of life. Their house, Anand Bhawan, which had been the select club of the élite of Allahabad became a caravan-serai, visited by humble-looking Congress workers. In December 1921 both father and son were imprisoned in Lucknow gaol.

The tide of the non-cooperation movement, after rising high in the early months of 1922, receded, in the wake of the Chauri Chaura tragedy. Jawaharlal was disappointed but not dismayed.

Even gaol life had its peculiar compensations. He wrote in a letter to his father on 1 September 1922:

Ever since my return from England I had done little reading, and I shudder to think what I was gradually becoming before politics and NCO [non-cooperation] snatched me away from the doom that befalls many of us. . . . The life I led and that so many of us led, the atmosphere of the lower courts . . . the continuous contact with the sordid side of human nature—all this and the absence of organized intellectual life—gradually kill . . . the power of free thought. We dare not think or follow up the consequences of our thought. We remain in the ruts and valleys, incapable almost of looking up towards the mountain tops. . . . And so we live out our lives with little said or little done that beautifies existence for us or for others, or that will be remembered by anyone after we are dead and gone. That was the fate reserved for us also, till the high gods took us in hand and removed us from the ruts and placed us on the mountainside. We may not reach the top yet awhile, but the glory of wide vision is ours. . . .

In gaol Jawaharlal embarked on a course of self-education which was not only to equip him for his role in the freedom struggle, but make him one of the most distinguished writers of his time. Among the books he sent for from the Anand Bhawan library were two on western Tibet and the borderland. He confided to his father his plans to undertake, along with a friend,

a long pilgrimage as soon as Swaraj is attained. We have chalked out a beautiful itinerary. We go to Kashmir and Ladakh and Tibet. We pay a visit to the lovely Mansarovar Lake and Mount Kailash. And then we go through the famous cities of Central Asia, may be Afghanistan and Iran, Arabia and go to the West. . . .

## III

The metaphor of the mountains and the valleys which recurs again and again in Jawaharlal's writings symbolized not only his love of mountains, but his inmost yearning for a life of high adventure. After he had cast in his lot with Gandhi, and freed himself from the humdrum life of a lawyer, his consuming passion was the struggle for the liberation of India. The non-cooperation movement had so wholly absorbed and enwrapped him that (to quote from *the Autobiography*) he 'gave up all other associations and contacts, old friends, books, even newspapers except in so far as they dealt with the work in hand. . . . I almost forgot my family, my wife, my daughter.'

By the mid-1920s the national movement was in the doldrums, and Jawaharlal felt suffocated in the political and social framework of the Congress party. A visit to Europe in 1926–7 for the treatment of his ailing wife gave him an opportunity to widen his horizons. The Brussels Congress of Oppressed Nationalities brought him into touch with representatives of other subject countries of Asia and Africa; it also brought him the attention of the British secret service. A four-day visit to Moscow in November 1927 gave him an insight into the constructive side of the Soviet experiment—the massive and planned assault on poverty, disease, and illiteracy, the tremendous push towards industrialization and away from cramping customs and obscurantism.

Jawaharlal returned to India in December 1927. During the next twelve months, he was at loggerheads with the Congress establishment. He addressed conferences of students, peasants, and workers, and frontally attacked feudalism, capitalism, and imperialism. His advocacy of complete independence in 1928 disconcerted not only the British, but the older leaders inside as well as outside the Congress. The founding fathers of the Congress, Dadabhai Naoroji, Pherozeshah Mehta, Surendranath Banerjea, Annie Besant, and even Tilak, had all believed that India could realize her political destiny as a self-governing dominion within the British Empire. In December 1921, Gandhi had frowned upon a motion at the Ahmedabad Congress in favour of complete independence, and reacted equally sharply six years later against a similar resolution passed by the Madras Congress at Jawaharlal's instance.

So when Jawaharlal advocated complete independence for India in 1928 he seemed a dangerous radical, the *enfant terrible* of Indian politics, who had dared to question the implicit belief of most Congressmen and to go against even the inclination of the Mahatma. Above all, he was embarrassing his own father, who had accepted Dominion Status as a basis of an All-Parties Constitution in the Nehru Report. As the time approached for the Calcutta Congress in December 1928, Motilal did not like the idea of his report being rejected. During the closing months of 1928, tension in Anand Bhawan was at its peak. Braj Kumar Nehru, who was then a student in Allahabad and stayed in Anand Bhawan, recalls that Motilal told him one day, 'Father and son are atilt, but Jawahar would not be my son if he did not stick to his guns'. Motilal's irritability was exacerbated by the seeming impetuosity of his son, who was taking extreme positions, associating with young firebrands, and making himself an easy target for the government. 'If Jawaharlal lives for ten years,' Motilal told Braj Kumar, 'he will change the face of India,' and then added plaintively, 'Such men do not usually live long, they are consumed by the fire within them'.

It required great intellectual and moral courage to fight for the substitution of complete independence for Dominion Status as the goal of the Congress, However, in retrospect, it seems fortunate that Jawaharlal, backed by Subhash Bose, did so. The immediate result of this controversy was a resolution passed by the Calcutta Congress, at Gandhi's instance, giving the British Government 'a year of grace' to concede Dominion Status, or to face mass civil disobedience under Gandhi's leadership. Indian politics were thus lifted out of the depression of the 1920s, into another militant, albeit non-violent, phase in 1929–30. Jawaharlal helped to liberate his seniors in the Congress party from the magic spell of Dominion Status, and the spider's web of the 'safeguards' relating to foreign affairs, defence and finance, the princes and minorities with which the British Government sought to hedge Indian freedom. The concept of complete independence also fitted in with the proposal, which Nehru was to popularize, of a constituent assembly (and not the British Parliament) framing the constitution of independent India. It is true that India joined the Commonwealth in 1949, but she did so on her own terms and as an equal partner, and thus changed the character of the Commonwealth of the Statute of Westminster from a White Man's Club into a multiracial and multinational association. Nehru had played for high stakes in 1928 and won twenty years later.

IV

The courage with which Jawaharlal gave a radical twist to the struggle for freedom stood him in good stead when in 1946–7 he set out to chart the course of independent India's foreign policy. Nehru perceived that the wartime alliance of the Allied Powers had collapsed after the defeat of Germany and Japan. The Soviet thrust into eastern Europe had aroused the suspicion and wrath of the

United States and her West European allies. The American policy had developed into a crusade to create bastions of anti-communism in Europe and Asia. The Americans and the British expected that Nehru, with his commitment to democracy and humanism, would join this crusade. Among his colleagues in the Cabinet, the Congress party and the higher echelons of the civil and military services, there were many who believed that India did not have the military and economic might to play an independent role on the world stage, and that she could best ensure her national security and economic development through an alliance with the Anglo-Saxon Powers.

Nehru spurned the immediate gains of a Western alliance. He saw the post-war situation in its historical context. The author of *Glimpses of World History* knew how the pursuit of short-term national self-interest by nation-states had ended in disasters; a much greater disaster seemed a certainty if the same policies were pursued in the post-Hiroshima era. India was not a Great Power, but she was too big a country to become the satellite of any other; her refusal to align herself with any ideological–military bloc was thus simply an assertion of her newly-won national freedom. India had the right to consider each international issue as it arose on its merits instead of binding herself to the policies of any of the Great Powers.

During these early years the Soviet Union under Stalin nurtured little friendship for India. Nehru's sister, Vijaya Lakshmi Pandit, who was India's first ambassador in Moscow, was not even accorded an audience with Stalin. Communist China under Mao Tse-tung was also far from cordial towards independent India: in the Chinese Press Nehru was being lampooned as a stooge of Western imperialism.

Nehru's decision not to align himself with either block was an act of faith—in other words a gamble. Nehru knew that his independent stance would earn him brickbats from both sides. As early as 2 January 1947, in a letter to K.P.S. Menon who was representing India in China, Nehru wrote:

Our general policy is to avoid entanglement in power blocs and not to join any group of powers against any other group. The two leading groups today are the Russian bloc and the Anglo–American bloc, both inimical and extraordinarily suspicious of each other as well as of other countries. This makes our path difficult and we may be suspected by each of leaning towards the other. This cannot be helped.

It took a long time for the two superpowers to recognize that India's independent foreign policy had a constructive purpose and a positive role to play in international relations. India's relations with the Soviet Union improved with the advent of the Khrushchev era. In the West, with the passage of years, non-alignment ceased to be a dirty word. In 1974 Henry Kissinger, the American Secretary of State, in a lecture in Delhi paid a tribute to Nehru for perceiving the 'impermanence of the postwar world into which India was born—of frozen hostility between the superpowers and their insistent efforts to enlist other nations on one side or the other'. Fourteen years later, the Reagan–Gorbachev accords vindicated Nehru's pleas for and predictions of a *détente* between the United States and the Soviet Union. In the early 1950s, Nehru had stood out as a heretic in international relations; forty years later his ideas on defusing tensions, building bridges, and widening the areas of peace were to find wide, almost universal, acceptance. Once again his gamble had paid off.

# 5

## Nehru and Bose

### I

Among the India's nationalist leaders in the inter-war years, Jawaharlal Nehru and Subhas Bose were, after the Mahatma, the most charismatic figures. They seemed to have much in common. Both came from westernized homes; both were sons of successful lawyers who could afford to give them the best education available in India or England. Nature endowed them both with good looks and brains; their Cambridge degrees enhanced their pride and self-confidence. Both managed to escape the comfortable anonymity of the Indian Civil Service—the El Dorado of brilliant and ambitious middle class youth. Jawaharlal entered the legal profession and became his father's junior at the Allahabad High Court; Bose successfully competed for the I.C.S., but resigned from it within a year, concluding that it was impossible 'to serve both masters at the same time, namely, the British Government and my country'.

Both Jawaharlal and Subhas Bose were imbued with strong nationalist fervour while still in their teens. Jawaharlal's letters from Harrow and Cambridge reveal a strong nationalist streak, and deep sympathy with the Tilak school of extremist politics. The passionate patriotism of Subhas Bose had led to a clash with his British professors and his rustication from Calcutta's Presidency College for two years.[1] Eighteen months at Cambridge did not dampen his nationalist ardour. Stirred to his depths by the accounts of the non-cooperation movement, he threw up his job in the I.C.S. and decided to take his place in the fight for the freedom of his country.

It is a singular fact that both Jawaharlal Nehru and Subhas Bose entered politics at a high level; young Nehru at once became a favourite disciple of the Mahatma, and Bose did not take long to become the political heir-apparent of C.R. Das, 'the uncrowned king of Bengal'. By the late twenties, both Jawaharlal and Subhas were the heroes of India's youth and the *bêtes noires* of the British authorities.

Subhas Bose once described Jawaharlal as 'his friend-in-arms'.[2] Jawaharlal and Bose could indeed have become 'friends-in-arms', but circumstances conspired to prevent this consummation. Apart from their intellectual and temperamental differences, what divided them was their response to Gandhi's personality and politics. The leadership of the Mahatma, which had originally sucked them both into the vortex of nationalist politics prevented them from coming together.

## II

After resigning from the Indian Civil Service, Bose sailed for India and landed at Bombay on 16 July 1921. The same afternoon, he called on Gandhi. As he sat uncomfortably cross-legged in his western clothes on the floor of Gandhi's room in Mani Bhawan, Bose fired a a volley of questions at the Mahatma on the strategy and tactics of the non-cooperation movement. Bose, who had been lately reading the history of the Irish, Russian, and Italian revolutions, expected precise answers to his pointed questions. He was disappointed; Gandhi seemed to him confused or deliberately evasive.[3] The Mahatma's reactions have not been recorded, but he could hardly have initiated the twenty-three year-old self-conscious youth, fresh from Cambridge, into the mysteries of satyagraha in a few minutes. He advised Bose to meet C.R. Das. It is clear from Bose's own account of the interview that it was an unmitigated disaster; he was never able to develop empathy with Gandhi during the next twenty years; his attitude was to remain usually clinical, often critical, and occasionally antipathetic.

Bose followed Gandhi's advice, and went to see C.R. Das. 'By the time our conversation came to an end,' Subhas Bose recalled many years later, 'my mind was made up. I felt that I had found a leader and I meant to follow him.'[4] C.R. Das was a member of the

Congress Working Committee and the leader of the non-cooperation movement in Bengal, but his conversion to Gandhi's leadership and programme had been a painful process. At the Calcutta
Congress in September 1920 Das had been the sharpest critic of
non-cooperation.[5] Three months later, at the Nagpur Congress, he
had fought a last-ditch battle against Gandhi's leadership, and then
astounded friends and foes alike by announcing his conversion to
non-cooperation.[6] Uncharitable critics attributed his *volte-face* to
his recognition that the tide of public opinion was irresistibly
running in Gandhi's favour, and opposition to the Mahatma
was tantamount to political harakiri. Das became Gandhi's chief
lieutenant in Bengal, but his relationship with him remained somewhat uneasy. Subhas Bose tells us how Das was beside himself with
rage when in December 1921 Gandhi did not accept the Viceroy's
offer of a Round Table Conference, and in February 1922 when,
after the Chauri Chaura riot, Gandhi suspended his plans of mass
civil disobedience. It was Das who, along with Motilal Nehru,
headed the Swarajist revolt in 1922–4.

Subhas Bose had boundless admiration for Das, and in his autobiography repeatedly refers to him as 'The Leader':

. . . He was clear-headed, his political instinct was sound and unerring
and, unlike the Mahatma, he was fully conscious of the role he was
to play in Indian politics. . . . He was a practical politician. He knew
more than anyone else, that situations favourable for wresting political
power from the enemy do not come often and when they do come,
they do not last long. While the crisis lasts, a bargain has to be struck.[7]

Identification with C.R. Das helped to deepen Bose's own initial
doubts about Gandhi's political wisdom and style, and to destroy
whatever chances there may have been of his developing rapport
with the Mahatma.

### III

Jawaharlal's experience with Gandhi was very different from Bose's.
'I was simply bowled over by Gandhi straight off,' was his description of Gandhi's first impact on him.[8] In his *Discovery of India*,
Jawaharlal likened Gandhi's advent into Indian politics to 'a powerful current of fresh air that made us stretch ourselves and take deep
breaths, like a beam of light, that pierced the darkness and removed

the scales from our eyes'.[9] Jawaharlal not only fell under Gandhi's spell, but drew his father, and indeed his whole family within the Mahatma's orbit. Despite the twenty years and differences in their intellectual make-up which divided young Nehru and Gandhi, a strong bond of deep affection developed between them.

Jawaharlal completely immersed himself in the non-cooperation movement. Gandhi's suspension of civil disobedience after Chauri Chaura in February 1922 came as a shock to him. He did not, however, align himself with the Swarajist revolt. After Gandhi's release from prison in 1924, he was continually in touch with him, taking part in the promotion of khadi, and other 'constructive' activities which happened to engage the Mahatma's attention.

After his visit to Europe in 1926–7, Jawaharlal visibly outgrew the social and political framework of the Congress party. He denounced feudalism, capitalism, and imperialism, and advocated the organization of workers, peasants, and students. Jawaharlal's radical utterances inevitably jarred on Gandhi and the Congress leaders, including his own father. The elder Nehru headed an All-Parties Committee in 1928 appointed, in response to a challenge from Lord Birkenhead, the British Secretary of State for India, to draft a constitution for a self-governing India. The committee accepted Dominion Status as the highest common denominator among the various parties; its report was to come up for approval before the Calcutta Congress in December 1928. Jawaharlal considered acceptance of Dominion Status a climb-down for the Congress, which as recently as December 1927, had, at his instance, voted for 'complete independence'. Subhas Bose agreed with him; and in November 1928 they formed the 'Independence for India League' to carry on propaganda in favour of complete independence. As the time for the Calcutta Congress approached, Motilal Nehru wondered whether he would have the mortification of seeing the report bearing his own name repudiated by the very session over which he was to preside. He summoned Gandhi to his rescue. The Mahatma was unwell, but on Motilal's insistence, agreed to attend the Calcutta Congress. The crucial issue of Dominion Status versus independence was discussed behind closed doors in the Subjects Committee. The discussions were long, heated, and bitter. Gandhi proposed a via media: the Congress should formally adopt the Nehru Report in its entirety, including Dominion Status, but if it was not accepted by the British Government within two years, the Congress should opt for complete independence, and fight for it by invoking the weapon of civil disobedience. In deference to the young radicals, Gandhi reduced the years of grace to the British from two to one; an amended resolution giving London only twelve months to concede Dominion Status to India was moved and passed in the Subjects Committee, but Jawaharlal was absent and Subhas Bose did not take part in the debate. Three days later, when Gandhi's resolution came before the plenary session, Bose opposed it and was supported rather halfheartedly by Jawaharlal. The voting, 1350 for and 973 against, gave a clear majority to the Mahatma, but the issue hung in the balance till almost the last moment.[10]

Bose regarded Gandhi's resolution as 'an anti-climax'. He felt that the Calcutta Congress had 'set the clock back'; it had shirked its duty of launching a struggle against the British imperialists. 'While the country was ready', Bose wrote, 'the leaders were not'.[11] Jawaharlal's reaction was different; it did not take him long to recognize that it was not the Congress old guard that had won at the Calcutta Congress. There was little likelihood of the British Government conceding Dominion Status within a year, and in any case, a year was not too long a period to prepare the country for civil disobedience. Complete independence, instead of being the catch-word of a few young radicals, bade fair to become the battle-cry of the Congress. Above all, the way had been cleared for Gandhi's return to active politics after a lapse of five years.

Subhas Bose felt sore that Jawaharlal had let him down by failing to oppose Gandhi vigorously at Calcutta, and the political partnership that had developed between the two young radicals did not survive that Congress. Jawaharlal's election to the presidency of the Lahore Congress the following year widened the gulf between them. The election itself seemed to Bose to be a clever stratagem of Gandhi's to wean Jawaharlal from the left wing of the Congress.[12] Bose also fell foul of Motilal Nehru who was calling upon Swarajists to tender their resignations from the legislatures as a prelude to the coming struggle.[13] Bose's belief that Gandhi had prompted the elder Nehru to boycott legislatures was baseless; the truth is that the elder Nehru himself had been disillusioned about the legislatures and had sought Gandhi's assistance, first to discipline the Swaraj Party and then to disband it.[14]

At the Lahore Congress Subhas Bose constituted himself as a one-man opposition to the Congress Establishment. He clashed with Motilal Nehru, who was chairing the meeting of the A.I.C.C. on 27 December 1929 on the admission of delegates elected from Bengal, and in protest, along with his supporters, staged a walk-out.[15] Five days later, at the plenary session, Bose was up in arms against the exclusion of three names—including his own—from the newly-formed Working Committee. He again staged a 'walk-out' and accused the leadership of partisanship and lack of fair play. In a press statement he made a blistering attack on Jawaharlal, who had presided over the plenary session:

The action of the President which forced us to withdraw from the house was not the first of its kind. It was the culmination of a series of unconstitutional and undemocratic acts which could no longer be tolerated. From the very beginning the President had taken up an attitude against certain members of the House which was not only unfair but also vindictive. . . . The services of Mahatmaji had to be commandeered in order to carry the prepared list of names, as had to be done in the case of practically all the important resolutions in the All India Congress Committee as well as in the open session of the Congress. . . . Pandit Jawaharlal Nehru has now more in common with erstwhile friends of Dominion Status school than with his erstwhile colleagues of the independence League.[16]

It was at the Lahore Congress, that Bose moved a resolution advocating the formation of a parallel government by the Congress. Gandhi considered the proposal completely impracticable:[17]

I ask you to reject summarily the resolution of Mr Subhas Chandra Bose . . . I know that he is a great worker in Bengal. . . . If you think that you can have a parallel government today then, let me tell you that the Congress flag does not at present fly even in one thousand villages. All honour to those who favour this amendment but it is not bravery, it is not prudence, it is not wisdom. . . . You will establish freedom not by words but by deeds.

Throughout the Congress session, Bose was openly critical and contemptuous of the Congress leadership, and accused it of stage-managing the show; he denounced 'woolly thinking'; he demanded a precise plan of action for the struggle. To the Congress leadership, he seemed impatient and impractical—an incorrigible dissident.

## IV

Bose had differed with the Congress leadership at the Lahore Congress, but he was arrested before the Salt Satyagraha was launched. He was released after the Gandhi–Irwin Pact, which struck him as a great blunder. At the Karachi Congress in March 1931 he was critical of the Mahatma,[18] he was unhappy with Gandhi's handling of the whole issue of Round Table Conference in London. Early in 1932 the Congress was outlawed, civil disobedience resumed, and Bose again imprisoned. A year later he was released after a medical board found that he was suffering from tuberculosis of the lungs, and was allowed to proceed to Europe for treatment. He entered a sanatorium in Vienna in poor health and low spirits. The news from India was depressing. The Congress was wilting under the sternest repression in its history; civil disobedience had declined, and the British bureaucracy in India seemed triumphant. As Bose brooded over the sequence of events, he could not help feeling that Gandhi was responsible for the sorry pass to which the country had come; his suspension of civil disobedience, when it was on the crest of a rising wave, his agreement with Lord Irwin and his abortive trip to London for the Round Table Conference had given time to the Government to plan its blitzkrieg against the Congress. His campaign against untouchability had diverted the energies of the people into non-political channels. Bose expressed his ambivalence about Gandhi to a German couple he came to know well:[19]

There is nobody I admire and respect more [than Gandhi]. He has changed the face of India . . . Politically, however, I cannot agree with him any more. He has certain ways of dealing with the British, a certain tendency to compromise, a way of reconciliation with them, which endangers our political progress. We need firmer methods to force the British from the Indian scene and to gain independence for our country.

Bose was not content to express his scepticism about Gandhi's methods in private. He issued a statement jointly with V.J. Patel (a former Speaker of the Central Legislative Assembly and the

brother of Vallabhbhai Patel), who also happened to be in Europe
for medical treatment, asserting that Gandhi as a political leader
had failed and the time had come for radical reorganization of the
Congress on new principles and methods for which a new leader
was essential,[20] and that if the Congress could not undergo such a
transformation, 'a new party would have to be formed composed of
radical elements'. A year later Bose developed this thesis in a book,
*The Indian Struggle*, which purported to be the history of the
nationalist movement, especially of the decade and half of Bose's
own association with it. He acknowledged that Gandhi had transformed the Indian National Congress 'from a talking body into a
live and fighting organization . . . the most representative political
organization in the country', but he pronounced him a failure.
Bose's chronicle reads as a sustained indictment of the Mahatma:

> The asceticism of Gandhiji, his simple life, his vegetarian diet, his
> adherence to truth and his consequent fearlessness—all combined to
> give him a halo of saintliness . . . Consciously or unconsciously, the
> Mahatma fully exploited the mass psychology of the people, just as
> Lenin did the same thing in Russia, Mussolini in Italy and Hitler in
> Germany. As for the doctrine of non-violence, it had evoked some
> response in India, but in any other country such as Italy, Germany and
> Russia, it would have led Gandhi to the Cross or to the mental
> hospital. . . . Gandhi has ceased to be a dynamic force; maybe it was
> the effect of age.[21]

Gandhi had failed, according to Bose, because while he understood
the character of his own people, he did not understand that of his
opponents. Gandhi's ethical qualms, his habit of placing all his
cards on the table, and his refusal to employ diplomacy and
propaganda abroad, had handicapped him in his struggle with the
imperial power. Bose deplored the religious and moral overtones of
satyagraha, and the campaign against untouchability which had
distracted the people from the main political issue. He considered
the reaction against Gandhi's leadership as a 'rationalist revolt', and
quoted with obvious approval a remark by a Bombay Congress
leader, K.F. Nariman: 'How can we induce Gandhiji to rid himself
of this almost incorrigible habit . . . this perpetual blundering and
blending of religion and politics?'[22]

  *The Indian Struggle*—which was intended for a foreign audience—portrayed the Mahatma as an astute politician, who

maintained his hold on the Congress through the exploitation of mass psychology, clever manoeuvre, wire-pulling, and stage-management. Bose alleged that Gandhi had deliberately suspended the satyagraha struggle in May 1933 'under cover' of his three weeks' fast; and altered the Congress constitution in the following year 'under cover' of his retirement from the Congress.[23] Bose dismissed Gandhi's retirement in 1934 as a 'strategic retreat'.[24]

It is clear that Bose's lack of empathy with Gandhi hindered his understanding of the nuances of satyagraha and of Gandhi's methods and motives, and distorted his judgements on men and events. The 1929 Congress at Lahore, which is regarded as one of the most inspiring episodes in the saga of Indian independence, figures in Bose's chronicle as a record of Gandhi's cunning, Nehru's opportunism, and the pusillanimity of other Congress leaders.[25] Bose regretted that the Congress no longer had men of the calibre of C.R. Das, Motilal Nehru, and Lajpat Rai to check Gandhi's whims and fads. The Congress Working Committee had men of 'character, courage, patriotism and sacrifice', but few among them had the capacity to think for themselves or to stand up to the Mahatma.[26]

*The Indian Struggle* was published in London in January 1935. It was banned in India, but it is likely that some copies were smuggled into the country. Nehru read it when he went to Europe in 1935. The book's principal thesis, however, appeared in an article by Bose in the *Modern Review* of Calcutta in September 1935. 'Satyagraha had failed,' Bose wrote, 'the King's Government in India went on much as usual.' The British people had remained unimpressed by Gandhi's ethical approach. Bose quoted with approval the opinion of Romain Rolland, Gandhi's long-time friend and admirer, that if satyagraha failed in India, 'then the hard facts of life would have to be faced, and the nationalist struggle 'conducted on other lines'.[27]

There is no doubt that by the end of 1934 Bose was convinced that India needed more resolute leadership than Gandhi was capable of providing. Bose was heartened by the recent emergence of the Congress Socialist Party. If only Nehru, an avowed socialist and anti-imperialist, could be won over to the radical (or what Bose described as the leftist) cause, there was hope for militant nationalism. But the problem was how to secure Nehru's support. 'Gandhi is too good and too moderate in his views and his action', Bose wrote to a friend in February 1934. 'We want a more radical and more militant policy. Nehru's ideas are more in our favour, but in *action* he gives full support to Gandhi. His head pulls one way and his heart in another direction. His heart is with Gandhi.'[28]

Fortunately, in the winter of 1935 Bose, while still an exile in Europe, had an opportunity to exchange views with Nehru, who had been released to join his ailing wife Kamala in Germany. Dr Atal, Nehru's family friend and physician, testified to 'the keen and affectionate interest which Bose took in Kamala's health'[29] before Nehru joined her. Bose saw in Nehru a potential ally for wresting control of the Congress from the Gandhiites. In 1928 Bose and Nehru had collaborated in challenging the Congress Establishment on the question of Dominion Status versus Independence; eight years later they could again be allies in moving the Congress away from its conservative moorings. Bose urged Nehru to seize the opportunity which the Lucknow Congress, over which he was to preside, offered:

*Subhas Bose to Jawaharlal Nehru, Vienna, 12 January 1936:* . . . Please let me know if you come to a decision about your future policy. I should like very much to be closely associated with you in our Congress work in future. . . . The long conversations we had gave me the impression that there is so much on which we agree and possibly so little on which we disagree. . . .[30]

*4 March 1936:* . . . Among the front-rank leaders of today—you are the one to whom we can look up to for leading the Congress in a progressive direction. Moreover, your position is unique, and I think that even Mahatma Gandhi will be more accommodating towards you than towards anybody else . . . Please don't consider your position to be weaker than it really is.[31]

## V

Bose's overtures to Nehru were not made a day too soon. Nehru himself was far from happy with the state of the Congress party. Imprisonment and domestic affliction had kept him out of the political arena for nearly four and a half years. Gandhi was conscious of Nehru's popularity as well as his differences with the

Congress leadership. His feeling was that much of Nehru's discontent was due to his having been out of touch with the realities of the political situation. 'I would like you to allow yourself to be elected president next year', Gandhi wrote to Nehru on 12 September 1935. 'Your acceptance will solve many difficulties.' Gandhi was only confirming the offer which he had conveyed to Nehru a few days earlier through Jamnalal Bajaj just when Nehru was about to fly to Europe.[32]

The atmosphere at Lucknow Congress in April 1936 was surcharged with tension. Nehru knew that his Socialist friends were in a minority in the party, and he therefore included only three of them, Jayaprakash Narayan, Achyut Patwardhan, and Narendra Deva in the 15-member Working Committee, leaving the remaining eleven seats to the old guard, the so-called Gandhiites. But the new Working Committee found it hard to work as a team.[33] By the end of June the crisis came to a head. Seven members of the Working Committee sent their resignations to Nehru. The argument of these members was that it was premature and even suicidal for the Congress to raise the social issue when the principal political issue, that of Indian freedom, remained unresolved. The Congress party was still illegal in some parts of the country; its organization was in disarray; it had to contend, on the one hand, with inertia and internal dissensions and, on the other, with British hostility. Anti-Congress forces, such as landlords and feudal elements in the UP, were being bolstered by the government. A general election was due at the end of the year. The socialist slogans of class struggle could damage the chances of the Congress, because barely 10 per cent of the population—and largely the propertied class—was entitled to vote.

Gandhi saw that the drift towards disintegration needed to be checked if the Congress was to survive as an efficient instrument of the anti-imperialist struggle. He insisted on the withdrawal of the resignations of the members of the Working Committee, and ruled out reference of the dispute to the All India Congress Committee. He pulled up Nehru for his irascibility and directed that all wranglings should cease.[34] Thanks to the Mahatma's skill, the crisis within the Congress in the summer of 1936 was resolved before causing much damage to the party.

## VI

Bose had hoped to team up with Jawaharlal Nehru at the Lucknow Congress, but had been arrested immediately after he set foot on Indian soil. The Lucknow Congress passed a resolution protesting against his arrest and detention. Nehru issued a press statement supporting the observance of 10 May 1936 as 'Subhas Day' in protest against his arrest. Nehru also included Bose in his Working Committee. There were some friendly exchanges between them; Bose borrowed books from the Anand Bhawan library, and Nehru gave a letter of introduction to help Bose's nephew who was going to join Cambridge University.[35]

Curiously enough, even at this time when there was a wave of sympathy for him, Bose could not resist the temptation of taking a swipe at the Congress leadership. Before his arrest he issued a press statement in which he complained that the Congress Working Committee had declined to vest him with representative capacity for carrying on Congress propaganda abroad. Nehru, as Congress President, hastened to rebut the charge; he pointed out that Dr Rajendra Prasad, who had been president of the Congress during the preceding eighteen months, was certain that no communication had been received from Bose on this subject and, therefore, the question of its rejection by the Congress Working Committee had never arisen.[36] A few months later, Sarat Bose, Subhas Bose's elder brother, in a letter to Nehru, accused the Congress Working Committee of playing off the two Congress factions in the Bengal Congress against one another. 'I think you are unjust to the Congress Working Committee, and that you have drawn wrong inferences from what they have done or not done,' Nehru protested, 'I can assure you that there is not the faintest idea in their minds of setting up one group against the other. The one thing they have aimed at, rather helplessly it is true, is to bring various groups together.'[37] In reality, the Bengal Provincial Congress Committee had long been a hotbed of factionalism and intrigue. The five-year long antagonism between J.M. Sen Gupta and Subhas Bose, which had hamstrung the Bengal Congress, ended only with the former's death in 1933. The situation was complicated by feuds between volatile groups of revolutionaries who supported the rival Congress factions. The endless election disputes, recriminations, and charges of partisanship which Bengal Congressmen traded against each other baffled the Congress Working Committee.

In March 1937 the Government released Subhas Bose on grounds of health. On his arrival in Calcutta after five and a half years of prison, exile, and detention, he received a magnificent welcome. 'In future,' he declared, 'I intend to devote a good portion of my time and energy to all-India problems and activities.' Fortunately for him, the attitude of Gandhi and the Congress leadership softened towards him. They knew that he had been more or less a dissident in nationalist politics, but he had made great sacrifices and undergone great sufferings for the national cause. Gandhi saw something of the Bose family in 1937 during his visits to Calcutta for negotiations with the Bengal Government on the release of political prisoners. Bengal had suffered much during the Willingdon regime; if Subhas Bose was elevated to the Congress presidency for the Haripura Congress in 1938, it would be a gesture to Bengal. Gandhi may also have hoped that responsibility might have a sobering influence on Subhas, as it had on Jawaharlal. The Mahatma had some lingering doubts about the wisdom of making Bose Congress president; this is evident from a note he wrote on 1 November 1937: 'I have observed that Subhas is not at all dependable. However, there is nobody [else] but he who can be the President.'[38] When Subhas returned from Europe in January 1938, there was a telegram awaiting him from the Mahatma: 'Welcome home. God give you strength to bear the weight of Jawaharlal's mantle. Love.'[39]

Bose presided over the Haripura Congress in February 1938. In his presidential address he expressed his desire to mobilize 'the left forces'. He urged Nehru to agree to become general secretary of the Congress. Nehru declined. 'I was pressed hard to become general secretary this year,' Nehru confided to Krishna Menon. 'I could not tolerate the idea of having to deal with a tremendous amount of routine work which would have left me with no leisure. It was as much as I could do to consent to remain a member of the Working Committee.'[40] Nehru had other reasons too for not identifying himself too closely with Bose. He had serious misgivings about the views Bose held about the international situation.[41] While in Europe, Bose had met Mussolini, Goering, and other Fascist and Nazi leaders. In *The Indian Struggle* and in articles in newspapers and journals, Bose had advocated an 'unsentimental approach' to world affairs: 'whatever strengthens Britain is bad for us; whatever weakens her is welcome. This is realpolitik as they say in Europe.' Bose hazarded the prediction that the 'next phase in world-history will produce a synthesis between Communism and Fascism. And will it be a surprise if that synthesis is produced in India?'[42]

Ostensibly, there was nothing much to distinguish Bose's term as president in 1938 from that of his predecessors. He functioned as chairman at the meetings of the Working Committee. Decisions were taken by consensus, and whenever there was a serious difference of opinion, Gandhi's advice was sought. Such critical issues as the release of political prisoners, and the Khare episode in the Central Provinces in 1938, were handled in this way.

Though the minutes of the Working Committee do not reveal any serious divergence of views, it seems Bose was unable to develop a rapport with most of his colleagues. He did not hit it off with J.B. Kripalani, the general secretary of the All India Congress Committee.[43] With Vallabhbhai Patel, Bose became involved in a tortuous litigation on the custody of the funds left by Vallabhbhai's elder brother Vithalbhai Patel for propaganda in Europe. Bose was also unable to make friends with Nehru. D.P. Mishra, a Congress minister in the Central Provinces during the years 1937–9, tells us that Bose used to stay with him at Nagpur on his way to Wardha, and that 'whenever he complained it was neither against Gandhi nor Gandhi's adherents in the Working Committee, but always against Nehru.'[44] We know now that Nehru was not impressed by Bose's style as Congress President. 'Apart from principles and policies,' Nehru confided to Krishna Menon, 'Subhas's methods of work are difficult to put up with. He has paralysed the A.I.C.C. office and passes orders over its head in all manner of election matters and local disputes—these orders being flagrantly partial and against our rules or procedure.'[45]

Towards the end of his term as Congress president Bose gratuitously offended Gandhi. It appears that he had persuaded Gandhi to agree to the Congress party forming a coalition ministry with Fazl-ul-Haq in Bengal, but the Mahatma changed his mind after a meeting with Abul Kalam Azad, G.D. Birla, and N.R. Sarkar. 'It has astonished me,' Bose wrote to the Mahatma, 'that you did not feel it necessary even to consult me before you arrived at a decision on such a serious matter. .... The position, therefore, is that you attach more importance to the views of these three gentlemen than to the views of those who are responsible for running the Congress organization in Bengal.'[46] In reply to this rebuke Gandhi told Bose that he had only expressed his opinion on the facts presented to him, that the opinion was not binding on him, and that he was free to act just as he liked so far as Bengal was concerned.

## VII

The Tripuri Congress was to be held in March 1939. In November 1938 Rabindranath Tagore wrote to Gandhi and Nehru suggesting that Subhas Bose should be re-elected as Congress president. Gandhi told the poet that Bose needed to be freed from presidential responsibilities so that he would have time to 'rid Bengal [Congress] of corruption.'[47] A.K. Chanda, Tagore's secretary, wrote to Nehru that the feeling in Santiniketan was that 'there are only two modernists in the High Command, you and Subhas Babu.'[48] Nehru replied: 'Gurudeva seems to attach more importance than is warranted to the office of the Congress president. No major policy has been determined by the Congress President for some time past.'[49] Nehru who had been almost a permanent member of the Working Committee, and thrice Congress president, knew full well that Congress policies and programmes were determined by the Congress Working Committee and not by the president, subject of course to the approval of the All India Congress Committee and the annual Congresses.

It may be safe to assume that Bose was aware of the correspondence which had passed between Tagore, on the one hand, and Gandhi and Nehru, on the other. Meanwhile, informal discussions were going on among Congress leaders on the choice of Bose's successor, and opinion crystallized in favour of Abul Kalam Azad. Azad agreed to stand, but then changed his mind and suggested that the honour should go to the Andhra leader, Pattabhi Sitaramayya. Bose then announced that he would seek re-election. The announcement created a sensation. Never before in the history of the Congress had there been a contested election for the Congress presidency. After the results of the voting by the provincial Congress Committees became known, the usual practice was to attempt a unanimous choice with the consent of the Mahatma, and the other candidates retired from the contest. This had happened in 1929 when Gandhi and Vallabhbhai Patel had withdrawn and made way for Jawaharlal's election as president of the Lahore Congress. In the entire history of the Congress there had been only one instance in which the presidency had gone to the same person for two consecutive years: Jawaharlal Nehru, who had presided over the Lucknow Congress in April 1936, was again chosen to preside over the Faizpur Congress in December 1936. This could be justified on the ground that Nehru had not served a full year's term; the imminence of the general elections towards the end of 1936 was perhaps another reason for not making a change.

In his election manifesto Bose justified his candidature for the Tripuri Congress on the plea of 'increasing international tension and the prospective fight over federation'. He alleged that he was being opposed by the 'Right Wing' of the Congress because it feared that a leftist President would obstruct its designs for a compromise with the British Government. His allegations were repudiated by eleven members of the Congress Working Committee in a joint statement issued at Gandhi's instance. Nehru issued a separate statement of his own repudiating Bose's thesis.

The question of left or right [Nehru wrote] did not arise. Indeed, so far as Gandhiji was concerned, he expressed his wish repeatedly in my presence that he would like a socialist as President. Apart from my own name, he mentioned Acharya Narendra Deva's name. But . . . I did not like the idea of a socialist being President at this stage. I wanted the burden to be shouldered by those who were primarily responsible for the policy to be followed . . . I insisted, therefore, on Maulana's [Azad] name. There was, so far as I know, no desire on anyone's part to keep out a leftist as such or to insist on a rightist President.[50]

Bose had darkly hinted at a conspiracy by the Congress 'Right Wing to accept federation and even plans for forming of ministries had been prepared'. 'So far as I know,' Nehru wrote, 'there was never any difference of opinion in regard to federation in the Working Committee. Indeed, there was hardly any marked difference over any other matter, except to some extent about the formation of coalition ministries, on which Subhas Babu held strong views, which I was unable wholly to share. But this was hardly a matter of principle.'[51]

Pattabhi Sitaramayya was a prominent Congress leader of Andhra, but he was not so well-known outside his own province, and lost the election, obtaining 1375 votes as against 1575 votes polled by Bose.

## VIII

'A Defeat for Wardha', was the British-owned *Statesman's* summing up of the results of the Congress presidential election.[52] 'I must confess,' Gandhi said in a press statement,

> that from the very beginning I was decidedly against his [Bose's] re-election . . . I do not subscribe to his facts or the arguments in his manifestoes . . . it is plain to me that the [Congress] delegates do not approve of the principles and policy for which I stand . . . Subhas Babu . . . is now president elected in a contested election. This enables him to choose a homogeneous cabinet and enforce his programme without let or hindrance.[53]

Gandhi informed Nehru that, after the election and the way in which it had been fought, he felt he could best serve the country better by absenting himself from the Tripuri Congress.[54] Little did Gandhi realize that he was about to be drawn into the dispute between the ruler of the small principality of Rajkot, backed by the 'Paramount Power', and his subjects.

Meanwhile events moved fast. On 22 February, a fortnight before the Tripuri Congress, twelve members of the Congress Working Committee, namely, Abul Kalam Azad, Vallabhbhai Patel, Rajendra Prasad, J.B. Kripalani, Sarojini Naidu, Bhulabhai Desai, H.K. Mahtab, Jamnalal Bajaj, Abdul Ghaffar Khan, Shankerrao Deo, Jairamdas Daulatram, and Pattabhi Sitaramayya tendered their resignations. Nehru did not resign, but neither did he support Bose. Subhas had only one member of the Working Committee with him: his brother Sarat Bose. As ill-luck would have it, at this juncture Subhas fell ill. Accompanied by a doctor and a nurse he was carried in an ambulance to Howrah railway station for his onward journey to Tripuri on the night of 6 March. The following day, reclining in an invalid's chair, with a damp cloth over his head, and attended by the ladies of the Bose family, he presided over the meeting of the All India Congress Committee.

The Tripuri session was one of the most turbulent sessions in the history of the Congress, in which battle lines were drawn between Bose and the Congress old guard. The most controversial resolution of the session was moved at the meeting of the All India Congress Committee by Pandit G.B. Pant, the UP Premier, expressing confidence in the old Working Committee and enjoining President Bose to nominate his Working Committee with Gandhi's approval. The resolution had been endorsed by 160 members—a majority of the members of the All India Congress Committee. Bose ruled the resolution out of order on the ground that there was nothing in the Congress constitution or past practice to permit it. However, when the A.I.C.C. reassembled as the Subjects Committee of the Tripuri Congress a little later, Bose allowed the resolution to be moved, but suggested that a way should be found to ensure that it was passed unanimously. A number of amendments moved on behalf of Bose's group and designed to water down the resolution were, however, rejected, and the original resolution was passed with 218 votes for and 135 against it.

Later, when the resolution came before the plenary session of the Congress, Bose was too ill to preside, and Abul Kalam Azad officiated on his behalf. The decision of the Congress Socialist Party to abstain from voting ensured an easy passage for the resolution. The debate was long, heated, and acrimonious. The delegates from Bengal were agitated and angry. There were disorderly scenes. Nehru was heckled and prevented from speaking for an hour and a half until Sarat Bose intervened. And when Congress leaders, including Nehru, came out of the Congress *pandal*, they were met with hostile demonstrations.

Pant's resolution, with a stroke of the pen, deprived Bose of the fruits of his electoral victory. The old guard had turned the tables on him by making it incumbent upon him to form his Working Committee with Gandhi's approval. Ironically, Gandhi had no hand in the drafting or passage of this resolution, being deeply involved at the time in the Rajkot imbroglio. When he read the resolution a few weeks later, he considered it ill-conceived.[55] He advised Bose to go ahead, appoint a Working Committee of his own choice, formulate his own policies and implement them. 'So far as Gandhiites (to use that wrong expression) are concerned,' Gandhi wrote to Bose, 'they will not obstruct you. They will help you where they can, they will abstain where they cannot.' Curiously, it was

Bose, who now insisted on the enforcement of the Pant resolution, and pleaded with Gandhi to nominate the Working Committee. 'Knowing your own views,' Gandhi told Bose, 'knowing how you and most of the members [of the outgoing Working Committee] differ on fundamentals, it seems to me that if I give you names, it would be an imposition on you.'[56]

The deadlock created by the Pant resolution continued for nearly two months and the Working Committee could not be formed. When the A.I.C.C. met at Calcutta towards the end of April, Bose resigned. His resignation was accepted and Rajendra Prasad was elected to succeed him. Bose formed a new party, the Forward Bloc, to rally 'all the progressive, radical and anti-imperialist elements in the Congress'.[57] Two months later, Bose was up in arms when the All India Congress Committee passed a resolution curbing the power of the provincial Congress committees, and refused to hold elections to the Bengal Provincial Congress Committee, of which he was president. The Congress Working Committee, with the approval of the Mahatma, acted firmly; it decided to disqualify him from holding any elective office for a period of three years. In July 1940 Bose was arrested and detained by the Government under the Defence of India Act. He was released early in December on medical grounds. In January 1941 he slipped out of his house in Calcutta, and was soon on his way to Germany and Japan to seek the assistance of the Axis Powers in the liberation of India from British rule.

## IX

Nehru had anxiously watched the political storm of 1939 raised by Bose's candidature for the Congress presidency, and advised Bose against precipitation of a crisis. Though Nehru was extremely unhappy when Bose threw down the gauntlet to the entire Congress leadership, he refused to endorse the joint statement which Vallabhbhai Patel and other members of the Working Committee issued at Gandhi's instance. However, Nehru's own separate statement was no less critical of Bose. 'Personally,' Nehru declared, 'I do not see what principles or programmes are at stake in this election.'[58] He felt that Bose was talking rather loosely of 'left' and 'right' wings in the Congress:

Broadly speaking, there are two divisions (and this has practically nothing to do with right or left); those who might be called the Gandhiites and those who consider themselves modernists. . . . These two broad divisions must not be confused with right and left. There are rightists and leftists in both groups, and there is no doubt that some of our best fighting elements are in the Gandhian group . . . there is a small rightist fringe, a left minority and a huge intermediate group or groups which approximate to left-centre. The Gandhian group would be considered to belong to this intermediate left-centre.[59]

Nehru had a strong suspicion that certain 'adventurist elements' were instigating Bose. 'Subhas has gone off the rails,' Nehru wrote to Krishna Menon, 'and has been behaving very badly in many ways. His principal supporters are very irresponsible and unreliable people and it is quite impossible for me to join this motley group with whose viewpoints on national and international politics I do not agree.'[60]

Despite misgivings about Bose's attitude, Nehru made a conscious effort to affect a neutral stance. Minoo Masani, who was one of the leading figures of the Congress Socialist Party at that time, and was present at the Tripuri Congress, tells us in his memoirs that Nehru was 'as vague as ever. When faced with a difficult choice, he would be non-aligned. Subhas Babu was quite cynical about such an attitude and told us that Nehru was an opportunist, who thought about his own position first and then about anything else.'[61]

Nehru's stand at Tripuri stemmed not from vacillation or opportunism, but from his anxiety to bring the two groups together and to avoid a split in the Congress. He counselled moderation on both sides. On 17 April 1939 he wrote to Rajendra Prasad, seeking his good offices 'in solving this present tangle . . . it is essential that something must be done before the A.I.C.C. meets and we quarrel amongst ourselves and in public view'.[62] On the same day he remonstrated with the Mahatma, who was still preoccupied with the Rajkot problem and inclined to absent himself from the A.I.C.C. meeting at Calcutta, which was being convened to resolve the crisis in the party:

I realize [Nehru wrote] the importance of Rajkot, but I think you will agree with me that the larger issue is infinitely more important. . . . The idea that you will not attend the A.I.C.C. is alarming. That simply means that conditions should go on deteriorating, and that the Congress should go to pieces.[63]

Two days later, Nehru called on Subhas Bose. 'We had a long friendly talk,' Nehru informed his daughter, 'and yet from time to time I had a sensation that he was not fully aware of what I was driving at. This lack of awareness and sensitiveness of some people is terrible.'[64]

Nehru's efforts at conciliation did not earn him Bose's gratitude. In a letter to his nephew in England, Bose complained: 'Nobody has done more harm to me personally and our cause than Pandit Nehru.' In his postscript to *The Indian Struggle*, written in Europe during World War II, Bose accused Nehru of vacillation and 'riding two horses', and then joining the Rightist camp. The fact is that Bose's feelings towards Nehru had always been extremely ambivalent: admiration for his ability was mingled with deep mistrust of his motives. It is instructive to compare the autobiographies of these two men, both written at about the same time. While there is not one word of criticism of Bose in Nehru's autobiography, Bose's chronicle is punctuated with the harshest verdicts on Nehru. At the height of the crisis in 1939 the Bose brothers, Subhas and Sarat, could not refrain from flaying Nehru in long letters addressed to him. All this did not, however, prevent Nehru from pleading behind-the-scenes with Gandhi and other Congress leaders not to push Bose to the wall. Later, when Bose's expulsion was being considered by the Working Committee, Nehru, though not a member of the Committee, tried to intercede on Bose's behalf but without success.

In the spring of 1939 Nehru's efforts at mediation proved abortive. His last effort was a resolution at the A.I.C.C. meeting at Calcutta, asking Bose not to resign from the Congress presidentship but to reappoint the old Working Committee, with the addition of two of his nominees to fill the vacancies caused by the ill-health of Jairamdas Daulatram and Jamnalal Bajaj. Bose refused to be fobbed off with two of his own men in a committee of fifteen. He had proposed to Gandhi a coalition cabinet: seven members of the Working Committee and the general secretary to be nominated by himself, and seven members and the treasurer to be nominated by Patel.[65] Gandhi did not agree. A 'coalition Working Committee' between two antagonistic factions in it would have been paralysed.

Moreover, it was clear that Bose wanted a decisive voice in the running of the Congress organization. He did not want, he said, to be a 'puppet president'.

## X

1939 had been a critical year for the Indian National Congress and for Subhas Chandra Bose. The year had begun triumphantly for him with his victory in the presidential election but ended disastrously with his expulsion from the Congress. Bose himself claimed that he had been a victim of a political vendetta by the 'Gandhiites'. But he knew full well that he had himself provoked a crisis in the party, the gravest in its history since the Surat Congress of 1907.[66] He was too seasoned a politician to act on a passing impulse, or in a fit of pique. For several years, especially since 1933, he had been openly criticizing Gandhi and those whom he called the 'rightists' in the Congress. It is difficult to resist the impression that Bose had come to believe that he was India's Man of Destiny, whose mission it was to rescue the Congress from the feeble and incompetent hands of Gandhi and to liberate India from the iron grip of British imperialism. He believed that the British could be expelled from India with a mass upsurge—a final struggle— and that a golden opportunity for this struggle would arise when Great Britain became involved in a European war.

Early in 1939 the clouds of war were gathering over Europe, and it seemed to Bose that he had no time to lose. The retirement of Abul Kalam Azad from the presidential contest in favour of the colourless Pattabhi Sitaramayya was a godsend to Bose. He had been impressed by C.R. Das's maxim that situations for wresting political power did not come often and when they did come, they did not last long. Bose saw in the election an opportunity to establish his own credentials, to put the Gandhiites in their place, and to boost the morale of the 'Congress Left'. Bose was well aware that it was not easy to dislodge the 'Gandhiites' without dislodging Gandhi. In *The Indian Struggle*, he had candidly analysed Gandhi's vulnerability to a challenge from the Congress Left. After conceding that the Mahatma's popularity and reputation were likely to be lifelong (because they depended not on his record as a political

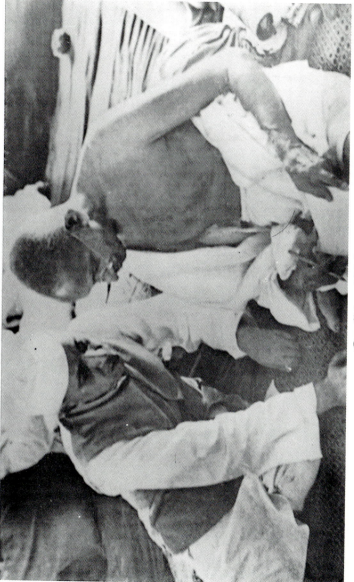

Gandhi and Nehru

Nehru and Subhas Chandra Bose

Nehru and Churchill entering
the House of Commons

Sarojini Naidu, Sardar Patel, Subhas Chandra Bose, Maulana Azad, Jawaharlal Nehru, *c.* 1939 (from left to right)

Nehru and Kennedy

Nehru with leaders of the Non-alignment Movement (from left)
Kwame Nkrumah (Ghana), Nasser (Egypt), Sukarno (Indonesia),
Tito (Yugoslavia)

Nehru with his daughter Indira holding a copy of the newly published
*Autobiography* (1936)

leader, but on his character), Bose discussed Gandhi's retirement and argued:

The Mahatma will not play second fiddle to anyone. As long as it will be possible for him to guide the political movement he will be there— but if the composition or the mentality of the Congress changes, he may possibly retire from active politics. . . . It is not improbable that in the event of the Left-wingers capturing the Congress . . . there will be a further secession from the Right. . . . But once the clarification [on an economic basis] takes place, his political following will be greatly affected.[67]

If Bose could win the election and give a demonstration of the strength of the Left-wing under his leadership, was it not possible that Gandhi would himself opt out of the Congress? Indeed this almost happened when, immediately after Bose's victory, Gandhi told Nehru that he would not attend the Tripuri Congress. If Gandhi had not been drawn into the Rajkot affair, he would have vetoed the Pant resolution. As it was, this resolution, sponsored by Patel and other members of the outgoing Working Committee, clipped Bose's wings by reducing the issue at the Tripuri Congress to a vote of confidence in the Mahatma's leadership. This strategy at once robbed Bose of the support of Congress Socialists which had tilted the balance in his favour in the election. The Socialists had no intention of challenging Gandhi's leadership and causing a breach in the Congress ranks. 'We Socialists,' J.P. Narayan remarked, 'do not want to create factions in the Congress, nor do we desire to displace the old leadership of the Congress and establish rival leadership. . . . We only want to influence the Congress decision.'[68] 'The Indian National Congress', he said on another occasion, 'was not a parliament, where opposing factions must oust each other; it was a "front" the unity of which could not be impaired.'[69]

If Bose hoped to repeat the feat of C.R. Das, the political mentor of his youth, by wresting control of the Congress from the Gandhiites, he had seriously miscalculated. The Swaraj Party was established while Gandhi was in jail, and two years later Gandhi handed over the reins of the Congress to Das and Motilal Nehru, not because he was in any danger of being outvoted in the All India Congress Committee or the plenary Congress, but because he wanted to avoid schism in the party at any cost.[70] Fifteen years later,

Gandhi's loyal lieutenants, 'the Gandhiites', were much more securely entrenched in the party, and the situation in India and abroad was much too grave to permit Gandhi to lightly walk away from politics. In the last resort, after two tense months, it was to Gandhi that all parties in the Congress—even Bose—looked for resolving the deadlock. Gandhi could do without the Congress, but the Congress could not do without him.

A letter written by Subhas Bose to his nephew at the height of the crisis in 1939 reveals both his initial sense of triumph after his victory in the election and his dismay after the Tripuri Congress:[71]

... you must have seen the accounts of the Tripuri Congress. The Old Guard had estimated that I would get 25 or 30 per cent votes at the [election] contest. ... They thought that [not] only was power (seven Provincial Governments) slipping out of their hands, but the Gandhiites as a body began to feel that their work of 20 years was undone in the course of a single day. ... Since Deshbhandu's time nobody had given them such a defeat. Then came Gandhiji's statement—he came to the rescue of the Old Guard and called their defeat his own defeat. Opinion among 'centrists' began to veer round. They were inclined to support us, but were not prepared to kick out Gandhiji—as they said.

In a résumé of these events, written in Europe three years later, Bose stated that by September 1938 he had become convinced that Gandhi had lost 'dynamism and initiative', and that India needed alternative leadership. Bose's comments on his victory in the presidential election were significant:

This was the first time since 1923–4 that the Mahatma suffered a public defeat and in his weekly paper, *Harijan*, he openly acknowledged the defeat. The election had served to show the wide and influential following that the writer [Subhas Bose] had, throughout the country, in open opposition to both Gandhi and Nehru.
... The Gandhi Wing was determined neither to accept the lead of the writer, nor to allow him to control the machinery of the Congress. ...[72]

Clearly, Bose had played for high stakes and lost. He had grossly overrated his capacity for effecting changes in the national leadership single-handed. There was no doubt about the immense popularity he enjoyed in his home province, but his sway even over the Bengal Provincial Congress had never been undisputed. In other provinces, while he had ardent admirers among the youth and leftist circles, he had very little support in the Congress organization. He failed to see the elementary fact that the vote in the presidential election against Pattabhi Sitaramayya was not a vote against Gandhi. Bose was justly sore at having been hamstrung at Tripuri by Pant's resolution. But when Gandhi unilaterally freed him[73] from the terms of that resolution, and allowed him unfettered choice of his team and policies to act on his own, he recognized that there was no possibility of his gaining a majority in the All India Congress Committee. He pleaded for a composite Working Committee in which he had an equal, if not predominant voice. But how did he expect those whom he had criticized day in and day out to work with him?

'If I had not taken to political life,' Bose wrote to a friend in 1934, 'I would probably have been a psychologist.'[74] The events in 1938–9, when Bose was in the centre of national politics, do not indicate that he possessed psychological insight of any depth. If he wanted to refashion the Indian National Congress, he had two options. The first was to influence the Congress from within, as Nehru was trying to do. The second was to attack the existing leadership and dislodge it. Subhas Bose was given an opportunity to adopt the first alternative in 1938, but he failed; he ended by alienating all his colleagues as well as the Mahatma. In 1939 Bose tried the second alternative, and again failed. He put the blame for his failure on his political opponents.

Of the fourteen members of the Congress Working Committee, Subhas Bose had been left with the support of only one—his own brother, Sarat. When he hinted at a conspiracy by his colleagues on the federation issue, Patel wrote to Nehru: 'The President . . . charged us with having entered into a conspiracy with the British Government. . . . Our enemies have . . . given credit for our honesty, not our President.'[75] In his letters to Gandhi, after the Tripuri Congress, Sarat Bose levelled wild charges against 'those whom the public look upon as your chosen disciples and representatives',[76] and accused them of carrying on propaganda, which was 'thoroughly mean, malicious and utterly devoid of even the semblance of truth and non-violence'. These rancorous diatribes revealed a curious lack of balance, and added to the difficulties of those who, like Nehru, were trying to arrive at a *modus vivendi* between Subhas Bose and the Congress Old Guard. And who were these men whose patriotism, courage, and bona fides were being called in question by the Bose brothers? They included Vallabh-bhai Patel, Rajendra Prasad, Abul Kalam Azad, Abdul Ghaffar Khan, and indeed all the stalwarts of the national movement. With Nehru, Bose's correspondence was so acrimonious that Nehru had to close it with the remark, 'I am sorry you find it difficult to understand me. Perhaps it is not worth trying.'[77]

## XI

The last word in this controversy rested with Gandhi. Kamaladevi Chattopadhyay, who had access to both Bose and Gandhi, tells us in her autobiography that 'obviously Gandhiji had developed deep suspicion of Subhas Babu, had probably heard that he could not be trusted, and decided he could not be expected to act with responsibility.'[78] Gandhi's distrust was based not on personal, but political considerations. As we have already seen, the Mahatma had some reservations about the offer of the Congress presidency to Bose in 1938; a year later, he was totally opposed to a second term for him.

The Congress leadership at the national level was a collective one, including as it did men of differing views, abilities, and temperaments, with Gandhi as an ultimate arbiter. In such a leadership, mutual compromises were inherent. Unfortunately, Bose had a rebellious streak in him which made it difficult for him to function as a member of a team. In Gandhi's view Bose lacked restraint and tact essential in the highest echelon of the party. Bose's previous record in Bengal had by no means been enviable; the Calcutta Corporation and the Bengal Provincial Congress Committee under his stewardship had continued to be a byword for factionalism and corruption. He was also handicapped by his delicate health and unmethodical ways.[79] Gandhi had a strong suspicion that Bose's belief in non-violence was tenuous,[80] and that his insistence on an immediate ultimatum to the British Government for the launching of a mass civil disobedience movement without adequate preparation exhibited a total lack of understanding of the technique of satyagraha. So little had Bose understood the nuances of satyagraha that in December 1929, at the Lahore Congress he had opposed Gandhi's resolution congratulating the Viceroy, Lord Irwin, on his providential escape when his train was bombed. Bose suspected that Gandhi's gesture had an ulterior motive: 'probably because he wanted to placate Lord Irwin and prepare the ground for a rapprochement in future'. Gandhi was exasperated by Bose's repeated calls for a mass struggle. On 2 April 1939 he wrote to Bose:

I see no atmosphere for non-violent mass action. An ultimatum without an effective sanction is worse than useless . . . But as I have told you, I am an old man, perhaps growing timid and over-cautious, and you have youth before you and reckless optimism born of youth. I hope you are right and I am wrong.[81]

Gandhi was convinced that Subhas Bose could not function within the ideology and discipline of the Congress. Bose's impression that Gandhi was being instigated against him by Patel[82] and others was mistaken. This was one crisis which Gandhi handled himself from beginning to end. When Bose was expelled from the Congress for indiscipline in August 1939, Gandhi made it a point to clarify in the *Harijan* that he had drafted the resolution (expelling Bose) for the Working Committee.[83] On the imperative need for discipline in the Congress, Gandhi had aired his unambiguous views on the Khare episode in the previous year when Bose was president of the Congress:[84]

Let us understand the functions of the Congress. For internal growth and administration, it is as good a democratic organization as any to be found in the world. But this democratic organization has been brought into being to fight the greatest imperialist power living. For this external work therefore it has to be likened to an army. . . . Therefore, the Congress, conceived as a fighting machine, has to centralize control and guide every department and every Congressman, however highly placed, and expects unquestioned obedience. The fight cannot be fought on any other terms.

After Gandhi inaugurated 'individual civil disobedience' in 1940, Bose wrote to him from prison offering the cooperation of his party, the Forward Bloc.[85] Gandhi turned down the offer. 'As for [the Forward] Bloc joining civil disobedience,' Gandhi replied, 'I think with the fundamental difference between you and me, it is not possible. Till one of us is converted to the other's view, we must sail in different boats, though their destination may appear, only appear, to be the same.'[86] Curiously, a few weeks before Bose offered his cooperation to Gandhi, he had confided to his brother Sarat, 'One is forced to wonder which is a greater menace to India's political future—the British bureaucracy or the Gandhian hierarchy'.[87]

Nirad C. Chaudhuri has suggested that Gandhi was the 'real inspiration and moving spirit behind the persecution of Bose', and was being driven by his 'insatiable love of power'.[88] The idea that Bose was the victim of a political vendetta was—and perhaps still is—widely current in Bengal where the conflict was seen primarily in personal terms—Gandhi versus Bose or Bose versus Nehru. This was not how the situation seemed to Gandhi, other Congress leaders, or even the British. It was not only Nehru who saw the Congress 'going to pieces'. The British-owned *Statesman* (28 April 1939) described the Congress as 'split from top to bottom'. The Viceroy, Lord Linlithgow, and his advisers expected—and indeed hoped for—a split in the Congress, and the emergence of the 'Right and Left Wing parties, working in somewhat different directions'.[89] For Gandhi the problem in 1939 was how to restore some coherence and discipline in the party, and to maintain it as an efficient instrument for the struggle against British imperialism. Gandhi, and indeed almost all the senior Congress leaders, agreed that Bose was not the right person to be at the helm.

Fifty years later, it is possible to take a more objective view of the crisis that rocked the Congress than it was for contemporary observers. Bose's decision to range himself against the entire Congress leadership of the day was a quixotic venture, foredoomed to failure given the alignment of political forces in the Congress party and the country. While Bose was second to none in his patriotism and self-sacrifice, he seems to have been deficient in political judgement, balance, and team spirit. Whether as mayor of Calcutta Corporation, as president of the Bengal Congress, or as president of the Indian National Congress, he tended to get bogged down in bitter and interminable, factional feuds, which detracted from his achievements. His grand plan for liberating India with the help of the Axis Powers was ill-conceived and did not work out as he had visualized; he discovered to his dismay that in the war strategies of the Fascist leaders of Germany and Japan, India's freedom was the lowest priority.[90]

Perhaps nothing conveys the heroism and pathos of Bose's life as a romantic revolutionary as his own comment on his first experience of leading a strike in his college at Calcutta for which he was rusticated for two years: 'I had a foretaste of leadership—though in a very restricted sphere—and of the martyrdom that it involves.'[91] For Bose it was to be martyrdom all the way.

## NOTES AND REFERENCES

1. Sisir K. Bose (ed.), *Netaji Collected Works* (henceforth *NCW*), vol. 1 (Calcutta, 1980), p. 78.
2. Subhas Bose to Mrs Kitty Kurti, 23 Feb. 1934, in Kitty Kurti, *Subhas Bose as I Knew Him* (Calcutta, 1966), p. 59.
3. Sisir Bose (ed.), *NCW*, vol. 2 (Calcutta, 1981), pp. 57–9.
4. Ibid., p. 60.
5. B.R. Nanda, *Gandhi, Pan-Islamism, Imperialism and Nationalism in India* (Bombay, 1989), pp. 232–6.
6. Ibid., pp. 237–8.
7. Sisir Bose (ed.), *NCW*, vol. 2, p. 123.
8. Tibor Mende, *Conversations with Mr Nehru* (London, 1956), p. 23.
9. J. Nehru, *Discovery of India* (Calcutta, 1946), p. 427.
10. B.R. Nanda, *The Nehrus* (London, 1962), p. 304.
11. Sisir Bose (ed.), *NCW*, vol. 2, p. 175.
12. Ibid., p. 188.
13. Ibid., p. 193.
14. B.R. Nanda, 'The Swarajist Interlude', in B.N. Pande (ed.), *A Centenary History of the Indian National Congress* (Delhi, 1985), vol. II, pp. 149–56.
15. Sisir Bose (ed.), *NCW*, vol. 6 (Calcutta, 1987), p. 102.
16. Ibid., pp. 105–8.
17. *Collected Works of Mahatma Gandhi* (henceforth, *CWMG*), vol. 42, p. 356.
18. Sisir Bose (ed.), *NCW*, vol. 2, p. 222.
19. Subhas Bose to Mrs Kitty Kurti, 23 Feb. 1934, in Kitty Kurti, op. cit., p. 59.
20. G.I. Patel, *Vithalbhai Patel (Life and Times)*, Book II (Bombay, 1950), p. 1219.
21. Sisir Bose (ed.), *NCW*, vol. 2, pp. 125–6.
22. Ibid., p. 295.

23. Ibid., pp. 290–1.
24. Ibid., p. 343.
25. Ibid., pp. 192–4.
26. Ibid., p. 67.
27. *Modern Review*, Sept. 1935, p. 322.
28. Kitty Kurti, op. cit., p. 59.
29. Dr Madan Atal to Jawaharlal Nehru, 24 April 1936 (NP).
30. NP.
31. Ibid.
32. B.R. Nanda, *In Gandhi's Footsteps, Life and Times of Jamnalal Bajaj* (Delhi, 1990), pp. 227–8.
33. Ibid., pp. 232–6.
34. Gandhi to J. Nehru, 8 July 1936 (NP).
35. Subhas Bose to J. Nehru, 9 March and 30 June 1937 (NP).
36. S. Gopal (ed.), *Selected Works of Jawaharlal Nehru* (henceforth, *SWJN*), vol. 7, pp. 205–6.
37. Ibid., p. 376.
38. *CWMG*, vol. 66, p. 285.
39. *Bombay Chronicle*, 26 Jan. 1938.
40. Nehru to Krishna Menon, 5 March 1938 (NP).
41. On 19 March 1935, Nehru noted in his prison diary: 'Subhas seems to be writing a deal of nonsense. He can only think in terms of being himself a Mussolini.'
42. Sisir Bose (ed.), *NCW*, vol. 2, p. 351.
43. J.B. Kripalani to Nehru, 14 March 1938 (NP).
44. D.P. Mishra, *Living An Era* (Delhi, 1975), vol. I, p. 307.
45. S. Gopal (ed.), *SWJN*, vol. 13, p. 711.
46. Bose to Gandhi, 21 Dec. 1938 in Nirad Chaudhuri, *Thy Hand Great Anarch* (London, 1987), pp. 480–1.
47. Gandhi to J. Nehru, 24 Nov. 1938 (NP).
48. A.K. Chanda to Nehru, 28 Nov. 1938 (NP).
49. J. Nehru to A.K. Chanda, 1 Dec. 1938 (NP).
50. S. Gopal (ed.), *SWJN*, vol. 9, p. 516.
51. Ibid., p. 517.
52. *Statesman*, 30 Jan. 1939.
53. *CWMG*, vol. 68, p. 359.
54. Gandhi to J. Nehru, 3 Feb. 1939 (NP).
55. *CWMG*, vol. 69, p. 207.
56. Gandhi to Subhas Bose, 29 April 1939 (*CWMG*), vol. 69, p. 180.
57. Subhas Bose, *Crossroads* (Bombay, 1962), pp. 179–80.
58. S. Gopal (ed.), *SWJN*, vol. 9, p. 516.
59. Ibid., pp. 511–2.
60. Nehru to Krishna Menon, 22 Feb. 1939 (NP).
61. Minoo Masani, *Bliss Was it in That Dawn* (New Delhi, 1977), p. 145.

62. J. Nehru to Rajendra Prasad, 17 April 1939.
63. J. Nehru to Gandhi, 17 April 1939 (NP).
64. J. Nehru to Indira Nehru, 22 April 1939 (NP).
65. Subhas Bose to Gandhi, 25 March 1939 (Gandhi Papers).
66. M.N. Roy wrote to Humayun Kabir on 30 July 1939 about 'Subhas Babu's ill-advised policy of forcing a premature split in the Congress' (M.N. Roy Papers).
67. Sisir Bose (ed.), *NCW*, vol. 2, pp. 330–3.
68. *Indian Annual Register*, 1939, vol. II, p. 5.
69. Ibid., p. 1.
70. B.R. Nanda, 'Swarajist Interlude' in B.N. Pande (ed.), *A Centenary History of the Indian National Congress*, vol. II, p. 129.
71. Subhas Bose, *Crossroads*, p. 112.
72. Sisir Bose, *NCW*, vol. 2, pp. 371–2.
73. Gandhi to Subhas Bose, 30 March 1939, *CWMG*, vol. 69, pp. 90–1.
74. Kitty Kurty, op. cit., p. 60.
75. Vallabhbhai Patel to J. Nehru, 5 Feb. 1939 (NP).
76. Sarat Bose to Gandhi, 21 March 1939 (NP).
77. J. Nehru to Subhas Bose, 11 July 1939 (NP).
78. Kamaladevi Chattopadhyay, *From Inner Recesses Outer Spaces* (New Delhi, 1986, p. 211.
79. Nirad Chaudhuri, who served as private secretary to Sarat Bose from 1937–41, tells us in his *Thy Hand Great Anarch* (p. 475) that 'no man could be more unmethodical in conducting business' than Subhas Bose. In Feb. 1929 Nehru wrote to N.S. Hardikar of the Congress Seva Dal: 'I am not surprised at Subhas Babu not answering your letters. He seldom does so. I have written to him at least five or six times in the course of last month, and I have had no reply. (*SWJN*, vol. 4, p. 130.)
80. Sisir Bose in his *Remembering My Father* (Calcutta, 1988, p. 99) tells us that in the 1930s, he had heard his father Sarat Bose and uncle Subhas Bose on 'the historical need of an armed struggle for the formal seizure of power.'

    D.P. Mishra who had been in Seoni prison with Subhas Bose in 1932 tells us that 'the only point on which we differed was the place of violence in our fight for independence. I could not share his view that terrorism could co-exist with Gandhian movements.'

    D.P. Mishra, *Living An Era* (Delhi, 1980), vol. 1, p. 211.
81. *CWMG*, vol. 69, p. 97.
82. Rani Dhavan Shankardass, *Vallabhbhai Patel, Power and Organization in the Indian National Congress* (Hyderabad, 1988), p. 182.
83. *Harijan*, 26 Aug. 1939.
84. Ibid., 6 Aug. 1938.
85. Subhas Bose to Gandhi, 23 Dec. 1940, *CWMG*, vol. 73, p. 457.

86. *CWMG*, vol. 73, p. 264.
87. Subhas Bose, *Crossroads*, pp. 326–8.
88. Nirad C. Chaudhuri, *Thy Hand Great Anarch* (London, 1987), pp. 527–8.
89. Linlithgow to Zetland, 30 Dec. 1939 (Zetland Papers).
90. This has been well brought out by H.N. Pandit in his *Netaji Subhas Chandra Bose from Kabul to Battle of Imphal* (Delhi, 1988).
91. *NCW*, vol. 1, p. 80.

# 6

## *Nehru and Religion*

### I

'English by education, Muslim by culture and Hindu by an accident of birth,' was a Hindu Mahasabha leader's description of Jawaharlal Nehru. Due allowance must of course be made for the malice of a political opponent, but the description has the plausibility of a half-truth. Jawaharlal himself made no secret of his antipathy to religion. 'I was born a Hindu,' he said in his presidential address to the Lahore Congress in 1929, 'but I do not know how far I am justified in calling myself one, or speaking on behalf of the Hindus.' Four years later, he confided to Gandhi that he was becoming more and more 'hostile to the religious idea' because it had become 'the negation of real spirituality' and 'a begetter of confusion and sentimentality.' He confessed that, out of deference to his old mother, he had occasionally participated in religious rites and ceremonials, but it had been 'an unwilling and ungracious participation'. Just then, he was having an argument with her over the choice of a bridegroom for his younger sister, Krishna. He did not see why she must marry a Kashmiri Brahman:

> The Kashmiri community, as a whole (there are exceptions of course in it) disgusts me; it is the very epitome of the petty bourgeois which I detest. I am not particularly interested in a person being a Brahman or a Non-Brahman or anything else. As a matter of fact I fail to see the relevance of all this; one marries an individual not a community.[1]

Jawaharlal was sharply critical of the Hindus' obsession with ceremonial purity, their 'touch-me-notism' and refusal to eat and drink with people of other castes. His hostility to the caste system was not surprising if we remember that his father, Pandit Motilal Nehru, had clashed with the orthodox section of the Kashmiri community in the 1890s. The elder Nehru had defied the caste taboos on foreign travel and, when threatened with social boycott, was disdainful, defiant, and even aggressive towards his critics. He kept open house for his European and Muslim friends as well as for high-born Hindu relatives and colleagues. He employed Muslim clerks and servants, had a smattering of Persian literature, and was fond of Urdu poetry. All this did not, however, add up to the adoption of 'Muslim culture', because during the two hundred years Motilal's ancestors had been settled at Delhi and Agra, and had imbibed the peculiar Indo–Muslim synthesis evolved during Mughal rule in dress and etiquette, art and literature, social customs—and even in superstitions.[2]

Specializing as he did in the law of Hindu inheritance, Motilal was not ignorant of the religion of his birth, but his was not a religious temperament; he was too absorbed by the daily struggle here and now to bother about the hereafter. He was a product of that late Victorian, free-thinking rationalism, which had learnt to dispense with divine explanations of the working of the universe, and pinned its faith on human intellect and on science to lead mankind along endless vistas of progress. His rationalism saved him from being swept off his feet by the tides of Hindu revivalism at the turn of the century.

If we must label Motilal, it would be safer to describe him as an agnostic rather than an atheist; his initial rebellion was not against the tenets of Hinduism, but against the superstitions and taboos with which it was encrusted. He would have wholeheartedly endorsed the reproof to Hindu orthodoxy administered by his great contemporary, Swami Vivekananda:

Our religion is in the kitchen. Our God is the cooking pot, and our religion is: 'don't touch me, I am holy'. I would rather see every one of you a rank atheist than superstitious fools, for the atheist is alive and you can make something of him.

Jawaharlal's mother, Swarup Rani was a deeply religious woman, as were two of his aunts who kept her company in the family home at Allahabad. The predominant influence on Jawaharlal, however, was that of his father. There was a brief interlude during which young Jawaharlal developed, under the influence of his tutor, Ferdinand T. Brooks, a fascination for theosophy, but he had already outgrown it by the time he left for England in 1905 at the age of sixteen.[3] The seven years he spent in that country decisively tilted the scales in favour of rationalism and agnosticism. His letters from Harrow and Cambridge do not betray the slightest interest in the religious or cultural lore of his homeland. When he returned to India in 1912 he was, in his own words, 'more an Englishman than an Indian'.[4]

Seven years later, after he fell under Gandhi's spell, Jawaharlal's life underwent a metamorphosis. He was (as he told the Hungarian journalist Tibor Mende many years later) 'bowled over straight off' by the Mahatma.[5] For a time it seemed that the transformation would not be confined to Jawaharlal's politics. He simplified his life, gave up smoking, turned vegetarian, and rediscovered a new fascination for the Gita. But his rationalist anchor held; we know that even during the euphoria of the non-cooperation and Khilafat movements their religious overtones jarred on him.

After the collapse of the non-cooperation movement, Jawaharlal was distressed by the religious tension and discord which disfigured the country. In prison he read and brooded over the problems of religion, culture, and politics, and sought to fill gaps in his own early education. By delving into the history of India he was re-rooting himself culturally, and at the same time bolstering his faith in Indian nationalism. He came to the conclusion that what had kept India going was not some secret doctrine or esoteric knowledge, but a varied and tolerant culture and a deep understanding of life. He dwelt with great pride on the philosophical and cultural achievements of his native land through the centuries, but was extremely wary of treading on metaphysical or spiritual terrain.

Any idea of a personal god [Nehru wrote] seems very odd to me. Intellectually, I can appreciate to some extent the conception of monism and I have been attracted towards the Advaita (non-dualist) philosophy of the Vedanta. . . . At the same time the Vedanta and other similar approaches, rather frighten me with their vague formless incursions into infinity.[6]

Was there such a thing as a soul? Was there survival after death? For Nehru this was mere intellectual speculation in an unknown region. Not that he did not sometimes have 'a sense of mysteries, of unknown depths, and the urge to understand it all', but he wanted to understand it 'rationally, through the methods of science'.[7] He could imagine himself feeling at home in 'the old Indian or Greek pagan or pantheistic atmosphere, minus the conception of god or gods that is attached to it'.[8] Equally attractive to him was the classical Chinese outlook, 'fundamentally ethical and yet irreligious or tinged with religious scepticism'.

It is significant that in his writings Nehru dwells on religion at length, but tends to treat it essentially as a vehicle of culture, not as an object of metaphysical exploration or spiritual seeking. He avows his admiration for the Gita, but qualifies it with the remark that it was not its religious, but ethical message which appealed to him. He writes of his love of the Ganga,[9] and in his will even asks for a portion of his ashes to be consigned to that river after his death; but he hastens to add that the suggestion was not inspired by any religious feeling, and that his fascination for the Ganga simply dated from his childhood days in his home town, Allahabad. Clearly, Nehru fights shy of acknowledging the slightest affinity to organized religion because it is equated in his mind with obscurantism. He deprecates all talk of going back to the Vedas by Hindus and of re-establishing Islamic theocracy by Muslims. These were 'idle fancies, for there is no going back to the past; there is no turning back even if this was thought desirable. There is only one way traffic in Time.'[10]

It is curious that Nehru's rationalism, verging on agnosticism and atheism, did not affect his proximity to Gandhi or detract from his popularity with the Indian masses. The Mahatma, who cared more for practice than the forms of religion, felt sure of a deep ethical streak in Jawaharlal. And as for the Indian masses, Nehru's integrity and repute as the Mahatma's chosen heir were sufficient credentials.

The question whether there was deep down in Nehru a hidden religious core would occur to any serious student of his life; it occurred to Dilip Kumar Roy, a disciple of Sri Aurobindo, soon after the publication of Nehru's autobiography in 1936. Roy felt a strong impulse to invite Nehru to Pondicherry to 'do yoga for a year to realize the divine harmony within him'. A similar offer to Subhas Chandra Bose had met with a rebuff. Roy feared that Nehru might react in the same way, and sought Sri Aurobindo's advice.[11] The reply of the sage of Pondicherry reveals a perceptive insight into Nehru's attitude to religion.

*Sri Aurobindo to Dilip Kumar Roy, 18 Sept. 1936*: He [Nehru] bears on himself a stamp of a very fine character, a nature of the highest *sattvic* kind, full of rectitude and a high sense of honour, a man of the finest brahman type with what is best in European education added. . . . But peace? Peace is never easy to get in the life of the world and never constant unless one lives deep within and bears the external activities as only a surface front of his being. And the work he [Nehru] has to do is the least peaceful of all. If Buddha had to lead the Indian National Congress—well! For the spiritual life there is perhaps no immediate possibility; his [Nehru's] mind stands in-between, for it has seized strongly the socialist dream of social perfection by outward change as the thing to be striven for, and has made that into a sort of religion. The best possible *on earth* has been made by his mind its credo; something beyond he does not believe in, something more here would seem to him a dream ·without basis I suppose.[12]

## II

'What is your religion?' Disraeli, the British statesman of the nineteenth century was asked. 'The religion of all sensible men', he replied. 'What is that?' Disraeli answered: 'Sensible men don't tell.' Jawaharlal Nehru might well have given the same answer if he had remained a private citizen. He might then have kept his disdain for religious orthodoxy and obscurantism to himself, or, as an Indian Bertrand Russell, vented it in barbed essays for the delectation of fellow rationalists. However, Nehru was destined to spend almost all his adult life at the centre of Indian politics, where it was impossible to ignore religious issues, because of their repercussions on the course of the nationalist struggle.

The Indian National Congress had from its inception claimed to speak for all the religious communities of India. This claim was disputed by the British authorities. What about the minorities? they queried. The British list of 'minorities' came in due course to include, besides Muslims, Christians, Anglo-Indians, Sikhs, Depressed classes, and even European commercial interests. The crux of the communal problem, however, was the future of the Muslim community. It was only natural that Muslims, the second largest religious community in India, should have entertained fears about their place in a self-governing and democratic India. It was also natural that the colonial regime should have played upon these fears. In the triangular battle of wits between British imperialism, Indian nationalism, and Muslim separatism, which began in the last quarter of the nineteenth century, the first round was won by the British with Lord Minto's assurances to a Muslim deputation in 1906 that led to the foundation of the All India Muslim League and the incorporation of separate electorates for Muslims in elected legislatures. However, in the second round, spanned by the Lucknow Pact and the non-cooperation movement, it was the Indian National Congress which had an edge on the government. The alliance between Gandhi's non-cooperation movement and the Khilafat agitation produced a spectacle of Hindu–Muslim unity which had never been seen before and was not to be seen again.

Jawaharlal Nehru did not like the religious overtones of the Khilafat movement and his worst fears were confirmed by its backlash in the form of communal tension and riots in the mid-twenties. When, at Gandhi's instance, he visited some trouble-spots in his home province, he realized his limitations as a mediator: his dispassionate and rational approach did not endear him to the warring groups. 'Whom would I represent?' Nehru wrote to Gandhi: 'the Hindus are not going to accept me, and why should the Muslims do so?'[13]

The Hindu–Muslim divide continued to weigh on young Nehru's mind, and he spoke and wrote about it time and again. He asserted that the cause of the rift was neither racial nor religious. There was, of course, great cultural diversity in India, but the differences were less on religious than on regional lines: a Bengali Muslim had more in common with a Bengali Hindu than with a Punjabi Muslim, and a Gujarati Muslim was probably closer to a Gujarati Hindu in his language, dress, habits, and customs than to his co-religionist in Tamil Nadu. Even the upper class Muslims in northern India, who seemed to think themselves apart from the rest of the country, bore, in Nehru's words, 'the impress of India on them all over the place, and were only superficially Persianized'.[14] Would any of them, he asked, be more at home or more in harmony with their surroundings in Persia, Arabia, or Turkey?

As Nehru saw it, the communal problem was the political creation of the upper class groups in various communities which had no relation to the basic needs of the masses. In the so-called 'unity conferences' in the 1920s and 1930s, leaders of various communities bickered over relative shares in jobs under the government and elective seats in legislatures, but they hardly ever got down to the consideration of the debt burdens on the agriculturists, the problems of the industrial workers, or the grievances of the lower middle class.

In thus dismissing religion as an irrelevant factor in national politics, it may seem that Nehru was impelled by his rationalist and—during the thirties—Marxist orientation. There was, however, little doubt that the communal problem in India was aggravated by the exploitation of religion for political ends. As Louis Dumont noted, the background of the men who organized the campaign for Pakistan was not Islamic law but Cambridge and Inns of Court;[15] at the other end of the political spectrum, the protagonists of Hindu nationalism were not overly religious. Indeed, V.D. Savarkar, for many years president of the Hindu Mahasabha in the pre-independence period, has left it on record that he was a practising atheist!

In his speeches and writings Nehru reverted again and again to the irrelevance of communal politics,[16] and looked forward to the day when religious labels would simply disappear, or at any rate cease to have any political significance. What had happened in Europe was likely to happen in India. Europe had had its wars of religion in which Christians had massacred Christians, but after attaining a measure of religious liberty, Europe had struggled for political liberty and legal equality; and then, finally, sought economic freedom and equality.[17] The real issues in India in the twentieth century were political independence and economic equality, but they were being obscured by the presence of the imperial power. Nehru believed that communalism had been overstressed and exploited for their own ends by the colonial rulers; it was synonymous with political and social reaction, and the British Government 'being the citadel of this reaction, naturally threw its sheltering wings over a useful ally'. The presence of the British, the 'third party', made an agreement between the two major communities difficult, because directly or indirectly it controlled all the levers of power and patronage.

Jawaharlal had a hand in the drafting of the Nehru Report in

1928, and had seen how difficult, indeed impossible, was 'the constitutional arithmetic' of reconciling rival claims by communal leaders to elective seats and government jobs in the future constitution of India. Several attempts at political 'pacts' between the communities having failed, Prime Minister Ramsay MacDonald gave a 'Communal Award' in 1932 which conceded almost all the claims of the Muslim minority. But as events were to show, even this Award did not end the controversies.

Nehru did not mince words in criticizing communalism, but his strongest denunciations were reserved for Hindu communal groups. In November 1933, he launched a blistering attack on the Hindu Mahasabha in a speech at the Banaras Hindu University. He accused it of cooperating with a foreign government for a few crumbs, and of bolstering the claims of Hindu princes and landlords. He could not, he said, imagine anything 'more degrading, reactionary, anti-national, anti-progressive and harmful than the present policy of the Hindu Mahasabha.'[18] Nehru's language may have been sharper, but his opposition to the Mahasabha had Gandhi's full support and that of the entire Congress leadership. The result was that the Congress was able to hold the Hindu Mahasabha and its allies at bay: they were unable to win a single seat in the 1937 general elections and their performance in 1946 elections, which influenced crucial decisions during the transfer of power, was equally dismal.

The more difficult problem, as Nehru and his colleagues were to discover, was that of containing Muslim communalism. Among Congress leaders no one was better equipped to win the confidence of the Muslim community than Nehru. His complete freedom from sectarian prejudice was well-known, as also his relentless opposition to Hindu communalism. He enjoyed the confidence of nationalist Muslim leaders such as Dr Ansari, Maulanas Mohamed Ali and Abul Kalam Azad, Asaf Ali, Syed Mahmud and Rafi Ahmed Kidwai. Young Muslim radicals, such as Sajjad Zaheer, Yusuf Meherally, and Z.A. Ahmad adored him. It was, however, not possible for a Hindu leader—even for Jawaharlal Nehru—to stem the tide of Muslim communalism all by himself. Nationalist Muslims included able and patriotic individuals, but they could not carry their community with them. Nehru had commented upon their limitations in his autobiography in 1934:

Many of those Congress Muslims organized themselves into a group called the 'Nationalist Muslim Party', and they combated the communal Muslim leaders. . . . But they were all upper middle-class folk, and there were no dynamic personalities amongst them. They took to their professions and their businesses, and lost touch with their masses. . . . Their method was one of drawing-room meetings and mutual arrangements and pacts, and at this game their rivals, the communal leaders, were greater adepts. Slowly the latter drove the Nationalist Muslims from one position to another, made them give up, one by one the principles for which they stood. Always the Nationalist Muslims tried to ward off further retreat and to consolidate their position by adopting the policy of the 'lesser evil', but always this led to another retreat. . . . There came a time when they had nothing left to call their own, no fundamental principle. . . .[19]

These limitations grew with the passage of time. Nehru did all he could to keep up their morale, and sometimes, went out of his way to do so, as is evident from a letter he wrote to Asaf Ali on Gandhi's campaign against untouchability.

*Jawaharlal Nehru to Asaf Ali, 12 Oct. 1933*: I am not at all enamoured of Harijan work though of course I am very keen on the abolition of untouchability. I realize that there is some feeling among the Muslims that the Harijan movement is aimed at strengthening Hindus politically. This is of course without foundation but nonetheless it is there. As a matter of fact the aspect of Harijan movement which appeals to me most is that it will weaken the Hindus in the sense that it will create split amongst them. I like such splits because they clear up the position and bring real issues before the public. It is a good thing that the orthodox section of the Hindus is showing its true colours and behaving politically as a most reactionary group.[20]

Nehru disputed the claim of Muslim communal parties, such as the Muslim League, to speak for the entire community, but he had to concede as early as 1933 that their views were of the 'dominant and politically clamorous groups among the Muslims . . . most of the leading members are government officials, ex-officials, ministers, would-be ministers, knights and title-holders, big landlords etc.'[21] Their leader was the Aga Khan, who combined in himself 'most remarkably the feudal order and the policies and habits of the British ruling class'.

Nehru put even Jinnah's leadership in the same category.

'Essentially, I think, the attitude of Jinnah and the Muslim League,' Nehru wrote to Syed Mahmud in 1942, 'is governed by the desire to prevent radical changes or the democratization of India, not because of a Hindu majority, but because the radical elements will put an end to semi-feudal privileges, etc.'[22] This might seem a harsh verdict on Jinnah but, if questioned, Nehru would have invoked some simple tests. Even if all of Jinnah's communal demands *vis-à-vis* the majority community were conceded, was he prepared to join a non-violent civil disobedience struggle, such as those the Congress had launched from time to time, to enforce the nationalist demands? Was he prepared to accept the principle of democratization of princely India and making all princes merely constitutional rulers of their States? Was he prepared to agree to the abolition of landlordism? Was he prepared to demand a constituent assembly to frame a constitution for India on the basis of adult franchise? Given the largely loyalist and feudal composition of the Muslim League leadership, it is doubtful if Jinnah's answers to any of these questions could have been in the affirmative in 1937 or even in 1942.

Meanwhile in 1933 Nehru had come out with a proposal whose novelty and the daring at first startled the government and most Indian politicians. It was, he said, for the people of India, not for the British Parliament to decide on the shape of things in independent India. He demanded a constituent assembly, elected on adult or semi-adult franchise, to frame a constitution for India. It was for this assembly to redefine the relations between India and Britain, and also to adjudicate on the claims of the minorities. Though he was opposed in principle to separate electorates, he was prepared to concede election to this assembly by separate electorates for those minorities who desired it. 'If the Muslim elected representatives for the constituent assembly', Nehru wrote, 'adhere to certain communal demands, I shall press for their acceptance.'[23]

Three years later, at the Lucknow and Faizpur Congress sessions over which Nehru presided, a campaign for the political education of the masses was launched, directed to all communities but especially to Muslims. 'Ours is a democratic association,' Nehru declared, 'and our objective is to fight the British imperialism'. The elections to the provincial legislatures in 1936–7 produced spectacular results, and enabled the Congress to form ministries in eight out of eleven provinces. The Congress did not, however, do well in Muslim constituencies; indeed it had contested very few Muslim seats. Nehru felt that the Congress had not done enough to put across its political and economic programme to the Muslim community and the political vacuum had been filled by communal and reactionary groups. In the event, his hopes from the mass-contact campaign were not to be realized, but for a while in 1937 the prospects of communal unity seemed to him promising. His optimism was reflected in an article he wrote in October 1937 for *Foreign Affairs*:

In India today no one, whatever his political views or religious persuasions might be, thinks in terms other than those of national unity. There are differences of course and certain separatist tendencies, but even these do not oppose national freedom or unity. They seek to gain a special favour for their group and because of this, they hinder sometimes the growth of the nationalist movement. Religious differences affect politics less and less, though still sometimes they distract attention. There is no religious or cultural problem in India. What is called the religious or communal problem is really a dispute among upper class people for a division of the spoils of office or of representation in a legislature. This will surely be settled amicably wherever it arises.[24]

Ironically, by the time article actually appeared in *Foreign Affairs* in January 1938, the process of the conversion of Muslim communalism into Muslim separatism had already begun. There was a widening of the gulf between the two communities, and an accentuation of the struggle between the Indian National Congress, British imperialism, and Muslim separatism which culminated in the simultaneous liquidation of British rule and the division of India in 1947. It is not necessary to recapitulate sequence of events in this last phase of the struggle and Nehru's role in them as they form the central theme of a separate chapter in this book.[25]

## III

Though Nehru had agreed to the partition of India under the compulsion of events in 1947 and did not accept Jinnah's two-nation theory, what resulted was the triumph of Muslim separatism and the defeat of nationalist and secular forces on the subcontinent. It did not take Nehru long to discover that the object for which the high price of partition had been paid was not achieved; the communal problem was no nearer a solution, and was indeed aggravated by the holocaust and mass migration of the minorities across the new borders between India and Pakistan, and by the armed conflict in Kashmir.

It was not surprising that, in the surcharged atmosphere immediately before and after the partition of the country, there was an upsurge of Hindu revivalism. Nehru became sharply aware of it when on 7 August 1947 he received a letter from Dr Rajendra Prasad, the President of the Constituent Assembly, on the widespread Hindu sentiment in favour of banning cow-slaughter.[26] This sentiment, Dr Prasad said, had reached a pitch at which it was difficult, if not impossible, to ignore it. Nehru replied to him the same day in a long letter explaining why he could not accept the suggestion. The fundamental issue, wrote Nehru, was whether independent India was to function as a 'composite country' or as a Hindu country. He did not deny the intensity of feeling among the Hindus on cow-protection, but rather than succumb to it, he was prepared to step down.[27] The threat seemed to have worked, and the crisis passed off without the public knowing about it.

The revivalist feeling in the majority community was continually fanned by the tensions with Pakistan during the early years of independence. It required great courage and tenacity for Nehru to fight this feeling in his Cabinet, the Congress party, and Parliament. 'India will be a land of many faiths,' he declared in January 1948, 'equally honoured and respected but of one national outlook'.[28] Three months later, the Constituent Assembly, which also acted as an interim Parliament, resolved that, for the proper functioning of democracy and the growth of national unity and solidarity, communalism must be eliminated from India's life. This was the time when the constitution of the Indian Republic was being framed by the Constituent Assembly; Nehru's influence was exercised in favour of giving it a secular basis. When it took final shape in 1949, it gave all citizens the right to freedom of religion, assembly, association, and movement. There was to be no official state religion; there was to be no provision for religious instruction in state schools, no taxes to support any religion, and no discrimination against any citizen on the grounds of religion, race, caste, sex, or place of birth. Any citizen of India could aspire to the highest office in the state; minorities were permitted to protect and conserve their language, script, and culture, and various means were provided enabling the citizen to move the courts for the enforcement of his fundamental rights.

After 1947 Nehru continued to concentrate his fire on Hindu communalism which he associated in his mind with bigotry, obscurantism, and social inequality. It was easier for him to attack Hindu communalism than Muslim communalism, but he may also have felt that after the establishment of Pakistan, Muslim communalism in India was likely to remain subdued. He was not deterred by his secular credentials from sponsoring legislation on the rights of Hindu women. He met with strong opposition, but with patience and persistence managed to push through the Hindu Code Bills. 'Our laws, our customs fall heavily on womenfolk,' Nehru observed, 'and the new laws would bring about certain equality between men and women'. It is significant that though he regarded the enactment of these laws as his greatest service to his country, he excluded the Muslim community from them on the ground that it was not yet ready for the reform.

In the early 1950s, it seemed to Nehru that Hindu–Muslim tensions were on the wane. But as the effects of the trauma of Partition wore off, the ostensible tranquillity on the communal plane was disturbed. From 1959 onwards communal riots began to disfigure the country, especially in Bihar, Uttar Pradesh, and Madhya Pradesh. There was 26 riots in 1960, 92 in 1961, 60 in 1962, and 61 in 1963. Nehru was bewildered and dismayed by these events; each time the communal problem looked like having been solved, it arose in an aggravated form. In September 1961, he convened a National Integration Conference, and asked the Chief Ministers to take strong administrative action and make district officers responsible for preserving communal peace. He came down heavily on the majority community whenever there were breaches of the peace, though he knew that Hindu communalism had its counterpart in Muslim communalism and not infrequently was a reaction to it.

Muslim communalism had been somewhat subdued by the guilt and remorse that many Indian Muslims felt for their aggressive postures before 1947 in precipitating division of the country. The Muslim League, the principal instrument of the division of the country, ceased to exist except in the southern state of Kerala. However, as Prof. Hasan says, it was only natural that a community 'nurtured in the tradition of political separatism and religious fundamentalism, exemplified by the Jamat-i-Islami and Muslim League movements, was rather slow in coming to terms with the secular framework of the Indian polity.'[29] As late as January 1962, M.C. Chagla, a member of Nehru's cabinet, noted that Indian Muslims had not yet fully adjusted themselves emotionally to a secular state.[30]

Nehru had been conscious of the psychological aspect of the problem, and in January 1948, when speaking at the Aligarh Muslim University, had dwelt on the cultural heritage:

I have said that I am proud of our inheritance and our ancestors who gave an intellectual and cultural pre-eminence to India. How do you feel about this past? Do you feel that you are also sharers in it and inheritors of it, and therefore, proud of something that belongs to you as much as to me? Or do you feel alien to it. . . . You are Muslims and I am a Hindu. We may adhere to any religious faith or even to none; but that does not take away from that cultural inheritance that is yours as well as mine. The past holds us together; why should the present or the future divide us in spirit?[31]

Eight years later, Aligarh was one of the several towns in northern India which witnessed communal violence in the wake of the reprinting in India of a book by two American authors entitled 'Biographies of Religious Leaders'. Dr Zakir Husain, the retiring Vice-Chancellor of Aligarh Muslim University, expressed his sense of shock at the 'disgraceful manner' in which the students of Aligarh Muslim University had behaved. 'I am sure', Zakir Husain said, 'that your reaction should have caused pain to the soul of the Prophet'.[32]

This exhibition of Muslim communalism disconcerted Nehru because it had also an anti-national slant. Nehru noted that newspapers were full of poison; that the members of the Jamat-i-Islami were aggressive, indulging in speeches and writings of 'a venomous kind'. And he noted sadly that 'the freedom of the press and of speech and our democratic Constitution spread out their wide umbrella to cover all this evil brood'.[33]

In retrospect it seems that the revival of communalism in the late fifties and early sixties was also the result of certain acts of omission and commission by the State. The 1949 constitution under the rubric of freedom of religion had allowed citizens not only the profession and the practice of their respective religions but also their propagation. Besides, it had allowed the establishment of educational institutions along communal lines by the minorities. Communalism of the minority communities had its reaction on the majority community and vice versa. The growth of Sikh and Muslim fundamentalism could not but have its repercussions on Hindu fundamentalism. The framers of the constitution had not foreseen that adult franchise would by itself give a boost to unscrupulous exploitation of caste, religion, and language for electoral purposes. Political parties compromised on communalism for immediate political gains. Even the Congress party did so by going into partnership with the Akali party in Punjab and the Muslim League in Kerala.

Nehru has been criticized for not lending state support to the principle of secularism such as Lenin and Kemal Ataturk had given in the Soviet Union and Turkey. A parliamentary democracy based on adult franchise could hardly adopt the stern methods of Lenin and Ataturk, but Nehru could have made a beginning with a common civil code applicable to all communities. By exempting the Muslim community from this code, Nehru left a nucleus for the growth of Muslim fundamentalism which, after his death, was to gather momentum. Similarly, a ban on parties based on religion could easily have been imposed in the 1950s.

The question has been asked whether Nehru's personal attitude to religion changed during his last years. He has been accused of being anti-Hindu. This was, of course, not true. Whenever he spoke on Ramakrishna and Swami Vivekananda he did so with great feeling. Ramakrishna had 'once again made the ancient Indian tradition of great savants and seers come alive . . . once again shown us that the search for truth has been the real and fundamental goal of our great men'. Of Vivekananda, Nehru always spoke in the highest terms; he had, he said, read his books and lectures for years and been profoundly impressed by him.[34]

Nehru was not against Hinduism but against such elements in it which in his view promoted weakness and disunity and impeded the progress of the country in the twentieth century. He was repelled by what passed for organized religion and rebelled against what seemed to him superstition or mere ritual. T.T. Krishnamachari, one of the Cabinet colleagues with whom Nehru had a rapport, has left it on record that in 1954 he had accompanied Nehru to a temple in Chidambaram:

I said 'you should take off your coat'. He said: 'I won't'. He did not go in, and it was noted. But I saw a change in him from about 1956–7. I think by that time he had left off his agnosticism. He probably did believe that there was something; that strong negative outlook had disappeared . . . You could put a 'tilak' on his head, he would not be angry.[35]

R.K. Karanjia in his book, *The Mind of Nehru*, tells us that Nehru spoke to him of ethical and spiritual solutions. 'What you say,' Karanjia said, 'raises the visions of Mr Nehru in search of God in the evening of his life.' 'Yes', said Nehru, 'I have changed . . . the old Hindu idea that there is a divine essence in the world, that every individual possesses something of it, and can develop it appeals to me.'[36]

One wonders whether this change came in the evening of Nehru's life through study and reflection or through the experience of governing the country for a decade and discovering that Gandhi had after all been right in his emphasis on the spiritual and ethical aspects of life.

Whether and how far Nehru moved away from his agnostic moorings we do not know, but his views on state policy remained unchanged to the last. He remained convinced that, in a multi-religious, pluralist, and democratic country like India, a secular framework was imperative. Three years before his death he put the problem in perspective. He conceded that where the great majority of the people in a country belonged to one religion, this fact alone was likely to colour to some extent its cultural climate, but the state itself could remain independent of any particular religion. He recognized that though the Indian constitution laid down that India was a secular state, it was not wholly reflected in the living and thinking of the people. In a country like England the state was under its constitution allied to the Church of England, but the state and the people largely functioned in a secular way. 'And the society, therefore, in England', Nehru wrote, 'is more advanced in this respect than in India, even though our constitution may be in this matter more advanced.'[37] This very idea had been expressed tersely by Nehru when a few years earlier, André Malraux had asked him what his greatest difficulty since Independence had been; 'Creating a just State by just means . . . perhaps, too, creating a secular State in a religious country.'[38]

## REFERENCES

1. Jawaharlal Nehru to Gandhi, 25 July 1933 (NP).
2. B.R. Nanda, *The Nehrus* (London, 1962), pp. 43–4.
3. Ibid.
4. *SWJN*, vol. I (Delhi, 1972), p. 252.
5. Tibor Mende, *Conversations with Mr. Nehru* (London, 1956), p. 23.
6. J. Nehru, *Discovery of India* (Calcutta, 1946), pp. 16–17.
7. Ibid.
8. J. Nehru, *An Autobiography* (London, 1958 edn), p. 377.
9. J. Nehru to Edward Thompson, 7 April 1940 (NP).
10. J. Nehru, *Discovery of India*, p. 633.
11. Dilip Kumar Roy to Sri Aurobindo, 17 Sept. 1936 (NP).
12. Sri Aurobindo to Dilip Kumar Roy, 18 Sept. 1936 (NP).
13. *SWJN*, vol. 2 (Delhi, 1972), p. 169.
14. *SWJN*, vol. 6 (Delhi, 1974), p. 176.
15. Louis Dumont, 'Religion, Politics and History in India' in *Collected Papers on Indian Sociology* (Paris, 1970), pp. 90–1.
16. *SWJN*, vol. 6 (Delhi, 1974), p. 181.
17. *SWJN*, vol. 4 (Delhi, 1973), p. 186.
18. J. Nehru, *Recent Essays and Writings* (Allahabad, 1934), pp. 45–6.
19. J. Nehru, *An Autobiography*, pp. 138–9.
20. NP.
21. *SWJN*, vol. 6 (Delhi 1974), p. 163.
22. J. Nehru to Syed Mahmud, 2 Feb. 1942, *SWJN*, vol. 12 (Delhi, 1979), p. 511.
23. *SWJN*, vol. 6 (Delhi, 1974), p. 181.
24. *SWJN*, vol. 8 (Delhi, 1976), p. 627.
25. *See* Chapter 7 on 'Nehru and the Partition of India'.
26. Rajendra Prasad to J. Nehru, 7 Aug. 1947 (NP).
27. J. Nehru to Rajendra Prasad, 7 Aug. 1947 (NP).
28. *Hindustan Times*, 25 Jan. 1948.
29. Mushirul Hasan, 'The Search for Integration and Identity, Indian

Muslims Since Independence', in *Economic & Political Weekly*, Special Number, Nov. 1988.

30. Ibid.
31. Convocation address at Aligarh University, 24 Jan. 1948, *Hindustan Times*, 25 Jan. 1948.
32. Letter dated 20 Sept. 1956, in G. Parthasarathy (ed.), Jawaharlal Nehru, *Letters to Chief Ministers*, vol. 4 (Delhi, 1988), pp. 436–7.
33. Ibid.
34. *SWJN*, vol. 10 (Delhi, 1977), p. 93.
35. Oral History Transcript (NMML), pp. 40–1.
36. R.K. Karanjia, *The Mind of Mr Nehru* (London, 1960), pp. 32–3.
37. Foreword to Raghunath Singh: *Dharm Nirpeksh Raj*, quoted in S. Gopal, *Jawaharlal Nehru: An Anthology* (Delhi, 1980), p. 331.
38. André Malraux, *Antimemoirs* (London, 1968), p. 145.

# 7

## *Jawaharlal Nehru and the Partition of India*

I

During the twelve years preceding the partition of India, Jawaharlal Nehru was one of the foremost leaders of the Indian National Congress, a member of its executive (the Working Committee), and presided at three of its annual sessions. He exercised considerable influence over the politics of the organization, but he did not by any means dictate them. In spite of the allegations of its political opponents at the time, the Congress organization was not monolithic, but collective in its leadership. No one individual, not even Gandhi, could bend the Congress to his will without carrying conviction to its leadership and educating its rank-and-file. The Congress Working Committee included members who diverged widely in temperament and political convictions, who argued, differed, and even quarrelled, but finally made up under the force of events or the benign influence of Gandhi.

Nehru's views on the communal problem were clearly thought out and strongly held, but they cannot be explained except with reference to the changing pattern of Indian politics, the pressures operating within and on the Congress, and the state of almost continual conflict between the Congress and the Government. Nehru did not see the communal problem and the challenge of the All India Muslim League as a thing apart; the communal issue seemed to him one aspect of the total situation with which nationalist India had to reckon. In this chapter an attempt has, therefore, been made to interpret the attitudes and actions of Nehru—

and the Congress leadership—to the challenge of Muslim separatism in the context of not only the Congress–Muslim League equation, but of the Congress–Government equation; the latter influenced, aggravated, and distorted the former.

## II

When the Government of India Bill was being piloted through the House of Commons during the winter of 1934–5, Jawaharlal Nehru was in gaol and writing his autobiography. 'It is an illusion to imagine', he wrote in this book, which was as much a personal chronicle as a political manifesto, 'that a dominant imperialist Power will give up its superior position and privileges unless effective pressure amounting to coercion is exercised.'[1] He quoted with approval the words of Reinhold Niebuhr: 'Since reason is always to some degree the servant of necessity in a social situation, social justice cannot be resolved by moral or rational suasion alone.'[2] In a country without a democratic constitution, 'constitutional' activity had little meaning: it was synonymous with what was 'legal', which in practice meant the will of the all-powerful executive. Nehru did not therefore set much store by the Government of India Act 1935: it was hedged in with too many 'safeguards', checks and balances: it was as if a motor vehicle was to be set in motion in low gear with the brakes on. In the federal legislature, the Princely States were to be allotted nearly one-third of the total seats; in the absence of elective bodies, the States' representatives were to be nominees of the Princes. Apart from this built-in conservatism of the federal legislature, its powers were severely circumscribed: matters relating to the military, the services, and the interest charges, for example, were outside its purview. In the Provinces, a wider field had been permitted to ministers responsible to elected legislatures, but even there the Governors were invested with overriding and preventive authority in financial and other matters.

These limitations led Nehru to describe the Act of 1935 as 'a Charter of Slavery'.[3] In his presidential address to the Lucknow session of the Indian National Congress in March 1936, he declared that the new constitution offered India only responsibility without power, and therefore, deserved to be rejected 'in its entirety'. Sensing the mood of the party, he did not oppose Congress participation in the elections. But he left his audience in no doubt that he did not expect India's salvation through the new constitution. On the other hand, he pinned his hopes on a:

Constituent Assembly elected on adult franchise and a mass basis. . . . That Assembly will not come into existence till at least a semi-revolutionary situation has been created in the country and the actual relationships of power, apart from paper constitutions, are such that the people of India can make their will felt.

When this was to happen he could not predict, but the world seemed to him 'too much in the grip of dynamic forces today to admit of static conditions in India or elsewhere for long'.[4]

Though Nehru had agreed that the Congress should contest the elections to prevent politically reactionary elements from capturing the new legislatures, the idea of his party holding office under the new constitution seemed unthinkable to him. He warned,

It is always dangerous to assume responsibility without power even in democratic countries; it will be far worse with this undemocratic constitution, hedged in with safeguards and reserved powers and mortgaged funds where we have to follow the rules and regulations of our opponent's making. . . . The big things for which we stand, will fade into the background and petty issues will absorb our attention and we shall lose ourselves in compromises and communal tangles and disillusion with us will spread over the land.[5]

Nehru's distrust of the Act of 1935 and of British intentions stemmed not only from the clauses of that Act, but from what he and the Congress had gone through at the hands of the Government. The Government of India under Lord Willingdon had waged total war on the Congress, gaoled its members by the thousand, sealed its offices, frozen its funds, choked its publicity media, and tried to crush it once and for all.[6] All this could not but leave a bitter taste in Nehru's mouth. In December 1935 he confessed to Lord Lothian:

I feel a certain hesitation in meeting people who have been officially associated with the Government of India during the past nightmare years. That period is full of horror to us and it is very difficult for me to understand how any sensitive person could tolerate it, much less give his approval to it. It is not so much the repression and suppression of much that was best in India that I refer to, but the manner of it. There was, and is, in it an indecency and vulgarity that I could hardly have conceived. And the wonder of it is that hardly anyone in England realizes this or has any idea of what is happening in India's mind and heart.[7]

## III

'The real problem before us', Jawaharlal Nehru had told the Lahore Congress in December 1929, 'is the conquest of power; and the withdrawal of the army of occupation and economic control by Britain.'[8] Seven years later, he held the same opinion. He was convinced that the communal problem had been overrated and overemphasized both by the Government and vested interests in the two countries.[9] He himself was remarkably free from religious passion and prejudice. His father, Pandit Motilal Nehru, had defied Hindu orthodoxy, employed Muslim clerks and servants, and avowed his love of Persian classics and Urdu poetry. Both father and son cherished Muslim friends and colleagues. Indeed, they were often accused of being objectionably pro-Muslim. The fact is that Jawaharlal was a rationalist and a humanist, and did not view cultural conflict in twentieth-century India in the same way as the leaders of communal parties did. The real struggle seemed to him not between Hindu and Muslim cultures, but between these two cultures and the conquering scientific culture of modern civilization. 'I have no doubt personally', he added, 'that all efforts, Hindu or Muslim, to oppose modern scientific and industrial civilization are doomed to failure and I shall watch this failure without regret.'[10] 'The communalism of today,' he told an English correspondent, 'is essentially political, economic and middle class.'[11] Of this communalism he had a good glimpse in 1928 when he helped his father in drafting the report of the All-Parties Committee, which came to be known as the Nehru Report. He saw how upper-class politicians, both Hindu and Muslim, with little contact with the masses or appreciation of the social and economic issues, wrangled endlessly over the distribution of seats in legislatures and jobs under the Government, which in any case could benefit only a tiny minority. It was a crazy political puzzle in which majorities in legislatures (such as in Punjab and Bengal) wanted to be protected, minorities asked for weightages, and rival claims of Muslims, Sikhs, Scheduled Castes, and others were irreconcilable. The protagonists of these claims had one eye on the unity conference they were attending, and the other on Whitehall or the Viceregal Lodge, the repositories of real power and patronage. This had led Motilal Nehru to lament at the Calcutta Congress in December 1928: 'It is difficult to stand against the foreigner without offering him a united front. It is not easy to offer a united front while the foreigner is in our midst domineering over us.'

Jawaharlal had thought deeply on the causes of the communal deadlock that frustrated the Nehru Report and blocked the Round-Table Conference, and came to the conclusion that the political bargaining and haggling could not take the country far, because 'whatever offer we make, however high our bid might be, there is always a third party which can bid higher and, what is more, give substance to its words. The third and controlling party inevitably plays the dominant role and hands out its gifts to the prize boys of its choice.'[12] It was only by visualizing a political structure without the British, and an economic structure orientated to the needs of the masses rather than to those of the upper and middle classes, that the communal problem could be lifted out of the grooves in which it had got stuck. This was the reason why Nehru was attracted to the idea of a Constituent Assembly elected on adult franchise to draw up the constitution of free India. By 1936 he had won over Gandhi and the Congress to this solution of both the political and communal problems. The demand for the Constituent Assembly figured prominently in the Congress election manifesto.

## IV

After the Lucknow Congress, Nehru was intimately concerned with the preparations for the election campaign. There was not much time to lose. The Congress Working Committee constituted a Parliamentary Board consisting of a number of national leaders and of presidents of all the provincial Congress committees. The Parliamentary Board met on 1 July 1936 and elected a executive committee of eleven members with Vallabhbhai Patel as President, and Rajendra Prasad and G.B. Pant as Secretaries. The burden of planning the election campaign and guiding the provincial committees fell on this executive committee.

Though most of the restrictions on its activities had been

withdrawn, the Congress organization was still illegal throughout the North-West Frontier Province, and in parts of Bengal. Elsewhere, it was not difficult to see that official sympathy—if not active support—went to parties opposing the Congress. In Nehru's home province, the United Provinces, the Governor and high British officials had encouraged the formation of the National Agriculturist Party in which Hindu and Muslim landlords combined to oppose the Congress.[13] In December 1936, the Chief Secretary to the UP Government reported to the Government of India:

Though the National Agriculturist Party do not appear to be functioning very effectively . . . they are concentrating on, and strengthening, their personal influence, relying on friendly visits and the feudal tie. The latter still seems fairly powerful and the Congress are not likely, even in districts where their forces are strongest, to have a walk-over.[14]

Nehru was aware of the fact that the Congress was anathema to the official world. In September 1936, he came across a copy of a circular letter from the Secretary of the Court of Wards, Allahabad, to all district officers advising them that it was

essential, in the interests of the class which the Court of Wards represents, and of agricultural interests generally, to inflict as crushing a defeat as possible on the Congress with its avowed socialistic principles. To this end, it is of the utmost importance to avoid to the greatest extent practicable, a split in the landlord vote, and a consequent dissipation of the voting power of the elements opposed to the Congress.[15]

It was after reading this letter that Nehru issued a statement to the press on 18 September 1936:

The real contest is between the two forces—the Congress as representing the will to freedom of the nation, and the British Government of India and its supporters who oppose this urge and try to suppress it. . . . Let this position be clearly understood by our people as it has been understood and acted upon by the Government. For the Government, there is only one principal opponent—the Congress.

This statement was directed not against the Muslim League—which later was to make much play with it—but against the Government. It is noteworthy that Nehru had described the contest as between 'two forces', not between 'two parties'. What he was stating was the obvious truth: the Congress represented the principal anti-imperialist force in India.

It was in this election that Nehru revealed for the first time his tremendous stamina and ability as a campaigner. During the eight months preceding the election, he covered over 50,000 miles by train, car, and aeroplane, addressed thousands of meetings and came into direct contact with about ten million people.

His labours and those of his colleagues were well-rewarded. The Congress won clear majorities in Bihar, United Provinces, Central Provinces, Madras, and Orissa. In Bombay it emerged as the largest party; in Assam and NWFP, it gave a very good account of itself. Nehru's own assessment of the election results was recorded in a letter to Sir Stafford Cripps on 11 February 1937:

Remarkable as this election victory has been, the really significant feature of the election campaign has been the shaking up of the masses. We carried our message not only to the thirty million and odd voters, but to the hundreds of millions of non-voters also. The whole campaign and the election itself have been a revelation of the widespread anti-imperialist spirit prevailing throughout the country. It has made clear the class cleavages among the people. The big landlord class and other vested interests were ranged against us. They were swept away in the flood, their most determined opponents being their own tenants. This class cleavage is very apparent in the comparison between the elections for the Provincial Assemblies [Lower Houses] and the Provincial Councils [Upper Houses]. In the former, the franchise was low and the electorates were large, the average constituency having as many as forty to sixty thousand voters. In the latter, the franchise was a high property one and the electorate was very small, usually some hundreds. In the Assembly elections we carried all before us and our majorities were prodigious. . . . In the Council elections we fared badly (though even here we won a few seats). The election made it perfectly clear that the wider the mass appeal, the greater was our success.

Nehru acknowledged that the Congress had not done so well in Muslim constituencies:

Partly, this is due to our own timidity as we ran few Muslim candidates. The burden of running over a thousand candidates (in the general constituencies) was great and we did not wish to add to it. If we had run more Muslim candidates, I trust we could have had a fair measure of success, especially in the rural areas. . . . It is true that the Muslim masses are more apathetic. They have been too long fed with communal cries. . . . Even these Muslim masses are getting out of the rut of communalism and are thinking along economic lines. Equally significant is the change that is coming over the younger generation of Muslims. These young people are definitely cutting themselves away from the old communal ways of thought. On the whole I think that the communal position is definitely brighter. The Hindu communalists have been largely swept away by the Congress and they count for little.[16] The Muslim communal leaders still function, but their position weakens, for they have no reply to the question of poverty, hunger and unemployment and independence that their own people put to them. They can only think in terms of jobs for the upper classes.

In the light of later history, it may seem that Nehru's optimism was premature, but early in 1937 he had reasons to hope that the Muslim intelligentsia and masses were acquiring keener consciousness of economic issues; he himself had done much to sharpen this consciousness.

The UP Government had indeed been alarmed by the impression that Nehru was beginning to make on the Muslim community and even on avowedly loyal elements. Commenting on Nehru's tour of the western districts, which had a sizeable Muslim population, the UP Government reported to the Government of India in September 1936:

What the tour makes evident for the first time in this province is the remarkable hold that Mr Nehru has obtained on the popular imagination. He has in fact become Mr Gandhi's successor as the popular leader. That the Municipal Board, Cawnpore, constituted of what was regarded as a strong anti-Congress majority, should have taken the lead in presenting him with an address was not perhaps extraordinary in view of Hindu feeling in urban areas; but it is remarkable that the Muslim Chairman of the Meerut District Board, a leader of the National Agriculturist Party, who was justifiably proud of his success in routing the Congress party at the local elections, should find it necessary to read an address to the arch-enemy of his party and class. Lawyers and businessmen who would be the first to suffer if Mr Nehru achieves his objects, which he makes but little attempt to disguise, joined in doing him honour. . . .[17]

In his 1,500-word survey of the election results to Cripps, Nehru did not so much as mention the Muslim League. Evidently, in

February 1937 Nehru had a low opinion of the League, but his opinion was not different from that Jinnah himself is reported to have expressed a year earlier. According to Khaliquzzaman, Jinnah told him in February 1936 that the Muslim League 'consisted mostly of big landlords, title-holders and selfish people who looked to their class and personal interests more than to communal and national interests and who had always been ready to sacrifice them to suit British policies'.[18] It is true that Jinnah had promised Khaliquzzaman that he would reform the League, of which he had been virtually a permanent president for twenty years. To the average observer in 1937 the composition of the League did not, however, seem to have changed much: the titled gentry, the Khan Bahadurs, the Nawabs, and the gallant knights still occupied important positions in it; former Congressmen like Khaliquzzaman, who had recently switched their allegiance to the League, were a small minority and viewed with some suspicion by their colleagues as well as by the Government. It is true that the League manifesto in 1936 had expressed some progressive views; but so did almost every other party. Neither the composition nor the past history of the League raised hopes of its capacity to pursue a radical course on political and economic issues.[19]

After the elections the question of office acceptance was fiercely debated in the Congress party. It was argued that if the Congress abstained from forming ministries, conservative elements favoured by the Government would step in. Gandhi's opinion tilted the scales in favour of office acceptance. The Mahatma himself had no ambition to be a legislator or a minister, but he wondered whether, with all its limitations, the new constitution could not be used to improve the lot of the people in India's villages: to encourage village industries, ensure supply of clean water, and an inexpensive and nutritious diet, reduce the burdens on the peasantry, promote the use of homespun cloth, and extend education. Those who opposed office acceptance—and Nehru was one of them—felt that nothing much could be got out of the new constitution, and that the Congress would have to bear the odium for the apparatus of imperialism without being in a position to be able to provide any tangible relief to the people. As a compromise between the two opposing groups it was decided by a convention of Congress members of the provincial legislatures, and members of the All

India Congress Committee held on 18 March 1937, that the Congress should form ministries, provided the leader of the Congress party in the provincial legislatures was satisfied and was able to state publicly that the Governor would not use his special powers of interference or set aside the advice of ministers 'in regard to their constitutional activities'. This assurance the Governors seemed unwilling to give. Official spokesmen took the line that the Governors could not contract themselves out of the terms of an Act of Parliament or 'Instrument of Instructions' issued to them. The Government called upon other parties in the legislature to form interim ministries. 'It is clear now', Patel wrote to Nehru on 29 March 1937, 'that there is going to be no Congress ministry anywhere'.

Not until 22 June 1937 did the Viceroy issue the statement which became the basis for acceptance of office by the Congress. The 'assurances' given by the Government were not very explicit, but it was evident that much would depend upon the strength and discipline of the Congress parties. The political situation was fraught with a great deal of uncertainty. No one could say in the summer of 1937 how much cooperation the Congress would get from the British bureaucracy, which until recently had been its arch enemy. The long record of antagonism between the two was not likely to be erased overnight. The Congress approach to office acceptance was, therefore, marked by a measure of caution and reserve. Nehru and his colleagues were apprehensive that, in the peculiar conditions prevailing in India, 'parliamentary activities' could lead to demoralization and division in nationalist ranks. In the 1920s, Motilal Nehru, his tremendous personality and prestige notwithstanding, had been unable to stop the rot in the Swaraj Party; some of his adherents had succumbed to official blandishments and communal pressures. Strong and disciplined parties in the provincial legislatures were, therefore, a necessity if the Congress was not to lose its character as a militant national party.

It is important to remember this background when reviewing the negotiations between the Congress and the Muslim League in the UP for the representation of the latter in the provincial cabinet. The crucial question in these negotiations was not whether the UP cabinet should have one or two representatives of the Muslim League,[20] but whether the provincial cabinet, after the induction of the League members, would be able to maintain its cohesion. Nehru was consulted by Abul Kalam Azad, who had been authorized by the Congress Working Committee to deal with Congress affairs in Bihar and UP, and who conducted the negotiations on behalf of the Congress, but the decision did not rest with Nehru alone. Indeed, G.B. Pant, Rafi Ahmed Kidwai, K.M. Ashraf, P.D. Tandon, and other members of the UP legislature exercised as much influence, if not more, on the ultimate result of the negotiations. The most important consideration with the provincial Congress leaders, as with Nehru, was that if the Muslim League with its landlord support came into the provincial cabinet, the Congress programme for agrarian reform, particularly the abolition of *zamindari*, would be jeopardized.[21] That this fear was not groundless is proved by the stubborn opposition of the Muslim League to land reform in the UP during the years 1937–46.[22]

Khaliquzzaman and Nawab Ismail Khan may have honestly felt that they could cooperate with the Congress in 1937; but it is doubtful if they would have been permitted to do so by the League leadership. On 25 April 1937, Khaliquzzaman and his friends were taken to task by the Working Committee of the UP Muslim League Parliamentary Board for their flirtations with the Congress.[23] Early in May, the Committee of the Bombay Provincial Muslim League, with Jinnah in the chair, appealed 'to the Muslim members of the UP Legislative Assembly who had been elected on the League ticket not to act in such a way as to cause disunion among Muslims of India by arranging sectional or provincial settlements with the Congress'.[24] 'We shall face the challenge of the Congress', Jinnah declared, 'if they think that the Muslims will accept their policy and programme, because our policy and programmes are different in vital respects.'[25]

A couple of days later, Jinnah visited Lucknow to assert his authority over the provincial party. He was reported to have rebuked Leaguers, who 'talked loosely of co-operating with the Congress', and affirmed that 'for the time being they would join hands neither with the Congress nor with the Government, but wait till they had gained strength by organizing the Muslims.'[26]

Such a minatory posture on the League leader's part was not calculated to reassure Congress leaders that a coalition with the League was workable. Indeed, in the negotiations for an understanding between the League and the Congress in Bombay, the Congress was willing to let Jinnah nominate two members of the provincial cabinet. But his conditions were such that the Congress could not accept them. According to K.M. Munshi (with whom Vallabhbhai Patel and Abul Kalam Azad were staying in Poona when Jinnah's terms were received) the 'position would have been that Mr Jinnah would have dictated the whole policy [of the Bombay cabinet] through one or two of his nominees who would threaten to resign at any moment they chose. . . . Such terms would have imposed the dictatorship of Mr Jinnah over every Congress Government in the country.'[27]

The Congress could not afford to make its first experiment in ministry-making vulnerable at the very outset. The party position in the UP legislature did not suggest any urgent need for, or the inevitability of, a coalition with the Muslim League.[28] In 1937 it was difficult for the Congress to foresee how the equation with the Government would work out. For nearly four months (March–June 1937) there seemed little prospect of the Congress being able to form ministries. Indeed, in April 1937—after the introduction of the new constitution—the Government of India at the highest level was considering the prosecution of Jawaharlal Nehru for the speeches he had delivered during the election campaign.[29] Even after the formation of the ministries in July, the Congress was not sure how far it would be allowed to carry out its programme in such matters as release of political prisoners and radical economic reforms. In these circumstances it is not difficult to see why the Congress should have been reluctant to admit the Muslim League (whose leader emphasized fundamental differences in outlook and programmes between the two organizations) into partnership in UP without ensuring that the cohesion of the cabinet would be maintained. The negotiations broke down on the insistence of the Congress that the League ministers joining the UP cabinet would adhere to the programme and discipline of the Congress party.

## V

Whatever the merits of the coalition controversy in UP, there is no doubt that the events of 1937 had a tremendous, almost a traumatic effect upon Jinnah.[30] The tide of provincial autonomy had come and gone, and left him becalmed. The real tragedy was not the failure of his party to secure two seats on its own terms in the UP cabinet, but the collapse of all the assumptions on which he had conducted his politics for twenty years. He had pinned his hopes on separate electorates and on organizing Muslims on a separate political platform, on the formation of as many Muslim majority provinces as possible by 'redrawing provincial boundaries', and on weighted representation for Muslims in provinces where they were in a minority. His 'Fourteen Points' had been practically conceded in the new constitution. But all these safeguards had not yielded the advantages he had hoped from them. In the Muslim majority provinces, where indeed the Muslim League could legitimately have hoped to be voted to office, it had met with an electoral disaster of the first magnitude. In the Sind Legislative Assembly the League had won three seats, in Punjab only one, and in North-West Frontier Province none at all. In Bengal it had won a third of the Muslim (and one-sixth of the total) seats in the Legislative Assembly, but it did not occupy a commanding position even in that province. Party alignments in Muslim majority provinces had cut across religion; Sir Sikandar Hyat Khan in the Punjab, Fazl-ul-Huq in Bengal, and Sir Ghulam Husain Hidayatullah in Sind had not responded to Jinnah's appeal for 'Muslim unity', and seemed to have been swayed by personal and class interests rather than by religious affiliations. The Muslim electorate had failed to vote the League to office in the Muslim majority provinces; in the Muslim minority provinces the League's performance was hardly less disappointing. It did not win a single seat in the Lower Houses of three provinces, Bihar, the Central Provinces, and Orissa. Only in two provinces did it do well, winning 27 out of 64 Muslim seats in UP and 20 out of 29 Muslim seats in Bombay. And it was only in these two provinces that the possibility of a coalition was seriously explored.

In the summer of 1937 Jinnah was faced with the stark reality that his party scarcely figured on the political map of India under the new constitution. While Gandhi and Nehru and the Congress leaders would guide and control six (and later eight) provincial ministries, there was not one ministry he could call his own, or in the formation of which he had a say. And it may have seemed that Jinnah could do little about this situation until the next round of elections. He was however not the man to let history pass over his head. 'In politics', he once said, 'one has to play one's game on the chess board.'[31] He made a masterly move calculated to achieve through a propaganda barrage what the ballot box had denied him.

The by-election to the Jhansi–Jalaun–Hamirpur Muslim seat in UP gave an inkling of the new strategy. In this by-election the Muslim League simply raised the cry of 'religion in danger'. Nehru was shocked by this unabashed exploitation of religious feeling; the appeal issued by Jinnah in support of the League candidate did not contain a single reference to political and economic issues. Nehru appealed to Jinnah to refrain from importing religious emotion into politics:

The leaders of the Muslim League have issued many . . . leaflets and appeals. I have read some of these, but in none of them have I found any reference to a political and economic issue. The cry raised is that Islam is in danger, that non-Muslim organizations have dared to put up candidates against the Muslim League. . . . Mr Jinnah has capped the sheaf of Muslim League leaflets and statements by his appeal in his capacity as the President of the Muslim League. He appeals in the name of Allah and the Holy Koran for support of the Muslim League candidate. Mr Jinnah knows well that many eminent Muslims, including leaders of the Jamiat-ul-Ulema like Maulana Hussain Ahmed, are supporting the Congress candidate. Have they ceased to be Muslims because of this? . . . To exploit the name of God and religion in an election contest is an extraordinary thing . . . even for a humble canvasser. For Mr Jinnah to do so is inexplicable. I would beg him to consider this aspect of the question. . . . It means rousing religious and communal passions in political matters; it means working for the Dark Age in India. Does not Mr Jinnah realize where this kind of communalism will lead us to?[32]

Nehru wrote to Khaliquzzaman, the UP League leader who was once his fellow-prisoner during the non-cooperation movement, protesting against the electioneering tactics of the League. Khaliquzzaman in his reply deplored these occurrences but explained how candidates had to proclaim themselves 'to be as good and pious Muslims as their opponents . . . and all the religious zeal of the belligerents must be brought into play to carry the electorate with them'.[33] This was an eloquent commentary on the effect of separate electorates on Muslim politics, particularly at election time, and on the difficulty of posing concrete political and economic issues to the electorate. The by-election was a pointer to the new strategy which unfolded itself at the Lucknow session of the All India Muslim League in October 1937. Not even three months had passed since the Congress had formed ministries, but Jinnah was already proclaiming that Muslims could 'not expect any justice or fair play at their hands'.[34] The majority community had clearly shown their hand by saying that 'Hindustan is for the Hindus. The result of the present Congress party policy will be, I venture to say, class bitterness and communal war.' There had not yet been time to circulate 'atrocity stories', but the League leader was warning his co-religionists: 'There are forces which may bully you, tyrannize over you and intimidate you . . . but it is by going through this crucible of fire of persecution which may be levelled against you . . . a nation will emerge worthy of its past glory . . . .'.[35] Writing in the British-owned *Pioneer*, a Muslim observer noted the heated atmosphere at the Lucknow meeting of the League:

The doctrine of aloofness was preached *ad nauseam* in a most unrestrained and irresponsible language. Out of the clouds of circumlocution and confusion arose the cry of 'Islam in danger'. The Muslims were told that they were disunited and about to be crucified by the Hindus. Religious fervour was raised to a degree when it exhibited itself in blind fanaticism. In the name of Muslim solidarity Mr Jinnah wants to divide India into Muslim India and Hindu India.[36]

Conscious humility had rarely characterized Jinnah's public utterances, but from the summer of 1937, they acquired a new edge of bitterness. Referring to Nehru in a press statement on 26 July he said: 'What can I say to that busybody President [of the Congress]. . . . He seems to carry the responsibility of the whole world on his shoulders and must poke his nose in everything except minding his own business.'[37] Commenting on a statement by Gandhi, he said: 'A more disingenuous statement it would be difficult to find, coming from Mr Gandhi, and it is a pity it comes from one who is a votary of truth![38] The Mahatma, Jinnah jeered on another occasion, was the 'oracle of Delphi'.[39] Light had not dawned upon Sevagram. Mr Gandhi was groping in the dark; he had designs to 'subjugate and vassalize the Muslims under a Hindu Raj'.[40] The Congress was trying to 'encircle' and 'annihilate' the

'Muslim nation'. For Muslim nationalists, who did not follow Jinnah's lead, the harshest epithets were reserved. Abul Kalam Azad was denounced as a 'puppet president' of the Congress.[41] Muslims differing with League programmes or policies were guilty of the 'grossest treachery' and 'betrayal', and stabbing their co-religionists in the back. Indian Muslims were warned to beware of 'Muslim agents of the Hindus' and 'Muslim agents of the British'. In spite of the not too distant discomfiture of his party at the polls, Jinnah was arrogating to himself the right to speak on behalf of the 100 million Muslims of India: 'When I say 100 million I mean that 99 per cent of them are with us—leaving aside some who are traitors, cranks, supermen or lunatics. . . .'[42]

When Nehru returned after a brief visit to Europe in 1938, he was struck by the similarity between the propaganda methods of the Muslim League in India and of the Nazis in Germany: 'The League leaders had begun to echo the Fascist tirade against democracy. . . . Nazis were wedded to a negative policy. So also was the League. The League was anti-Hindu, anti-Congress, anti-national. . . . The Nazis raised the cry of hatred against the Jews, the League [had] raised [its] cry against the Hindus.'[43] The denunciation of democracy as a form of government, the right of a racial minority to blackmail and disrupt the State, the claim by sub-national groups to self-determination, the reiteration of wildly exaggerated and usually fictitious 'atrocity stories' were all the common coinage of German propaganda in 1937–8, and to all appearances the Nazis were earning good dividends from it. If the Sudetan Germans could embarrass the Czech majority and dismember the state of Czechoslovakia, could not the Muslim minority do the same to the Hindus in India? At a meeting of the Sind Muslim League Provincial Conference in October 1938, Abdulla Haroon, the Chairman of the Reception Committee, warned Hindus that if the League's demand was not conceded, 'Czechoslovakian happenings would find an echo in India as well'.[44] The warning was repeated by Jinnah. Syed Wazir Hasan (a former Chief Judge of the Oudh Chief Court, who had presided at the 1936 session of the All-India Muslim League) warned Nehru of 'the propaganda of misrepresentation, lies, and religious and communal hatred, not only between Mussalmans and Hindus, but also between Mussalmans and

Mussalmans' which had been set off at the Lucknow session of the League.[45]

VI

Nehru was shocked by the propaganda of the League, but he did not take long to realize its explosive possibilities. When riots broke out in Allahabad in April 1938, he rushed to his home town and helped to restore peace. He urged the UP Premier, Pant, not to spare any official, high or low, who was guilty of partiality in communal riots. Nehru knew that the communal temperature had risen not because of local grievances, but through the political heat generated by the League.[46] He tried to remove the misunderstanding by opening correspondence with Jinnah and explaining to him Congress attitudes and policies. Jinnah's response was cold, formal, legalistic. At the same time, Nehru wrote at great length to Nawab Muhammad Ismail, a League leader of UP, to clear doubts on such general questions as the 'mass-contact movement', the national anthem, and the national flag which had become the targets of League criticism.[47] The Congress 'mass-contact movement', he told the Nawab, was not directed against the Muslim League; it had never been thought of in terms of Muslims alone, nor was it confined to them. The Congress had worked among the Hindu masses and 'disabled the Hindu Mahasabha politically'; it had carried out effective and successful work among the Christian masses of the South, the Parsis, the Jews, and the Sikhs. The 'Bande Mataram' song, Nehru recalled, had first become popular during the agitation against the partition of Bengal, when it came to be regarded by the British as a symbol of sedition. From 1905 to 1920, the song had been sung at innumerable meetings at some of which Jinnah himself was present. The Congress flag had been born during the days of the Khilafat Movement, and its colours had been determined to represent the various communities: saffron for Hindus, green for Muslims, and white for other minorities. Had not Maulana Muhammad Ali, the Khilafat leader, delivered scores of speeches on the 'national flag' as representing the unity of India? As for the Wardha Scheme of basic education, it was no diabolical plot against Muslim children; it had been devised by two eminent

Muslim educationists, Zakir Husain and K.G. Saiyidain, to substitute coordinated training in the use of the hand and the eye for a notoriously bookish and volatile learning which village children unlearned after leaving school.

The Congress leaders were distressed by the widening of the communal rift and discussed all aspects of it, from the choice of Muslim ministers to that of a national anthem. How far the Congress leadership was prepared to go to soothe Muslim feelings is shown by the fact that a committee went into the question of national anthem and, on its recommendation, it was decided that, out of deference to Muslim susceptibilities, only the first two stanzas should be sung on ceremonial occasions.

Not content with making general allegations, the Muslim League brought forward charges of cruelty and tyranny against Congress ministries: the *Pirpur Report* and *Shareef Report* listed these charges in highly coloured language. Some of the allegations in these reports were discussed in provincial legislatures; some were inquired into by British officers and refuted in press communiqués. The Bihar Government issued a detailed and (as Professor Coupland described it)[48] a reasoned reply to the *Pirpur Report*. Nevertheless, the charges continued to be repeated against the Congress ministries by Muslim League politicians and newspapers. Nehru vainly appealed to Jinnah to agree to an impartial inquiry. Rajendra Prasad suggested an inquiry by Sir Maurice Gwyer, the Chief Justice of the Federal Court: this suggestion was rejected by Jinnah on the ground that the matter was under His Excellency the Viceroy's consideration. Later, in December 1939, Jinnah called for a Royal Commission, a demand which the British Government were hardly likely to concede in wartime and for raking up such a controversy.

'It has been our misfortune', Nehru wrote to Jinnah on 14 December 1939, 'that charges are made in a one-sided way and they are never inquired into or disposed of. You will appreciate that it is very easy to make complaints and very unsafe to rely upon them without inquiry.'

While isolated acts of petty tyranny by local officials may have occurred in remote villages and towns in Congress (as well as in non-Congress) provinces, the theory of a concerted tyranny directed against the Muslim community in the Congress provinces in 1937–9 would be difficult to sustain. It is important to recall that during these years nearly half of the members of the ICS were still British.[49] They occupied almost all the key positions in the secretariat, besides holding charge of important districts. Almost all the Inspectors-General of Police were British,[50] and so were most of the police superintendents. There was a fair sprinkling of Muslims and Christians in the ICS and in the Indian Police, and Muslims were well represented in the middle and lower ranks of the police. It is also significant that there is no evidence in the records of the Home Department of the Government of India to support the theory of a Hindu Raj in Congress-governed provinces. Law and order was of course a provincial subject, but the channels of communication between the Viceroy and his colleagues in the Executive Council, on the one hand, and the British Governors and Chief Secretaries, on the other, had not dried up.[51] It is impossible to believe that deliberate ill-treatment of the Muslim minority could have gone unnoticed and unrecorded by the representatives of the Raj even in their confidential correspondence.[52]

That the Muslim League should have thrown cold water on proposals for holding judicial inquires into its allegations against the Congress ministries is understandable. The League was not trying to convince the British or the Hindus: its propaganda was meant for 'home consumption', for the Muslim community, and in this it achieved remarkable success. The spectre of a Hindu Raj roused the deepest fears of the Muslim intelligentsia: religious emotion was worked up to a high pitch; political and economic issues receded to the background. The effect of this propaganda was felt not only in the Hindu majority provinces, but in the Muslim majority provinces where the Muslim League had cut no ice in the 1937 elections.

At the Patna session of the Muslim League (December 1938) a threat of direct action was held out against the Congress, and even the soft-spoken Sir Sikandar Hyat Khan, the Premier of Punjab, offered to join this agitation. 'Such an offer', Nehru wrote to Sir Sikandar, 'by a Prime Minister of a provincial government is unusual and if seriously meant, likely to lead to grave consequences'.[53] In adopting this heroic posture, Sir Sikandar may have been swept off his feet by the overheated atmosphere at Patna, but it is not unlikely that he was acting under the impulse of self-preservation. He was aware of the deep religious feeling which was being roused among his co-religionists, and of the fact that with its help the Muslim League could cut the ground from under his feet in Punjab. Sir Sikandar had therefore no objection to joining in the tirade against the Congress if in return he was left alone in his own province. Similar considerations seem to have influenced Fazl-ul-Huq, the Prime Minister of Bengal, who had been at first unresponsive to Jinnah's overtures.

Nehru and his colleagues in the Congress Working Committee were distressed by the League's propaganda which was bound to provoke a reaction from Hindu communal groups. As President of the Congress, Nehru had tried, and so had Subhas Chandra Bose after him, to open negotiations with Jinnah. Neither of them could progress beyond the preliminary stage. Jinnah insisted that before the dialogue started, the Muslim League must be recognized as the sole representative organization of Muslims. This was a novel demand and had not been raised earlier when Jinnah had discussed the Communal Award with Rajendra Prasad, who was Congress President in 1935. At that time he had insisted that the agreement with the Congress should also be endorsed by the Hindu Mahasabha.[54] From 1937 onwards, Jinnah branded the Congress as a Hindu organization and denied its right to speak for any other community. The Congress was of course not a homogeneous organization and included in its ranks members of different communities as well as different schools of thought, but the divisions within it did not run along religious lines. If the Congress was to accept Jinnah's condition and accept the status of a communal body, what was it to do with the hundred thousand Muslim members on its rolls, with the Christians, the Jews, the Sikhs, and the Parsis who had served it devotedly for many years? And what was to be done about trade unions, peasant unions, chambers of commerce, employers' associations, and others which cut across communal lines and looked up to the Congress for political leadership?

In retrospect it would seem as if this precondition for the recognition of the Muslim League as the sole organization representing all Muslims was laid down by Jinnah to avoid coming to the negotiating table. In March 1938 when Nehru had urged the League leader to spell out the demands of the League, all that he could do was to refer Nehru to the Fourteen Points and to an anonymous article in the *Statesman* dated 12 February 1938, another article in the *New Times* of 1 March 1938, and to a statement by M.S. Aney, the Nationalist Party leader. The truth is that almost all the political demands of the Muslim community embodied in the Fourteen Points had been conceded in the constitution which had come into force in 1937, and Jinnah had no concrete demands to make. This interpretation is supported by the confession of Khaliquzzaman that if the negotiations between the Congress and the League had really got off the ground during the years 1938–9, he (Khaliquzzaman):

wondered what positive demands we could have then made. The Communal Award had been conceded. There was no demand by the Hindu community for its abrogation after 1936. ... Both Nawab Ismail Khan and I were at a loss to find any substantial radical demand on the Congress to satisfy us and our community.

It is an interesting thought that during the years 1937–9, when the Congress ministries offered the handiest peg on which the Muslim League could hang its strictures, it really had no political demands to make on the Congress.

## VII

The brief partnership between the Congress and the Government inaugurated by the installation of Congress ministries in eight provinces, ended with the outbreak of the Second World War in September 1939.

Nehru's lead ensured that the Indian National Congress consistently and emphatically expressed its sympathy in favour of the Allies and denounced every act of aggression by Japan, Italy, and Germany. Nehru, who had visited Europe in 1936 and 1938, reacted strongly against the make-believe policy of 'appeasement'. When the war broke out, he was touring China. He hurried back to India and declared that in the conflict between democracy and freedom, on the one hand, and Fascism and aggression, on the other, 'our sympathies must inevitably be on the side of democracy ... I should like India to play her full part and throw all her resources into the struggle for a new order'.[55]

The Congress Working Committee met soon afterwards and offered its cooperation in the struggle against Fascism, but it was to be 'a co-operation between equals by mutual consent for a cause which both considered to be worthy'. This was in Nehru's view, the only honourable course for the Congress to adopt. How could India hold aloft the banner of freedom and democracy in Czechoslovakia or Poland while she was herself in bondage? Apart from the moral aspect, there was an important and practical consideration. Wars were no longer bouts between professional armies in distant battlefields; entire nations had to be mobilized as workers or soldiers; unless Britain could release India's energies by treating her as an equal partner in a common struggle, it was hardly possible for her to play her full part in the world struggle.

What was required in the autumn of 1939 was a little imagination and a little courage: these qualities were not forthcoming from the Government of India headed by Lord Linlithgow and the British Government headed by Neville Chamberlain. The Viceroy made the blunder of issuing a declaration of war on India's behalf without any form of consultation with Indian opinion. He tried to make up for this omission by inviting Indian leaders to meet him, but he had virtually nothing to tell them. During the early weeks of the war, Linlithgow was extraordinarily cautious; he seems to have been lulled into a false sense of security by the 'phoney war'. In his assessment of the political implications of the war, he lagged behind even the India Office. He underrated the gravity of the international situation and misread the mood of the Congress. The Congress plea for a declaration that after the war Britain would concede Indians 'the right of self-determination by framing their own constitution through a Constituent Assembly', left him cold. Nor was he willing to let the Congress and other political parties have an effective voice in the administration at the centre. It had never been the British policy in the past (he told the Secretary of State) 'to expedite in India constitutional changes for their own sake or gratuitously to hurry the handing over of controls to Indian hands'.[56] The continuing discords between the communities, he thought, would strengthen Britain's hold on India for many years.[57] Among the minorities and special interests which stood in the way of accepting the Congress demand, the Viceroy listed not only 'the great communities of India' but European business interests and the Indian Princes.[58] As he waded through interminable negotiations with numerous parties and individuals, it was obvious that he was finding arguments for maintaining the political status quo.

'The same old game is played again', Nehru wrote to Gandhi, 'the background is the same, the various epithets are the same, and the actors are the same, and the results must be the same.'

Having failed to get any response from the Government, the Congress decided to withdraw its ministries in eight provinces. The suspension of the provincial part of the constitution was a serious step, but to the British officials in Delhi it may not have been entirely unwelcome; unhampered by the Indian politicians they could now concentrate on beating the Germans.

Nehru had realized at an early stage of the war that it could flare up at any time and envelop India. The old issues had suddenly become outdated. The crisis called for new initiatives. It was this feeling which had led the Congress Working Committee to invite Jinnah to attend its first meeting after the outbreak of the war in September 1939. Jinnah did not of course avail himself of the invitation, but Nehru wrote to him on 18 October, after learning from a common friend (Raghunandan Saran) that the Muslim League leader seemed to be in a cooperative mood. Nehru made as cordial an overture as he could:

I entirely agree with you that it is a tragedy that the Hindu–Muslim problem has not been settled in a satisfactory way. . . . With your goodwill and commanding position in the Muslim League a solution should not be as difficult as people imagine . . . for after all the actual matters under dispute should be, and indeed are, easily capable of adjustment.

He begged Jinnah to join the Congress in protesting against India being plunged into the war without her consent. He appealed to Jinnah's patriotism: 'Our dignity and self-respect as Indians has been insulted.' For once Jinnah seemed interested and even cordial, but he did not commit himself to any course of action, agreeing only to continue the discussions.

There were good reasons for Jinnah to adopt this position. The war had created a new situation: the Congress and Government were drifting apart, but there was still a possibility of a *modus vivendi* between them. It was only when the talks between the Government and the Congress broke down that he showed his hand. In December 1939, just when Nehru was preparing to leave for Bombay to meet him, the League leader called upon Indian Muslims to observe 22 December as a 'Day of Deliverance' from the Congress Ministries, 'from tyranny, oppression and injustice during the last two and a half years'. The aggressiveness of this gesture left Nehru gasping, but it also took many people, including members of the League, by surprise. Some observers felt that Jinnah had overreached himself, and that his extreme tactics might even split the League.[59]

Jinnah's statement on Deliverance Day was a vitriolic attack on the Congress party; after reading it Nehru could not bring himself to meet the League leader. He began to wonder if there was any common ground at all between them. Nehru's heart was set on political independence and a socialist society, and the instrument of the new order was to be a Constituent Assembly elected by the people on the basis of adult franchise.

To Jinnah, the proposal for the Constituent Assembly seemed wholly utopian. 'It is puerile', he said, 'to ask the British Government to call a Constituent Assembly of another nation and afterwards to have the honour and privilege of placing the Constitution framed by this supreme assembly of India on the Statute Book of the British Government.'[60] On social and economic problems Jinnah spoke rarely, but he had no sympathy with Nehru's radical economics: 'All talk of hunger and poverty', he declared, 'is intended to lead the people to socialistic and communistic ideas for which India is far from prepared.'[61]

## VIII

By December 1939 it was clear to Nehru that Jinnah would neither settle with the Congress nor embroil himself with the Government. What Nehru did not quite foresee was Jinnah's ability to turn to his advantage the growing rift between the Congress and the Government. The observance of Deliverance Day had created a new gulf between the League and the Congress. Three months later, the Lahore session of the League in March 1940 made the gulf wider. It was at this session that the League resolved that:

. . . no constitutional plan will be workable in the country or acceptable to the Muslims unless it is designed on the following basic principles, viz., that geographically contiguous units are demarcated into regions which should be so constituted, with such territorial readjustments as may be necessary, that the areas in which the Muslims are numerically in the majority as the north-western and eastern zones of India should be grouped to constitute 'Independent States' in which the constituent assemblies are autonomous and sovereign.

The 'Pakistan resolution', as it came to be known, gave a new twist to the communal problem. All the solutions hitherto thought of—separate electorates, composite cabinets, reservation of posts—suddenly became out of date.

Fifty-three years after the passage of this resolution, nearly fifty years after the emergence of Pakistan as an independent State, it is difficult to realize that it came as a bombshell not only to Congressmen, but to almost everyone outside the inner circles of the Muslim League.

Nehru's immediate reaction was that

all the old problems . . . pale into insignificance before the latest stand taken by the Muslim League leaders at Lahore. The whole problem has taken a new complexion and there is no question of settlement or negotiations now.

Nehru was not alone in reacting sharply to the League's new stand. Gandhi described the two-nation theory as 'an untruth', the strongest word in his dictionary. Rajagopalachari called it 'a medieval conception',[62] Abul Kalam Azad described it as 'meaningless and absurd'.[63] Sir Sikander Hyat Khan, Premier of Punjab,[64] and Sir Ghulam Husain Hidayatullah, Premier of Sind,[65] rejected outright the idea of partition of India. Abdul Qaiyum Khan, who was later to be a lieutenant of Jinnah, declared that 'the Frontier Province will resist [partition of India] with its blood'.[66] Syed Habibul Rahman, a leader of the Bengal Krishak Proja Party, said that the proposal was not only absurd, chimerical, and visionary, but

. . . will for ever remain a castle in the air . . . Indians, both Hindus and Muslims, live in a common motherland, use the offshoots of a common language and literature, and are proud of the noble heritage of a common Hindu and Muslim culture, developed through centuries of residence in a common land. There is no one among the Hindus and Muslims who will be prepared to sacrifice all this in order to accept what is demanded by Mr Jinnah.[67]

'For the moment', wrote the *Manchester Guardian*, 'Mr Jinnah has re-established the reign of chaos in India.'[68]

In the spring of 1940, most serious observers of the Indian scene would have described the Pakistan plan as 'chimerical and impractical', words used by prominent Muslim witnesses before the Joint Parliamentary Committee in August 1933.[69] Even after the Pakistan proposal had been embodied in a resolution of the All India Muslim League, it was no more than a political phantom. It was left to the spokesmen of the British Government to give it body and soul.

We know now that in March 1939, two Muslim League politicians, Khaliquzzaman and Abdul Rahman Siddiqui, met Lieutenant Colonel Muirhead, the Under-Secretary of State, and Lord Zetland, the Secretary of State for India, and got the impression that if the proposal for a separate Muslim State in the north-west and east of India was put forward the British would 'ultimately concede'[70] it. This impression was conveyed to Jinnah and may have influenced him in formulating the Pakistan demand in 1940. There is also evidence to show that Jinnah took the Viceroy into confidence and mentioned the Pakistan resolution to him several weeks before the League held its Lahore session.[71] In private the Viceroy may have described the Pakistan proposal as an extreme and 'preposterous claim', which had been put forward for 'bargaining purposes', but he did more than any other person to lend it the air of feasibility which was needed before it could gather support even among the Muslims. In his long-awaited public statement of 8 August 1940, the Viceroy included a remarkable passage:

It goes without saying that they [His Majesty's Government] could not contemplate the transfer of their present responsibilities for the peace and welfare of India to any system of government whose authority is directly denied by large and powerful elements in the Indian national life, nor could be a party to the coercion of such elements into submission to such a government.

Evidently this passage had been included out of deference to Jinnah.

It is a curious fact that the Indian National Congress had to agitate for thirty-two years before securing Edwin Montagu's declaration of 1917 about 'responsible government' being the goal of British policy in India. Another twelve years elapsed before the phrase Dominion Status was used with reference to India. But it took the Muslim League exactly four and half months to secure an indirect endorsement of a novel and—in the light of Indian constitutional evolution until 1940—drastic doctrine for the solution of the Indian constitutional problem.

A further encouragement to the Pakistan proposal came in a speech delivered by Amery, the Secretary of State in the House of Commons:

The foremost among these elements stands the great Muslim community, ninety million strong and constituting a majority both in north-western and north-eastern India, but scattered as a minority over the whole sub-continent. In religious and social outlook, in historic tradition and culture, the difference between them and their Hindu fellow countrymen goes as deep, if not deeper than any similar difference in Europe. . . .

These two statements by the Viceroy and the Secretary of State were later cited by Jinnah as 'solemn declarations' on the part of the British Government endorsing the two-nation theory and Pakistan.[72] The Viceroy and the Secretary of State could not have been unaware of the implications of the League's demand. But they had their own reasons for not antagonizing the Muslim League. On the very day the August offer was announced by Lord Linlithgow, he had signed a secret letter to the Governors informing them of the plans which had been perfected in the Home Department of the Government of India for a knock-out blow at the Congress, 'a declared determination to crush that organization as a whole'.[73] Having written off the Congress, the Viceroy and his advisers could hardly resist the temptation of backing its principal opponent. 'Some British officials', says Tinker, 'welcomed this [Pakistan] plan as a means of checkmating Congress demands.'[74] Testimony has been borne by at least one League leader to the support received from senior British officers;[75] it is difficult to say how far this support was due to their affinity with the Muslim Leaguers, whose loyalty had never been in doubt, and with whom they could meet on friendly terms, and how far to their antipathy to the khadi-clad, vegetarian, gaol-going Congressmen who were the avowed enemies of the British Raj. In 1940 many of these British officers may not have troubled themselves about the merits of the proposal for the partition of India; it was enough for them that there was little chance of other parties accepting the proposal, that the political deadlock was likely to last indefinitely, and that the only alternative was continuance of British rule.

## IX

The circle of mistrust between the Congress and the Government which had begun with Linlithgow's declaration of war in September 1939 was to be completed with the passage of the 'Quit India' resolution by the All India Congress Committee in August 1942. Congress leaders realized during the first two years of the war that the British Government, headed by Winston Churchill in Britain and by Linlithgow in India, was reluctant to pledge itself to Indian freedom after the war, or to take the Congress and other political parties into effective partnership during the war. All that the Indian National Congress was offered was membership of advisory committees and seats in the Viceroy's Executive Council without an effective voice in the administration. This was a passive role which a militant nationalist party, with twenty years of struggle behind it, could not accept. It could hardly sit back with folded hands as a spectator of events, while the future of nations was at stake. Pressures began to build up within the Congress for a mass civil disobedience movement. Gandhi resisted these pressures as long as he could, and then diverted them into the relatively innocuous channels of 'individual satyagraha'. This was conceived as a token protest without seriously embarrassing the war-effort, but nearly 30,000 prominent Congressmen courted imprisonment during the years 1940–1. Gandhi's firm faith in non-violence and his refusal to countenance anything but non-violence even against external aggression created some complications at the time. His pacifism was not, however, shared by Nehru or, indeed, the majority in the Congress Working Committee. On two occasions, after the fall of France and the entry of Japan in the war, when a National Government in favour of vigorously prosecuting the war seemed to be a possibility, Gandhi did not stand in the way of his colleagues and stepped aside to let them cooperate with the Government, if honourable terms were forthcoming. At the beginning of 1942, as the Japanese swept everything before them in South-East Asia, and eastern India came perilously close to the theatre of war, a section in the Congress, led by Nehru, Azad, and Rajagopalachari, felt that it was time to mobilize national resources to the utmost for defence against Japan.

The critical war situation also had its impact on the British War Cabinet, and resulted in the despatch of Sir Stafford Cripps to India. His Draft Declaration was a great step forward in so far as it recognized India's right after the war to frame a constitution through a Constituent Assembly. The basic demand of the Congress had been conceded, but vitiated by certain provisions introduced out of deference to the Muslim League, the Indian princes, and British Tories. This clause in the Draft Declaration laid down that any province or provinces, which did not acquiesce in the new constitution, would be entitled to frame a constitution of their own, giving them 'the same full status as the Indian Union'. This clause threatened to convert India into a political chequer-board, containing scores of princely states and independent provinces, or groups of provinces which would make short work of India as a political and economic entity—a prospect which made every Indian nationalist shudder. Gandhi, who had been specially invited from Wardha to see Cripps, after reading the proposals, advised him to take the first plane home. Nehru's feelings on 'balkanization' were equally strong; in a telegram to Krishna Menon in England he criticized the 'whole conception leading [to the] break up of India with British forces guarding States, interfering [with] freedom [of the] Union, encouraging disruptive tendencies'.

In his press conferences and broadcasts, Cripps defended the provision for non-accession of provinces on the ground that it would, by reassuring Muslims, make the drastic step of secession superfluous. 'The door must be left open', Cripps said in one of his broadcasts. 'If you want to persuade a number of people who are inclined to be antagonistic to enter the same room, it is unwise to tell them that once they go in, there is no way out.'[76] Cripps failed to foresee that this approach would have a contrary effect upon the Muslim League. Jinnah welcomed the non-accession clause as a 'recognition given to the principle of partition'. His only grievance was that it was a 'veiled recognition', and in equivocal terms.[77] He demanded amendments in the details of the constitution-making process, which would ensure beyond doubt the secession of the provinces he claimed for Pakistan. In the event, Cripps succeeded not in weaning Jinnah from his secessionist aims, but in encouraging him in the belief that the partition of India would be conceded by Britain, if the League persisted in its campaign.

In its resolution of 2 April 1942, on the Cripps proposals, the Congress Working Committee criticized the 'novel principle of non-accession for a Province', but affirmed 'nevertheless the Committee cannot think in terms of compelling the people of any territorial unit to remain in an Indian Union against their declared and established will'. As an organization pledged to democratic principles and non-violent methods, the Congress may have felt justified in making such a declaration, but it was an indirect endorsement of the possibility of secession by a territorial unit, which could not but be a source of encouragement to the Muslim League. The immediate effect of the Cripps Mission was therefore to give a boost to the movement for Pakistan and to lower the morale of those, particularly nationalist Muslims, who had stood against it.[78]

For Jawaharlal Nehru, as for his colleagues in the Working Committee, the long-term proposals of Sir Stafford Cripps had serious snags, but he was prepared to shelve the constitutional issue and to concentrate on the formation of a National Government to resist the Japanese, who were battering at the gates of India. Nehru's mind was full of plans for raising national militias to fight the invader, should he get a foothold on Indian soil. No agreement could, however, be reached on the formation of a National Government owing to the basic hostility not only of the Viceroy, but also of Prime Minister Churchill, to bringing the Congress o r, as he had frankly described it, 'hostile elements into the defence machine'. While the British Government was unwilling to admit the Congress as a partner in the defence against Japan, the Muslim League maintained its hostility to the Congress despite the immediate peril from Japan. When Nehru suggested that the Muslim League would have joined a 'national government' if it had been possible to form one, Jinnah immediately refuted the statement. 'I assert', he said, 'that if the Congress demand [for national government] had been accepted, it would have been the death-knell to the Mussalmans of India'.[79] We know now that there was a school of thought in the Muslim League Council which opposed participation in a national government at the centre even during the war, lest this participation in a unitary government should prejudice the demand for Pakistan.[80]

In the weeks following the failure of the Cripps Mission, Gandhi was driven to the conclusion that something had to be done to save India from going the way of Malaya and Burma, by giving to the Indian people a stake in the defence of their country. He became convinced that no solution of the communal problem was possible so long as Hindus and Muslims had a third party—the British—to look up to. These convictions provided the main impulse behind the 'Quit India' resolution which the All India Congress Committee passed at its Bombay meeting on 8 August 1942. This meeting was preceded by hectic political activity. The Congress leaders felt that their organization faced the greatest crisis in its long history. In this crisis they were prepared to review relations not only with the British Government but with other political parties, particularly the Muslim League. They were imprisoned immediately after the 'Quit India' resolution was passed, but there is evidence to show that if they had been allowed time to do so, they would have tried to reach an agreement with the League. Testimony to this is borne by Dr Abdul Latif of Hyderabad who had been meeting and corresponding with Nehru and Azad at this time. In a letter dated 6 August 1942, Nehru explained his views on the Pakistan issue to Dr Latif:

India, as it is, contains nearly all the important elements and resources that can make her a strong and more or less self-sufficient nation. To cut her up will be, from the economic point of view as well as others, a fatal thing, breaking up that national economic unity and weakening each part.

All these arguments are reinforced by recent world history, and in fact by the course of the war itself.

This has shown that small nations have no future before them, except as hangers-on of larger nations. We do not want India or any part of India to be such a hanger-on or a kind of semi-dependency, political or economic, of any other nation. . . . In fact the tendency in the world is for large federation to come into existence.

The All India Congress Committee's principal resolution of

8 August had pledged the Congress to a federal constitution, 'with the largest autonomy for the federating units and with the residuary powers vested in these units'. Dr Latif, who had talked to Congress leaders during these critical days before their arrest, was convinced that they were willing to go to the farthest limit to satisfy the political aspirations of the Muslim community and to remove its misgivings. Gandhi had in fact gone so far as to propose that the British should quit India by transferring power exclusively to the All India Muslim League.

Dr Latif was not an adherent of the Congress; indeed, in his correspondence with Nehru he had started as a sharp critic. But by the summer of 1942 he had realized that the Congress was prepared to concede to the provinces the widest autonomy with a limited centre—'the substance of Pakistan'. He begged Jinnah to respond to the Congress gestures; the division of India, he argued, would not solve the communal problem, but only aggravate it. Jinnah dismissed Latif's correspondence with the Congress leaders as 'contradictory, disingenuous and dubious'. Latif replied that:

Arguments as these only go to confirm the view held by the Congressites that Mr Jinnah was never serious about a settlement with the Congress. For aught I can say, it is clear to my mind, from my talks with its leaders that the Congress on its part appeared sincerely anxious to settle its differences with the League and with its help and willing co-operation to rally the people of India for the defence of the country by forming an interim popular government.[81]

Latif observed later,

I have reasons to believe that he [Jinnah] and his Working Committee had neither studied nor attempted to grasp the full implications of Pakistan. He had unfortunately lulled himself into the belief that if he could only carve out two small so-called independent states for the Mussalmans in the north-west and north-east, he would have solved for all times, the problems of Indian Muslims.

The real Muslim problem does not concern so much the Muslims of those parts where they form a majority, and where they can look after themselves in any constitution, as it concerns the Muslim minority from Delhi, Lucknow, Patna towns to Cape Comorin, who would be rendered eternal orphans under Mr Jinnah's plan. . . . I have found Mr Jinnah incapable of conceiving the hundred million Muslims in

India as an indivisible entity and that we can secure all the advantages of his Pakistan without having to labour under its inevitable disadvantages by setting the scheme against an all-India background.[82]

Dr Latif's plea to Jinnah to grasp the hand of friendship that the Congress leaders were extending before they were removed from the political scene did not evoke a response. The arrest of the Congress leaders immediately after the meeting of the All India Congress Committee, mob violence in some parts of the country, and the swift and strong repression by the Government brought Government–Congress relations to the lowest ebb ever, and created a situation which the Muslim League immediately turned to its advantage.

The Muslim League Working Committee hastened to denounce the 'Quit India' movement as an attempt to establish 'Hindu Raj' and 'to deal a death-blow to the Muslim goal of Pakistan.' The League's tirade against the Congress was useful to the Government of India which had aimed the full force of its war-publicity machine against the Congress, in a bid to represent it as anti-British, anti-national, and pro-Axis.

With the Congress outlawed, its leaders in prison, its publicity media silenced, the stage was clear for the Muslim League. 'The Government have no love for the League', a Congress leader wrote, 'less for its leader. For them, the League and its leader are the enemy's enemy, the common enemy being the national forces represented by the Congress.'[83] Engaged in the task of an all-out offensive against the Congress, the British Governors and officials were glad to see an ally in the most vociferous opponent of the Congress.

The political gains of the League's new position were not long in coming. In August 1942, Sir Saadullah Khan formed a League ministry in Assam. A month later, Allah Baksh, the Premier of Sind (whose sympathy with the Congress was an open secret) renounced his title of Khan Bahadur and OBE; for these offences he was dismissed from his office even though he commanded a majority in the Legislative Assembly. A League ministry was formed in Sind. In March 1943, Nazimuddin, Jinnah's loyal supporter in Bengal, formed a ministry with the help of the European group. In May 1943, the Muslim League was able to form a ministry in

North-West Frontier Province, as most of the Congress members
were in gaol.

'The middle years of the war', a British historian has recently
pointed out, 'saw the consolidation of the Muslim League in the
Muslim majority provinces.'[84] This consolidation was a direct
result of the breach between the Congress and the Government,
and Jinnah's skill in making political capital out of it. This was not
a new technique: he had practised it since the outbreak of war.[85] It
was only when the estrangement between the Congress and the
Government reached its peak that the dividends to the League were
the highest in the form of League ministries in provinces which it
claimed for Pakistan.

## X

As the tide of war turned against the Axis Powers in 1944 there
were indications that the Indian political deadlock might relax.
C. Rajagopalachari, who had been pleading for two years with his
colleagues in the Congress party for the 'recognition of the right of
separation of certain areas from united India', presented to Jinnah
in April 1944 a formula which became the basis of talks between
Jinnah and Gandhi in September 1944. Gandhi had been released
from prison on grounds of health in May 1944 and was persuaded
to take the initiative in seeking an understanding with Jinnah on the
issue of Pakistan. Gandhi did not accept the two-nation theory, but
agreed that after the war a commission should demarcate contiguous districts in the north-west and north-east of India where the
Muslim population was in absolute majority, and the wishes of the
inhabitants of these areas be ascertained through the votes of the
adult population. If the vote went in favour of separation, these
areas were to be formed into a separate state as soon as possible after
India was free from foreign domination. However, there was to be
a Treaty of Separation between the successor states in the subcontinent, 'for satisfactory administration of foreign affairs, defence,
internal communications, customs, commerce, and the like, which
must necessarily continue to be matters of common interest between the contracting parties'.

That Gandhi should have offered these terms to Jinnah in
September 1944, would have been unthinkable four years earlier

when he had described Pakistan as an 'untruth'. Gandhi had not merely recognized the principle of partition, but even suggested a mechanism for it. It is important to note that while Gandhi suggested links between the two states, he did not insist on a Central Government. He was content to have 'a Board of Representatives of both the states' for certain common purposes and services. He could not, he confessed to Jinnah, envisage the two [successor] states after the partition 'as if there was nothing common between . . . [them] except enmity'. The search for cultural and economic autonomy was legitimate enough, but some safeguards were in Gandhi's view imperative to prevent an armament race and an armed conflict between the two states.

Jinnah rejected Gandhi's offer. The demarcation of boundaries by districts was unacceptable to him, though he was to accept it in 1947. He would have nothing less than the 'full' six provinces for Pakistan, even though in two of them (Punjab and Bengal) the Muslim majority was marginal, and in one province, Assam, it was non-existent. Jinnah did not see why non-Muslim population in these provinces should have a voice in determining their own fate: if there was to be a plebiscite or referendum, it was to be confined to Muslims. Nor would Jinnah agree to any common links between India and Pakistan in such matters as foreign affairs, defence, or customs. Nor would he agree that 'marriage should precede divorce', that partition should come, if at all, after the British departure and after the two communities had an opportunity to coexist. While these conversations were no more than a kind of re-education for Gandhi, they brought an accession of political strength to Jinnah. That Gandhi had knocked at his door raised Jinnah's prestige in the eyes of Indian Muslims. The fact that the Mahatma had relented so far as to discuss the machinery for the exercise of 'the right of self-determination' by Muslims was a feather in Jinnah's cap.

Two efforts at a short-term solution in 1944–5 met with no more success than Gandhi's attempt at a long-term solution. Early in 1944, the 'Bhulabhai Desai–Liaquat Ali Pact' for Congress–League cooperation in an Interim Government at the centre was published. Liaquat Ali backed out. Desai burnt his fingers in these parleys; the pact was rejected out of hand by Jinnah, but it nevertheless introduced the idea of parity between the Congress and the League in the formation of a national government. At the Simla Conference summoned by Lord Wavell in June 1945, this parity was almost taken for granted: by the time the conference ended, Jinnah had raised his price by demanding parity between the Muslim League and all other parties. The Simla Conference broke down because Jinnah would not permit the Viceroy to nominate to the Executive Council any Muslim member—not even a non-Congress Muslim 'Unionist' from Punjab—who did not owe allegiance to the League.

## XI

The Simla Conference had failed to break the deadlock. But two important events occurred in the wake of the Conference which made a new initiative possible. With the surrender of Japan on 15 August 1945, the war came to an end, and the Labour Party came into power. Lord Wavell went to London, and on his return to India announced on 19 September that the British Government was still working in the spirit of the Cripps offer and intended to convene a constitution-making body. Elections to the central and provincial legislatures, which were in any case overdue, were announced. Indian politics were again deeply stirred and entered a period of intense excitement, interminable negotiations, and bitter controversy.

In the early months of 1945, the Congress leaders could see the beginnings of a change in British policy, but they were not yet convinced of the British bona fides. This was understandable in view of what they had gone through. Nehru himself had spent 3,251 days in British prisons; his latest term from 9 August 1942 to 15 June 1945 had been the longest. A member of the parliamentary delegation has recorded how the members of the Congress Working Committee, 'all ex-prisoners, regarded the British Parliamentarians with a suspicious reserve behind a veil of courtesy'. Nehru had been quoted in the British press as having called the delegation 'a huge hoax'; he had not used these words, but neither he nor his colleagues were impressed by the gesture of a goodwill delegation. Indeed, it was not only the Congress leaders, who had lost faith in British sincerity; the veteran Liberal leader Srinivas

Sastri, who was on his deathbed, told Gandhi in January 1946, 'We know nothing can come out of it [the British parliamentary delegation]. Labour or Conservative so far as India is concerned, they are all one and the same.' That this melancholy judgement should have been passed at a time when the transfer of power was imminent, and by one who had always been a friend of the British connection, showed that the representatives of the British Raj in India, with whom the Indians came into contact, gave no inkling of an early departure.

The Cabinet Mission reached Delhi on 24 March 1946. Nearly fifty persons were summoned for exchanges of views with the Mission. 'It is difficult to understand', Vallabhbhai Patel wrote to Nehru on 27 March, 'why this procedure has been adopted and what useful purpose can be served by calling such a group again. It looks as if they are pursuing the same old process to which this country is accustomed, and it leads one to believe that the local bureaucracy must be behind it.'

As the negotiations with the Cabinet Mission proceeded, the Congress distrust of the British diminished, but it never entirely disappeared. It was not a question of the sincerity of Pethick-Lawrence, Cripps, Alexander, and Wavell. They seemed anxious to do the right thing, but they were surrounded by men—senior officials—who could hardly be expected to suddenly unlearn the history of the previous three decades. To the sympathy of some of the senior British officers with the League, testimony has been provided by one of its prominent members.[86] There were, it seemed to Congress leaders, 'English Mullahs' around the Viceroy who were not sorry to give a parting kick to the party who had been primarily responsible for challenging and liquidating the Raj and for wrecking promising British careers in the I.C.S. and the Indian army.

As the negotiations with the Cabinet Mission got under way, it became evident that the main confrontation was between the Congress and the League. For the first time Jinnah had been brought to the negotiating table, made to stay there, and to spell out his terms. Nehru and his colleagues were naturally cautious in dealing with him. For eight years he had defied all attempts at a direct and fruitful discussion. In one important respect, the situation had of course changed. The rift between the Congress and the Government which had given Jinnah his favourable bargaining position was closing. 'It would not be right to allow any minority, however large and important', Sir Stafford Cripps had declared in July 1945, 'to hold up the attainment of self-government in India, any more than it would be right to force the Muslim majority provinces into a new constitutional arrangement . . .'.[87] The Churchill–Amery–Linlithgow team which in the early years of the war had been so sympathetic to the League had been substituted by the Attlee–Pethick-Lawrence–Wavell team, which could be expected to take a more objective view of the Indian political situation.

The Muslim League seems to have realized this; from the beginning of 1946 it increasingly stressed dangers of civil war and issued threats which were calculated to rouse the Muslims, frighten the Hindus, and impress the British. In March 1946, Abdur Rab Nishtar, later a League nominee to the Interim Government, declared: 'The real fact is that Mussalmans belong to a martial race and are no believers of the non-violent principles of Mr Gandhi'.[88] Abdul Qaiyum Khan, the League leader of NWFP, threatened that the people in the tribal areas 'who were all armed' were for Pakistan. He was asked by many Muslim students and men in uniform of the time when 'marching orders would be given by the Qaid-e-Azam . . . if they [the British] decide there should be one Constituent Assembly, then the Muslims will have no other alternative but to take out the sword and rebel against it'.[89] Sir Firoz Khan Noon, whose loyalty to the British Raj had never been in doubt, threatened on 9 April: 'I tell you this much. If we find that we have to fight Great Britain for placing us under one Central Government or Hindu Raj, then the havoc which the Muslims will play will put to shame what Chengiz Khan and Halaku did.' Sir Firoz said that if the Hindus and the British did not concede Pakistan, 'the only course left to Muslims was to look to Russia. There was already a great movement in Punjab, including landlords, in favour of Communism.'[90] This menacing position was a novel one for a political party which had always been careful not to embroil itself with the Government and included among its leaders men who had been instruments, if not pillars, of the Raj.

It was to the accompaniment of this tearing propaganda campaign that the Cabinet Mission commenced its work in March 1946. From the record of the negotiations, it is obvious that the Congress Working Committee was subject to three divergent, and to some extent contradictory, pulls, making decisions painfully difficult. In the first place, the Congress was eager to be rid of foreign rule, and constructively respond to the gesture of the Labour Government in sending a high-powered mission to India. Secondly, the Congress was prepared to make the widest concessions to the minorities, particularly the Muslims, in the future constitution of India by agreeing to a limited centre, residuary powers in the provinces, and the maximum constitutional safeguards for protection of religious and cultural rights. These two considerations had, however, to be balanced against another: the Congress wanted to avoid pitfalls which the ingenuity of the Muslim League or the astuteness of the 'English Mullahs', operating behind the scenes, might devise: it was important not to accept constitutional formulae which would not work, or which would do permanent damage to the future of the country.

The three-month long negotiations in the trying Delhi summer were indeed a great strain on the British ministers. We know that Pethick-Lawrence was exhausted, Cripps became ill, and Alexander was exasperated. But the strain on Gandhi, Nehru, Azad, and Patel was no less serious. They knew they were engaged in not only a battle of wits but of wills with Jinnah. By sheer tenacity and refusal to make any concession, the League leader had built up his position and made the constitutional problem almost intractable. His price for settlement had progressively risen. It had begun with separate electorates in 1916, gone up to Fourteen points in 1929, to composite ministries in 1937, and finally to the partition of the country in 1940. The six provinces he claimed for his Pakistan included Assam, where the Muslim population was 33 per cent, and Punjab and Bengal where the Muslim majority was extremely slight. The League's insistence on holding a position which seemed untenable, intrigued and exasperated the Congress leaders. They felt that the League was out to achieve its objective by a combination of intransigence and threats of civil war. Why did the League want to include in its homeland predominantly non-Muslim areas?

The mental processes of the advocates of partition are illuminated by a letter written on 7 October 1942 by a prominent member of the League Council to Jinnah:

Further, one of the basic principles lying behind the Pakistan idea is that of keeping hostages in Muslim provinces as against the Muslims in the Hindu provinces. . . . If we allow millions of Hindus to go out of the orbit of our influence, the security of the Mussalmans in the minority provinces will be greatly minimized . . . complete segregation of the Muslim and Hindu population as at present situated is impossible, but there may come a time when it may become feasible. If we allow large territories to go out of our hands in the process of readjustment [of territories] such an exchange of population would be impossible, because the territories which will be left over with us will not be sufficient to receive and maintain large populations migrating from the other land. . . . There is one other factor which should be taken into account. If the whole of Punjab becomes a part of Pakistan zone, Kashmere and other Punjab native states will have no direct communication left with the non-Muslim provinces. They will naturally desire union with them and shall be forced to ask the Pakistan Union for a right of transit. In that event, the Pakistan Government can fairly claim the same right for Hyderabad and other Muslim estates [*sic*] to establish contact with the Pakistan Union.[91]

## XII

The negotiations with the Cabinet Mission were conducted by Azad on behalf of the Congress, though Nehru, Patel, and Abdul Ghaffar Khan were associated with him. The Working Committee was continually in session and Gandhi was available for consultations. Nehru was very much in the picture, but it was Gandhi whose scepticism, particularly about the grouping of provinces, influenced the Congress attitude in the early stages of the negotiations.

Torn between their desire for an early end to British rule and their anxiety about being outmanoeuvred by the Muslim League into a wrong decision, the Congress Working Committee had many an agonizing reappraisal before it passed its resolution on 25 June 1946 accepting the long-term Cabinet Plan. In the final decision, Vallabhbhai Patel's influence was probably dominant, but he was able to carry with him his colleagues in the Working

Committee, including Nehru. Gandhi's doubts were not entirely resolved, but when the time came for ratification by the All India Congress Committee, Gandhi threw his weight behind the Working Committee. The All India Congress Committee met at Bombay on 7 July 1946. It was at this meeting that Nehru took charge of the Congress presidency from Abul Kalam Azad and delivered a speech which has been described as a 'serious tactical blunder'[92] and even an act of direct sabotage of the Cabinet Mission Plan. This speech is alleged to have wrecked the Cabinet Mission Plan, and the last hope of preserving the unity of the Indian subcontinent. The charge is based on some remarks made by Nehru, but without reference to the context in which he spoke. Nehru was replying to the attacks made by socialist speakers. One of them, Achyut Patwardhan, had argued that 'the Cabinet Mission Plan foreboded ill both for Congress integrity and the communal problem',[93] and suspected the influence of 'Clive Street European capitalists' in the proposals for grouping of provinces. Another speaker, Aruna Asaf Ali, pointed to the 'traps laid by British imperialists', and called for a mass civil disobedience struggle to throw out the alien rulers.[94] A number of critics had cast doubts on the status and power of the Constituent Assembly, which was to be convened by the Government and could exist only at its sufferance. It was this criticism that Nehru attempted to answer in his speech of 7 July. The oft-quoted sentence from this speech: 'We are not bound by a single thing except that we have decided to go to the Constituent Assembly', was not the most important part of it. The whole tenor of his 6000-word speech was to justify the acceptance of the Cabinet Mission Plan. 'We cannot forget', he pleaded with his socialist critics, 'that while we have to be revolutionary, we also have to think in terms of statesmanship—not in shouting slogans and escaping responsibility but in terms of facing the big problems. The world looks to you and the Congress for great decisions and it is no use to sit cursing, fuming and fretting. . . .'[95] Nehru refuted the charge that the Constituent Assembly would be a 'sham', or a nursery game at which India politicians would play while the British Government supervised them. This was why he declared that no 'dictation' from the British Government would be tolerated.[96]

Three days later, on 10 July, Nehru covered the same ground at a press conference in Bombay. Here again, while he emphasized the sovereign character of the Constituent Assembly, he affirmed that the Congress was determined to make a success of the constitutional mechanism outlined by the Cabinet Mission. 'Once the Congress went into the [Constituent] Assembly', Nehru said, 'its main objective would be to see how to make it a success . . . and in so doing the Congress would certainly have to take into consideration the situation created by the Cabinet statement of 16 May.[97]

With some emphasis he added,

the Constituent Assembly would never accept any dictation or any other directive from the British Government in regard to its work. The only two factors which limit the sovereignty of the Constituent Assembly are those relating to the minorities and the Indo-British treaty. . . . When the Congress had stated that the Constituent Assembly was a sovereign body, the Cabinet Mission replied, 'Yes, more or less subject to two considerations. Firstly, proper arrangement for minorities; and the other, treaty between India and Britain.' I wish the Mission had stated both these matters are not controversial. It is obvious that the minorities question has to be settled satisfactorily. It is also obvious that if there is any kind of peaceful change-over in India, it is bound to result in some kind of a treaty with Great Britain.[98]

Clearly, Nehru had no intention of repudiating the framework of the Cabinet Mission Plan. All the available evidence points to his anxiety to arrive at a satisfactory solution of the minority problem, and of Indo–British relations after the withdrawal of British power. In so far as Nehru was outspoken, even provocative, in his utterances at Bombay on 7 and 10 July, his words were directed not to the Muslim League, but to the critics of the Congress policy within the Congress organization or to the British Government.

On the grouping of provinces in the Cabinet Mission Plan, Nehru told the press conference that,

the probability is, from any approach to the question, that there will be no grouping. . . . Section A would decide against grouping. There was but little chance of the NWFP supporting grouping. . . . Further, there was a good deal of feeling against grouping in the Punjab, in the NWFP and in Sind for economic and other reasons. . . . Both these provinces were afraid of being swamped by the Punjab.

This statement has often been cited as a destructive piece of work. In fact Nehru was doing no more than stating the political probabilities as they appeared to him in July 1946: the lack of majority support in Punjab (which had a non-League coalition ministry), the natural reluctance of even Muslims in Sind to be swamped by the Punjabis; the presence of a Congress government in NWFP with its solid base in the Muslim community, and opposition to the League, to grouping, and to Pakistan.

It is arguable that Nehru should have avoided a public discussion of political probabilities, which were likely to provoke the League. But he was committing neither a breach of faith with the Cabinet Mission, nor an act of sabotage. Neither in his speech at the All India Congress Committee, nor at the press conference did he intend to wreck the Cabinet Mission Plan. His ideas on how the Constituent Assembly would function were given in his broadcast on 7 September 1946 after the formation of the Interim Government. In this he said,

There has been much heated argument about sections and groupings in the Constituent Assembly. We are perfectly prepared to, and have accepted, the position of formation of groups. . . . We do not look upon the Constituent Assembly as an arena for conflict or the forcible imposition of one view-point on another. That would not be the way to build up a contented and united India. We seek agreed and inte-grated solutions with the largest measure of goodwill behind them. We shall go to the Constituent Assembly with the fixed determination of finding a common basis for agreement on all controversial issues.

And so, in spite of all that has happened and the hard words that have been said . . . we invite even those who differ from us to enter the Constituent Assembly as equals and partners with us with no binding commitments. It may well be that when we meet and face common tasks, our present difficulties will fade away.[99]

The meeting of the All India Muslim League Council, which was to withdraw acceptance of the Cabinet Mission Plan, had been called by Nawabzada Liaqat Ali Khan, its General Secretary, *before* Nehru held the press conference in Bombay. The Nawabzada's statement announcing the meeting referred to 'the grave possibility of All-India Muslim League not participating in the Constituent Assembly for lack of assurance that the fundamental principles of the Cabinet Mission Scheme will be adhered to'. The League had been sore at not being invited to form the Interim Government though it had conveyed its acceptance of the Cabinet Mission Plan, while the Congress had not. The Nawabzada charged the Viceroy and Cabinet ministers with breaking their pledge.[100] 'I ask the Muslims', he said, 'to be prepared and ready. We want peace with honour, but if there is to be war, we should accept the challenge.' Nehru's remarks at Bombay were thus not the initial, or even the primary factor in provoking the League to revoke its earlier resolution. As Pethic-Lawrence told an Indian visitor, 'those remarks gave Jinnah the excuse he was looking for to get out of the Constituent Assembly and the Cabinet Mission Plan'.[101]

In the resolution which the All India Muslim League passed on 29 July, countermanding its acceptance of the Cabinet Mission Plan, it asserted that 'of the two major parties, the Muslim League alone has accepted the statements of 16 and 25 May according to the spirit and letter of the proposals embodied therein'. The assertion is not borne out by the very terms of the resolution passed by the League's Council on 6 June 1946. One of the reasons given in this resolution for the acceptance of the Cabinet Mission Plan was that the League saw in it 'the basis and the foundation of Pakistan . . . [which] are inherent in the Mission plan by virtue of the compulsory grouping of six Muslim provinces in Sections B and C'. The resolution went on to affirm that the Muslim League agreed 'to co-operate with the constitution-making machinery proposed in the scheme outlined by the Mission in the hope that it would ultimately result in the establishment of [a] complete[ly] sovereign Pakistan'.[102]

Clearly, the League did not consider the Cabinet Mission Plan, with its three-tier structure, as a final compromise between the Congress ideal of a strong and united India and the League objective of two separate sovereign states. On the contrary, the League made no secret of its hopes and plans that the Cabinet Mission Plan would be a stepping-stone to an independent Pakistan. In his speech to the Muslim League Council on 5 June, Jinnah made no secret of his intentions or tactics:

Let me tell you that Muslim India will not rest content until we have established full, complete and sovereign Pakistan. . . . The Lahore Resolution [of March 1940] did not mean that, when Muslims put forward their demand, it must be accepted at once. . . . It is a big struggle and continued struggle. The first struggle was to get the representative character of the League accepted. That fight they had started and they had won. Acceptance of the Mission's proposal was not the end of their struggle for Pakistan. They should continue their struggle till Pakistan is achieved.[103]

As for 'groups of provinces', Jinnah told his Council, they 'should have powers on all subjects except defence, communications, and foreign affairs. But so far as defence was concerned, it would remain in the hands of the British till the new constitution was enforced. They would fight in the Constituent Assembly to restrict communications to what was absolutely necessary for defence only.'[104] The Cabinet Mission Plan was thus to be made a prelude to Pakistan in two ways. In the first place, the 'grouping' of provinces in the east and the west was to be made compulsory, the widest powers were to be conferred on the 'groups', and provincial autonomy was practically to cease to exist. In the second place, the Central Government was to be made as weak and ineffective as possible, by the narrowest interpretation of its functions and by denying it any right of taxation. A Central Government which lived on doles, had no say in trade, industry, and communications (except for defence) and was composed of representatives of antagonistic units in its executive and legislature, could scarcely be expected to prevent the secession of the League's groups of provinces in the north-west and east.[105]

A three-tier constitution, such as the Cabinet Mission had outlined, was a delicate mechanism with numerous checks and balances. Unless the two major parties, the Congress and the League, entered the Constituent Assembly with tremendous goodwill and determination to cooperate, it was impossible to draft a workable constitution, much less to enforce it. In retrospect, it is clear that the Muslim League's idea of a Central Government for a subcontinent like India, in the mid-twentieth century was completely out-of-date. A weak Central Government might endanger the security of the country and its economic growth, but was likely to create the ideal conditions in which units could break off.[106] The Congress had, of course, no intention of letting the League get away with the Pakistan of its own conception, with 'full' six provinces by disguising them as groups of provinces in the first instance. This was the background of the opposition by Gandhi, Nehru, Patel, and indeed the entire Congress leadership, to compulsory grouping of provinces. This opposition could have been softened if Jinnah had tried to assure the Hindus of Assam and West Bengal, the Congress Muslims of NWFP, and the Sikhs of Punjab, that grouping of provinces was a voluntary and constructive association of neighbouring provinces for mutual advantage, and that it would not involve coercion of minorities. By failing to give this assurance, Jinnah sealed the fate of the grouping scheme, and thus of the Cabinet Mission Plan: it is true he thereby ensured Pakistan, but it was to be a Pakistan minus East Punjab, West Bengal, and the major portion of Assam.[107]

## XIII

After the rejection of the Cabinet Mission Plan by the Muslim League, events moved fast. The Congress Working Committee passed a resolution, reaffirming its acceptance 'in its entirety' of the Cabinet Mission Plan. The Viceroy, who had invited both the parties to join an Interim Government, decided to go ahead with the proposal even though the Muslim League refused to be party to it. Nehru went to see Jinnah, but the League leader was adamant.

The formation of the Interim Government raised the frustration and bitterness of the League to a high pitch. Its leader spoke of 'the Caste Hindu, Fascist Congress and their few individual henchmen of other communities who wanted to be installed in power and authority in the Government of India to dominate and rule over Mussalmans . . . with the aid of British bayonets'.[108] The Congress knew what it was to be in the wilderness: that had been its lot for a quarter of a century. But for the League it was the first occasion when it was on the wrong side of the Government.

The resolution withdrawing the League's acceptance of the Cabinet Mission proposals had included a threat of 'direct action'. 'This day we bid good-bye to constitutional methods', Jinnah had told the League Council on 29 July, 'Today we have also forged a pistol and are in a position to use it'.[109] The League declared 16 August as a 'Direct Action Day', and asked Muslims to observe it all over India. One wonders whether League leaders had thought out the implications of 'direct action'. This was a technique the Congress had employed against the Government on a number of occasions, but in each case it had been under the leadership of Gandhi for whom satyagraha had been a lifelong discipline. No other Congress leader had ventured to launch a mass movement. Evidently, League leaders did not realize that 'a direct action movement' required more than angry feelings and strong words.

It is not necessary here to go into the details of the communal riots which began at Calcutta on 16 August with the observance of the 'Direct Action Day', and spread like a chain-reaction from Calcutta to East Bengal, from East Bengal to Bihar, and from Bihar to Punjab. Unfortunately, the League leaders reacted to the riots with a political rather than a human bias. Even though a League ministry was in office in Calcutta, Jinnah blamed the riots on 'Gandhi, the Viceroy and the British'. Each communal outbreak was cited as a further endorsement of the two-nation theory, and of the inevitability of the partition of the country.

Shaken by the Calcutta riots, the Viceroy, Lord Wavell, decided to bring the Muslim League into the Interim Government where the League members functioned from the outset as an opposition bloc. As one of them put it: 'We are going into the Interim Government to get a foothold to fight for our cherished goal of Pakistan.'[110] This meant disruption of the Interim Government from within. There was scarcely an issue of domestic and foreign policy on which the representatives of the two parties saw eye to eye. An unfortunate result of this antagonism was that the civil service was infected by the communal virus.

By March 1947, when Mountbatten replaced Wavell, the Congress leadership had been sobered by its experience in the Interim Government as well as by the growing lawlessness in the country. A *modus vivendi* with the League seemed not remote, but impossible. Partition of India, demanded by the League, was bad enough, but even worse possibilities had begun to loom ahead. In the twilight of the British Empire in India, some of the Indian princes were nursing new ambitions. The Political Department of the Government of India was proceeding on the assumption that British paramountcy over the Indian States would lapse with the withdrawal of British power, and each of the rulers of 562 states would be free to decide his future. The princes of western and central India, under the inspiration of some of the larger states, especially Bhopal, were thinking in terms of leagues of princes. It was the intrigue by the ruler of Bastar, a small state in central India with the Nizam of Hyderabad, and the attitude of the Political

Department to it, which finally convinced Patel that it was imperative to secure immediate British withdrawal even if it meant
acceptance of the partition of India. A similar conclusion was
reached by Nehru after the frustrating experience of the working of
the Interim Government, where he noticed a 'mental alliance'
between British officials and members of the League.

It has been suggested that Nehru and Patel agreed to the partition
of India because they were avid for power. It is important to recall
that the decision in favour of partition was not that of Patel and
Nehru alone; it was endorsed by the Working Committee; and
in the All India Congress Committee 157 voted for it and only 15
against. It was a painful decision taken with a heavy heart, but there
seemed no alternative at the time. The immediate problem, as
Nehru saw, it, was 'to arrest the swift drift to anarchy and chaos'.

In retrospect it appears that Congress acceptance of partition was
not such a sudden development as it may have seemed at the time.
It was the culmination of a process which had begun immediately
after the passage of the Pakistan resolution by the Lahore session of
the All India Muslim League. Gandhi had opposed the two-nation
theory and the 'vivisection' of India, but he had nevertheless written
as early as April 1940:

I know no non-violent method of compelling the obedience of eight
crores of Muslims to the will of the rest of India, however powerful
a majority the rest may represent. The Muslims must have the same
right of self-determination that the rest of India has. We are at present
a joint family. Any member may claim a division.[111]

This was perhaps an inevitable position for a leader committed
to non-violence, but another leader such as Abraham Lincoln could
have insisted that there could be no compromise on the unity of
country. Two years later, the Congress Working Committee in its
resolution on the Cripps proposals affirmed that 'it cannot think in
terms of compelling the people of any territorial unit to remain in
the Indian Union against their declared and established will'.[112]
Under the impact of League propaganda and the political deadlock
with the Government, the Congress position on the question
of Partition was gradually softening.[113] In 1944, Gandhi in his
talks with Jinnah not only accepted the principle of partition, but
even discussed the mechanism for the demarcation of boundaries.
In 1946 the Congress, after much heart-searching, accepted the

Cabinet Mission Plan with its loose three-tier structure, and a Central Government which was unlikely to have the powers or the resources to maintain the unity of the subcontinent.

The Cabinet Mission Plan proved stillborn. The Interim Government revealed the incompatibility of the two major parties. Henceforth, there were only two options: partition of the country as demanded by the League, or a moratorium on political controversy and conflict for a couple of years to allow tempers to cool and to produce the climate in which a compromise solution could be secured. Unfortunately, the widespread communal rioting that began in August 1946 made respite impossible. In April 1947, when the situation looked grim, one man still hoped to build bridges of understanding between the communities. Gandhi toured the villages and towns of Bengal and Bihar, condemning violence irrespective of who perpetrated it, rehabilitating refugees, restoring confidence, and preaching the brotherhood of man. His greatest triumphs in this self-imposed mission lay ahead: in Calcutta in August 1947 and in Delhi in January 1948. But he was convinced that the tension, however serious it might appear, was a temporary phase, and that the British had no right to impose partition 'on an India temporarily gone mad'.[114] He suggested to Mountbatten that Jinnah should be invited to form a Muslim League Government; by this supreme gesture the Mahatma hoped to win over the League leader. The proposal was not taken seriously by the Viceroy. Nor were Nehru, Patel, and their colleagues, who had the frustrating experience of the Interim Government, prepared to hand over all power to the League. As for Jinnah's reaction to Gandhi's proposal (if it had been transmitted to him), it is doubtful whether it would have been different from what he had said about a similar proposal made by Gandhi in August 1942.

If they [the Congress] are sincere I should welcome it. If the British Government accepts the solemn declaration of Mr Gandhi and by an arrangement hands over the government of the country to the Muslim League, I am sure that under Muslim rule non-Muslims would be treated fairly, justly, nay, generously; and further the British will be making full amends to the Muslims by restoring the Government of India to them from whom they have taken it.[115]

The crux of the problem was whether the delay, such as Gandhi envisaged, could have staved off Partition. The political temperature had risen; it did not suit the Muslim League to have it lowered; for the League it was a case of 'now or never'. Gandhi's plea that there should be 'peace before Pakistan' did not impress the League. Indeed, the League's argument was that there could be no peace until Pakistan was established; that it was either to be a 'divided or destroyed India'. Having declared their resolve to leave India by June 1948, the British Government did not want to and perhaps could not antagonize the Muslim League, or compel it to a particular course of action. Three or four years earlier the British could have exercised a moderating influence on the League; in 1947 the scope for this was limited, especially after the 1946 elections, based on separate electorates in which all the 30 Muslim seats in the Central Legislative Assembly and 439 out of 494 seats in the provincial assemblies had been won by the Muslim League. The sins of Linlithgow were visited on Wavell and Mountbatten.

It is arguable that communal tension or disorder could not have lasted indefinitely. But it is difficult to judge such situations with any degree of confidence in the midst of fast-moving events. The mounting tension in 1947 could have touched off a civil war; alternatively it could have been brought to an abrupt end by some unforeseen, and spectacular incident, such as a fast by Gandhi. In the event, Mountbatten's judgement in the summer of 1947 that division of the country was the only practical solution was accepted by the three main parties to the decision: the British Government, the Indian National Congress, and the All India Muslim League.

## XIV

The final result, the partition of India, was a personal triumph for Jinnah. By arousing deep emotions, by skirting the details of his demand for Pakistan, and by concentrating on a tirade against 'Hindu Raj' and 'Congress tyranny', Jinnah was able to sustain a large consensus in his own community; by keeping his cards close to his chest, he was able to keep his following in good order. Such was the magical effect of his insistence on the full six provinces— Pakistan—that large numbers of his adherents in Bengal and Punjab failed to see the consequences of the division of the country. Even a seasoned politician like Suhrawardy confessed later that he had never expected the partition of Bengal.[116] As for Muslims in the

Hindu majority provinces, they had in any case nothing to gain from the secession of provinces in the east and west; the two-nation theory and the theory of hostages were to do them no good at all. Jinnah had played his cards skilfully. From near political eclipse in 1937 he had brought his party to a position where it could decisively influence events. His success was, however, due not only to his skill and tenacity, but to the tension between the Congress and the Government which prevailed throughout this period, except perhaps for the two years in which the Congress held office in the provinces.

The Government of India Act of 1935 was not the radical measure of constitutional reform it is being made out to be by some historians. The levers of ultimate authority remained in British hands; the federal structure, with its communal and princely checks and balances, if it had come into being, could have been capable of sustaining British rule for many years. In 1939 the British hierarchy in India may not have had the optimism of earlier generations of the ICS, but the Raj seemed a solid enough structure. Sir S.P. Sinha, an able and patriotic man, the first Indian to be appointed to the Viceroy's Executive Council, had estimated before the First World War that British rule would last 400 years. Twenty-five years later, on the eve of the Second World War, most Britons in India would have confidently predicted a lease of fifty years if not longer for the Raj. It was the aim of the Indian National Congress to wear down the British reluctance to part with power. The antagonism between Indian nationalism and British rule was inherent in the unnatural relation between the two countries. This antagonism helped the Muslim League in two ways: in securing it at crucial moments the support of certain British politicians and civil servants who were embittered with the Congress, and in ensuring to the League virtually exclusive possession of the political platform when the Congress was not only out of office, but outlawed. The brunt of the struggle for the liberation of India was borne by the Congress. The Muslim League had no role or part in this struggle, of which the establishment of Pakistan was a by-product. Others forced open the doors through which Jinnah walked to his goal.

Nehru has been criticized by latter-day writers for estranging the Muslim League and for driving it to extremist policies. Some of this criticism is due to an inadequate appreciation of Nehru's ideas and attitudes, and of the political framework within which he and the Congress party had to function.

Nehru's secularism was not a tactic against the Muslim League, but a deep conviction he held in his years of office with the same tenacity as in the years of opposition. The 'mass contact movement' was not a conspiracy against the Muslim League, but an integral part of the Congress programme since 1920 to educate people of all communities in all parts of India on political and economic issues. There were good reasons for stressing mass contact in the late-thirties—the electorate had expanded from 2 to 10 per cent of the population, and was bound to increase further if the Congress aim of adult franchise was to be realized. The idea that only the Muslim League had the right to approach Muslim masses was a totalitarian doctrine which made nonsense of democracy and political life, as they were commonly understood.

It has already been indicated that the failure of the coalition talks in UP in 1937 was in the circumstances of the time almost inevitable: in the face of Jinnah's minatory posture, the Congress could hardly have hamstrung itself in its very first attempt at ministry-making. It was not failure of these talks, but the electoral disaster of 1937, which seems to have driven Jinnah—who had his roots in the Victorian age and was trained as a rationalist and constitutionalist in the school of Dadabhai Naoroji and Gokhale—to use the dynamite of religious emotion for blasting his way to political influence and power. The new strategy brought quick results. The cry of religion in danger, the reiteration of 'Congress tyranny', and the spectre of 'Hindu Raj' roused the Muslims, widened the communal gulf, and created the climate in which the proposal for the partition of the country could be mooted.

It is difficult even today to contest the validity of the argument of Nehru and his colleagues, that religion is not a satisfactory basis for nationality in the modern world, that multi-religious, multilingual, and even multiracial societies should seek a political solution within the framework of a federal structure. This is what has been done under widely different conditions by the USSR, USA, Canada, and South Africa.

No serious attempt at a compromise solution could, however, be made. From 1937 to 1940, Jinnah refused to begin a dialogue with the Congress until it conceded the League's right to be the exclusive representative of the Muslim community. From 1940 onwards, he refused to begin a dialogue until the Congress conceded the principle of the partition of India. He did not elaborate the constitutional, economic, and even geographic content of his proposal.[117] While the Congress attitude towards the constitutional future of India underwent important changes between 1939 and 1946, Jinnah did not meet the Congress halfway, not even quarter-way, not budging an inch from the position he had adopted. Every overture was rejected; every concession treated as a bargaining counter for a better deal. Only once, in June 1946, he seemed to agree to a compromise by accepting the Cabinet Mission Plan; but his acceptance (as shown earlier in this chapter) was more apparent than real; in any case it was withdrawn within seven weeks.

If Jinnah's position had little flexibility, his political style was hardly calculated to assist in a compromise. He heaped ridicule and scorn on all Congress leaders, from Gandhi and Nehru down-wards. Some critics have suggested that Nehru was on occasion too theoretical, too proud and impatient to deal with Jinnah success-fully. It is well to remember that the patience and humility of Gandhi, the cool calculation of Rajagopalachari, the militant radicalism of Subhas Chandra Bose, the sedate realism of Abul Kalam Azad, and the gentleness of Rajendra Prasad equally failed to work on the League leader.

## NOTES AND REFERENCES

1. J. Nehru, *An Autobiography* (London, 1958 rpt), p. 544.
2. Ibid.
3. J. Nehru, *India and the World* (London, 1936), p. 86.
4. Ibid.
5. Ibid., pp. 91–2.
6. For details, *see* B.R. Nanda, *Mahatma Gandhi* (London, 1958), pp. 332–44.
7. J. Nehru to Lord Lothian, 9 Dec. 1935 (NP).
8. *Congress Presidential Addresses*, 1911–34 (Madras, 1934), 2nd Srs., p. 893.
9. J. Nehru to Lord Lothian, 17 Jan. 1936 (NP).
10. J. Nehru, *An Autobiography*, p. 470.

11. J. Nehru to Lord Lothian, 17 Jan. 1936 (NP).
12. J. Nehru, *An Autobiography*, p. 137.
13. C. Khaliquzzaman, *Pathway to Pakistan* (Lahore, 1961), p. 153.
14. UP Government Fortnightly Report on the Political situation for the first half of Dec. 1936, Govt of India Home Dept File 18, Dec. 1936 Poll.
15. Circular No. K-70/C.W. 886/34 dated 9 July 1936 from Secy, Court of Wards, UP, Allahabad to all district officers in the UP, except Kumaun (NP).
16. The Hindu Mahasabha did not win a single seat in the UP Legislative Assembly.
17. UP Govt Fortnightly Report on the Political Situation for the first half of Sept. 1936, Govt of India Home Dept File 18, Sept. 1936 Poll.
18. Khaliquzzaman, *Pathway to Pakistan*, p. 141.
19. According to Stanley Wolpert, 'the one clear divergence between the League and the Congress . . . dividing Jinnah from Nehru and Subhas Bose, was the League's firm opposition to any movement that aims at expropriation of private property'. Stanley Wolpert, *Jinnah of Pakistan* (New York, 1984), p. 144.
20. As suggested in Abul Kalam Azad's *India Wins Freedom* (Calcutta, 1959), p. 161.
21. Ramnarayan Chaudhary, *Nehru in His Own Words* (Ahmedabad, 1964), p. 87.
22. Sajjad Zaheer, a young left-wing Congress Muslim in 1937, has recorded that he pleaded with Abul Kalam Azad 'against any kind of compromise with the Muslim League, which in our view was a reactionary organization . . . ridden as it was at the time with jaded Muslim landlords and Nawabs . . .' Quoted from 'Notes on Hindu–Muslim Unity', *Mainstream*, 17 June 1967.
23. *Leader*, 28 April 1937.
24. Ibid., 6 May 1937.
25. Ibid.
26. Ibid., 9–10 May 1937.
27. Interview with the writer, 18 Oct. 1966, Oral History Transcript (NMML).
28. Total strength of the UP Legislative Assembly was 228, as shown below:

| General (including 20 seats reserved for Scheduled Castes and 4 for women) | 144 |
|---|---|
| Muslims | 66 |
| Anglo-Indians | 1 |
| Europeans | 2 |
| Indian Christians | 2 |
| Commerce | 3 |

| | |
|---|---|
| Landholders | 6 |
| University | 1 |
| Labour | 3 |
| | 228 |

The state of parties in the UP Legislative Assembly in 1937 was as follows:

| | |
|---|---|
| Congress | 134 |
| National Agriculturist Party | 29 |
| Hindu Sabha | 0 |
| Muslim League | 26 |
| Liberal | 1 |
| Independent Hindus | 8 |
| Independent Muslims | 24 |
| Independent Christians | 2 |
| Europeans and Anglo-Indians | 4 |
| | 228 |

29. Notes in the Home Dept, Govt of India File, 4 Oct. 1937 Poll, NAI.
30. In Aug. 1938, Lord Brabourne, the acting Viceroy, reported to Secretary of State for India an account of the interview Jinnah had with him. Jinnah ended up with the startling suggestion that 'we should keep the centre as it is now, that we should make friends with the Muslims by *protecting* them in the Congress provinces and that if we did that, the Muslims would *protect* us at the Centre.' Zetland, *Essayez* (London, 1956), p. 247.
31. *Star of India*, 31 Dec. 1938.
32. Press statement, Allahabad, 30 June 1937, *Tribune*, 2 July 1937.
33. Khaliquzzaman, *Pathway to Pakistan*, p. 175.
34. Jamil-ud-Din Ahmad, *Some Recent Speeches and Writings of Mr Jinnah* (Lahore, 1946), p. 30.
35. Ibid., p. 40.
36. Dr Mahmudullah Jung in the *Pioneer*, 7 Nov. 1937.
37. Jamil-ud-Din Ahmad, *Some Recent Speeches*, p. 25.
38. Ibid., p. 122.
39. Ibid., p. 225.
40. Ibid., p. 154.
41. Ibid., p. 426.
42. Ibid., p. 567.
43. Dorothy Norman, *Nehru: The First Sixty Years*, vol. II, pp. 344–5. *Hindustan Times*, 4 Oct. 1947.
44. *Star of India*, 15 Oct. 1938.
45. S. Wazir Hasan to Jawaharlal Nehru, 11 Feb. 1938 (NP).
46. Haig, the Governor of UP wrote to the Viceroy on 23 Oct. 1938,

'Finding themselves unable to effect much by parliamentary methods, they [the Muslim League] are inevitably tempted to create unrest and disturbances outside the legislature, and there is no doubt that the Muslim League have set themselves quite deliberately to this policy.' Haig to Linlithgow, 23 Oct. 1938, Haig Corres.

47. Jawaharlal Nehru to Nawab Muhammad Ismail Khan, 4 and 5 Feb. 1938 (NP).
48. R. Coupland, *Indian Politics*, 1936–42 (Madras, 1944), p. 187.
49. 'In 1938, of the members of the ICS serving in the Provinces, 490 were British and 529 were Indians', R. Coupland, *Indian Politics, 1936–42*, pp. 118–19.
50. Of the eight Inspectors-General of Police who attended the Home Ministers' Conference in May 1939, only one was Indian.
51. The Viceroy, in a White Paper, stated in Oct. 1939 that the Congress ministers had conducted their affairs 'with great success'. For details *see* Cmd Paper 6121.

   Compliments to the Congress ministers' administrative ability and general impartiality were paid by Sir Harry Haig, Governor of the United Provinces 1934–9, in an article entitled 'The United Provinces and the New Constitution', in the *Asiatic Review* (July 1940); and by Lord Erskine, Governor of Madras, in an article entitled 'Madras and the New Constitution' in *Asiatic Review* (Jan. 1941).
52. Sir Maurice Hallett, Governor of Bihar, wrote to the Viceroy on 8 May 1939 that he did not know of any case in which government or local officials had failed to take action against aggressors in communal riots. Muslims, whom the Governor had met, 'had admitted their inability to bring any charges of anti-Muslim prejudice against Government' (Linlithgow Papers).

   On 5 Oct. 1939, when Jinnah raised this subject during his interview with the Viceroy, Lord Linlithgow frankly informed him that after studying the charges of persecution in Congress Provinces he could 'find no specific instances of oppression' (Lord Glendevon, *The Viceroy at Bay* [London, 1971], p. 150).
53. J. Nehru to Sir Sikandar Hyat Khan, 4 Jan. 1939 (NP).
54. Rajendra Prasad, *India Divided* (Bombay, 1946), p. 155.
55. V.P. Menon, *Transfer of Power* (Calcutta, 1957), p. 60.
56. Lord Linlithgow to Lord Zetland, 28 Dec. 1939, quoted in Zetland, *Essayez* (London, 1956), p. 277.
57. *See* R.J. Moore's paper 'British Policy and the Indian Problem 1936–40', in C.H. Phillips and M.D. Wainwright (eds), *The Partition of India* (London, 1970), pp. 79–94.
58. Gwyer and Appadorai, *Speeches and Documents on the Indian Constitution* (London, 1957), vol. 2, p. 492.
59. Report from the UP Govt to the Govt of India, 5 Jan. 1940, Govt of India, Home Dept File 18; Dec. 1939, Poll (NAI).

60. Jamil-ud-Din Ahmad, *Some Recent Speeches*, p. 126.
61. Ibid., p. 36.
62. *The Hindu*, 27 March 1940.
63. Ibid., 8 April 1940.
64. *The Tribune*, 11 Sept. 1940.
65. *The Hindu*, 17 Apr. 1940.
66. *The Tribune*, 29 March 1940.
67. *The Hindu*, 4 Apr. 1940.
68. *Manchester Guardian*, 2 Apr. 1940.
69. A. Yusuf Ali, Sir Muhammad Zafrullah Khan and Dr Shuja-ud-Din cited in Rajendra Prasad, *India Divided*, p. 207.
70. Khaliquzzaman, *Pathway to Pakistan*, p. 211.
71. Ibid., p. 234.
72. *Dawn*, 23 March 1946, and Jamil-ud-Din Ahmad, *Some Recent Speeches*, p. 443.
73. B.R. Nanda, *Mahatma Gandhi* (London, 1958), p. 440.
74. Hugh Tinker, *Experiment with Freedom* (London, 1967), p. 24.
75. Khaliquzzaman, *Pathway to Pakistan*, p. 257.
76. Gwyer and Appadorai, *Speeches and Documents*, vol. 2, p. 522.
77. Jamil-ud-Din Ahmad, *Some Recent Speeches*, pp. 418–20.
78. R.F. Mudie, Chief Secy to the UP Govt's comment on the Cripps proposals was that 'Pakistan has advanced one stage further' (Fortnightly Report for first half of Apr. 1942 in Home Pol. File 18–4–42).
79. Jamil-ud-Din Ahmad, op. cit., p. 423.
80. C. Khaliquzzaman, *Pathway to Pakistan*, p. 288.
81. Nazir Yar Jung (ed.), *The Pakistan Issue* (Lahore, 1943), p. 125.
82. Ibid., pp. 137–8.
83. J.B. Kripalani, 'League and War Effort', in *National Herald*, 5 Oct. 1941.
84. Tinker, *Experiment with Freedom*, p. 30.
85. V.P. Menon records that in Feb. 1940 Jinnah, in the course of an interview with Lord Linlithgow, sought the support of the Governor Sir George Cunningham in teaching 'a salutary lesson to the Congress' by forming a League ministry in the NWFP, the Congress ministry having resigned a few months earlier. See V.P. Menon, *Transfer of Power*, p. 78.
86. Khaliquzzaman, *Pathway to Pakistan*, p. 333.
87. Gwyer and Appadorai, *Speeches and Documents*, vol. 2, p. 566.
88. *Dawn*, 26 March 1946.
89. *The Indian Annual Register*, Jan.–June 1946, p. 197. See also *Dawn*, 26 March and 8 Apr. 1946.
90. Ibid., p. 196; see also *Dawn*, 11 April 1946.
91. Khaliquzzaman, *Pathway to Pakistan*, pp. 425–7.
92. Michael Brecher, *Nehru: A Political Biography* (London, 1959), p. 317.
93. *Bombay Chronicle*, 8 July 1946.

94. Ibid.
95. Ibid.
96. 'What for the Congress implied British dictation to the Constituent Assembly was for the League a British guarantee against Congress dominance' (Anita Inder Singh, *The Origins of the Partition of India* [Delhi, 1987], p. 197).
97. *Bombay Chronicle*, 11 July 1946.
98. Ibid.
99. Dorothy Norman, *Nehru: The First Sixty Years*, vol. 2 (Bombay, 1965), p. 251.
100. *Statesman*, 1 July 1946.
101. Sudhir Ghosh, *Gandhi's Emissary* (London, 1967), p. 180.
102. Gwyer and Appadorai, *Speeches and Documents*, vol. 2, p. 601.
103. *The Indian Annual Register*, Jan.–June 1946, vol. 1, p. 181.
104. Ibid., p. 182.
105. For Muslim League's conception of the functions and resources of the Central Government, *see* the 'Terms of the offer made by the Muslim League as a basis of agreement 12 May 1946', reproduced in Gwyer and Appadorai, *Speeches and Documents*, vol. 2, pp. 573–4.
106. That the Congress fears were not groundless is shown by what Jamil-ud-Din Ahmad, Convenor of the League Committee of Writers, wrote to Jinnah on 29 May 1946:

'. . . we work the Plan up to the Group stage and then create a situation to force the hands of the Hindus and the British to concede Pakistan of our conception. . . .' Quoted in R.J. Moore, *Escape from Empire* (London, 1982), p. 123.
107. 'The two-nation theory with which Jinnah had hoped to get a share of power at the centre was the sword which was now cutting his Pakistan down to size.' Ayesha Jalal, *The Sole Spokesman, Jinnah, the Muslim League and the Demand for Pakistan* (Cambridge, 1985), p. 255.
108. *Indian Annual Register*, July–Dec. 1946, p. 226.
109. Ibid., p. 178.
110. Ibid., p. 79.
111. D.G. Tendulkar, *Mahatma: Life of Mohandas Karamchand Gandhi* (Bombay, 1952), vol. 5, pp. 333–4.
112. Khaliquzzaman's thesis in Apr. 1944 was that Congress would eventually accept any British award, even if it was made without their consent—they had done so in 1909, 1932, and 1935. 'That is what Jinnah is playing for.' Quoted in Anita Inder Singh, *The Origins of the Partition of India*, Delhi, 1987), p. 108.
113. Gwyer and Appadorai, *Speeches and Documents*, p. 525.
114. Pyarelal, *Mahatma Gandhi: The Last Phase* (Ahmedabad, 1958), vol. 2, p. 208.

115. Jamil-ud-Din Ahmad, *Some Recent Speeches*, p. 447.
116. Khaliquzzaman, *Pathway to Pakistan*, p. 397.
117. 'At no point between 1940 and the Cabinet Mission's arrival in 1946, did the League expand, revise or make more specific, the incomplete and contradictory statement (the March 1940 Lahore resolution of the All India Muslim League)' (Ayesha Jalal, *The Sole Spokesman: Jinnah, . the Muslim League and the Demand for Pakistan* [Cambridge, 1985], p. 59.)

# 8

# Azad, Nehru, and Partition

I

The title of Maulana Abul Kalam Azad's book, *India Wins Freedom*[1] is a misnomer. Autobiography is hardly a suitable medium for writing history, especially of such a turbulent period as the last decade of British rule in India. Even thirty years ago there was a vast reservoir of source material, but it is doubtful whether the Maulana or Humayun Kabir, who collaborated with him in the writing of the book, had the opportunity or the time to draw upon it. Since then both published and unpublished material on this theme have multiplied enormously. The Maulana evidently wrote—or rather dictated—from memory. His treatment is far too sketchy and subjective to pass as history, but even as the personal record of an eminent political leader and a major player in the political drama of those years, it is flawed by numerous errors of fact as well as of judgement. J.B. Kripalani, who was the General Secretary of the Congress during this period, writing in 1970, described the Maulana's account as a 'curious mixture of facts and fancies. His memory too seems to have been failing. It is not a question of correcting a passage here and there. It would require a volume as big as he has written to correct all his misstatements and misconceptions.'[2] Some critics have suggested that the book may have suffered from a communication gap between its co-authors; Humayun Kabir's grasp of the nuances of the Urdu language was as shaky as the Maulana's grasp of the nuances of English. Or, perhaps Kripalani was right: the book was completed in the last years of the Maulana's life when he was (to quote Kabir's words from the preface) 'in shattered health', and his memory may have been failing.

It is impossible not to notice a certain bitterness with which the Maulana's account is tinged. This bitterness is understandable. The partition of India was a traumatic experience for him. He had begun his journalistic and political career before the First World War as a pan-Islamist, but after coming into contact with Gandhi in 1920 he quickly completed his transition to secular nationalism. For the rest of his life he was a staunch nationalist. In the late 1930s, after the defection of the Ali Brothers and the death of Dr Ansari, the Maulana was indisputably the most important nationalist Muslim leader in the country. It was therefore not surprising that the events leading to Partition should have left scars on his mind and heart which never healed.

A certain amount of egotism is inherent in an autobiography, and indeed is part of the fascination of this literary genre. The author is naturally at the centre of events he describes; everything is refracted through the prism of his memory; there is an irresistable temptation to exaggerate his own role in the shaping of events. The Maulana was a good 'committee man', an excellent chairman, who could be depended upon to find a via media when there was an acute difference of opinion. He was conscious of this particular talent, but he seems to have overrated its potential. His feeling that in 1937 or in 1946–7 he could have negotiated a settlement with the British and the Muslim League, which was also acceptable from the nationalist point of view, was illusory. Diplomacy has its limits. It was not easy to argue the British out of their imperialist strategy, or to reason Jinnah out of, what K.B. Sayeed graphically described, his 'chess-board strategy'. The non-violent bombshells of the Mahatma, which took the form of fasts or satyagraha, the impulsive (or even calculated) militancy of Jawaharlal Nehru, and the 'no-nonsense' stubbornness of Vallabhbhai Patel, which seem to jar so much on the Maulana in this book, were in fact necessary weapons in the nationalist armoury to cope with the dual challenge the Congress faced from imperialist and separatist forces.

The Maulana has arraigned Gandhi for not accepting the proposal for a Round Table Conference which Malaviya had proposed to Lord Reading in December 1921, and thus for missing 'a golden opportunity for a political settlement'. We know now from the

British Cabinet records that there was no possibility of a political settlement at the time, and that Lord Reading was reprimanded by his superiors in London for even seeming to make an overture to Gandhi.[3] The Maulana criticizes Gandhi's handling of the Congress policies during the Second World War. The Maulana was sceptical both about individual civil disobedience and the Quit India movement, though eventually he fell in line with Gandhi's views. The Mahatma was not deterred by the Maulana's scepticism; he was accustomed to scepticism from his colleagues whenever he took a new initiative. In December 1929, at the Lahore Congress, Sarojini Naidu and Dr Ansari had advised him against launching civil disobedience which was to take the form of Salt satyagraha. Ten years earlier, at the Calcutta Congress, the entire old guard of the Congress, including C.R. Das, Malaviya, Lajpat Rai, Annie Besant, and Jinnah had opposed the non-cooperation movement. If Gandhi had listened to words of 'sanity' and 'moderation', and pinned his faith solely on negotiations with the British, Congress politics would have been indistinguishable from those of the Liberal Party, there would have been no satyagraha campaigns, and the British would perhaps still be ruling over India.

The mass media have, for obvious reasons, concentrated on the Maulana's indictment in his book against Jawaharlal Nehru and Vallabhbhai Patel for the partition of India. It is a highly complex and controversial issue, but with the wealth of the contemporary evidence available, it is now possible to set the record straight.

The Maulana tells us that Nehru's opposition to the inclusion of two (instead of one) Muslim League legislators in the Congress ministry in UP in 1937 was a blunder. 'If the [UP] League's offer of cooperation had been accepted', the Maulana writes, 'the Muslim League party would for all practical purposes have merged in the Congress. Jawaharlal's action gave the Muslim League in the UP, a new lease of life . . . Mr Jinnah took full advantage of the situation and started an offensive which ultimately led to Partition.' The reasoning is naïve, but it has had such wide currency that it needs to be examined in some detail.

In the 1937 elections the Congress won majorities in six provinces and was the largest party in two provinces; it was eventually able to form ministries in eight out of eleven provinces. The Muslim League led by Jinnah had met with electoral disaster. It won 39 out of 107 Muslim seats in Bengal; 2 out of 87 Muslim seats

in the Punjab; 3 out of 33 Muslim seats in Sind; 10 Muslim seats
in Madras. It did not win a single Muslim seat in the legislatures
of Bihar, CP, Orissa and N.W.F.P. In UP and Bombay it did
relatively better, winning 27 out of 69 Muslim seats in the former
province, and 20 out of 29 in the latter province. With this poor
showing the League hardly qualified for a coalition with the Congress in most of the provinces. Indeed, only in one province, UP,
were there serious negotiations for a coalition. These negotiations
were conducted on behalf of the Congress by Maulana Azad, who
had been authorized by the Congress Working Committee to deal
with Congress affairs in UP and Bihar. The Maulana was in charge
of negotiations in UP and nothing seems to have been done against
his wishes. Fortunately, we have a letter written by Jawaharlal
Nehru to Dr Rajendra Prasad on 21 July 1937 which gives a fairly
full account of the negotiations:

Maulana and Pant went to Lucknow. There were talks with Khaliq[uzza-
man] who agreed with all the conditions except two: the winding up
of the parliamentary board [of the Muslim League] and not to set up
separate candidates at by-elections. . . . Ultimately we sent word that
we regretted we could not alter our previous conditions at all; if they
were accepted in toto we would agree, not otherwise. We had no
authority to go beyond this without consulting the Working Committee. So the matter dropped and Maulana Azad went off to Bombay.
Khaliq said he was unable to agree.

The problem thus was not, as the Maulana makes out in *India
Wins Freedom*, of including one or two Muslim Leaguers in the
Congress ministry, but of the adherence of the League ministers to
the programme and discipline of the Congress party. That this was
so is confirmed by Khaliquzzaman, the UP League leader in his
book *Pathway to Pakistan*:

Azad returned to Lucknow on July 15. This time he came with Pant.
Azad handed over to me a two page note which I was supposed to sign
as a price for the Muslim League coalition with the Congress. This was
immediately rejected. I said, 'You want me to sign the death warrant
of the Muslim League Parliamentary Board as well as the Muslim
League organization, which I am representing here . . . I cannot sign
this document'.

Nehru's own part in these negotiations was relatively small. Soon
after the elections he had one of his rare spells of ill-health. He was,

of course, being consulted by Azad, who was in touch with G.B. Pant, R.A. Kidwai, K.M. Ashraf, P.D. Tandon, and other important members of the Congress party in the UP Council. The most important consideration with the provincial Congress leaders, as with Nehru, was that if the Muslim League, dominated as it was by the landlords, came into the cabinet, the Congress programme for agrarian reform, particularly the abolition of *zamindari*, would be blocked. That this fear was justified is proved by Khaliquzzaman's statement before the Cabinet Mission in 1946 that to strike at the *zamindari* in UP was 'to strike at the root of Muslim existence'. Moreover, it is not improbable that if the Congress had formed a coalition ministry with the Muslim League in 1937 in UP and other provinces on Jinnah's terms, the paralysis which struck the Interim Government at the centre in 1946–7 would have overtaken the Congress ministries ten years earlier. That Jinnah was in no mood to genuinely cooperate with the Congress was noted by Lord Brabourne, the Governor of Bombay, who wrote to Lord Linlithgow on 5 June 1937:

Jinnah went on to tell me some of his plans for consolidating the Muslim League throughout India. . . . His policy is to preach communalism , noon and night, and endeavour to found more schools, to open purely Muhammadan hostels, children's Homes and teach them generally to stand on their own feet and make themselves independent of the Hindus.

## II

In *India Wins Freedom*, some of the severest strictures have been reserved for Nehru for making certain comments at a press conference in Bombay on 10 July 1946. According to Azad, this was 'one of those unfortunate events which change the course of history', because Nehru's remarks 'provoked Jinnah', and led to the withdrawal of the Muslim League from the Cabinet Mission Plan, and thus ultimately to the partition of India. The Maulana further tells us that all this would not have happened if he had not made the 'greatest blunder' of his life in proposing Nehru's name for the presidentship of the Congress in 1946:

I came to the conclusion [the Mualana writes] that since I had been President for seven years from 1939 to 1946, I must now retire. I therefore decided that I shall not permit my name to be proposed. The next point I had to decide was the choice of my successor . . . it seemed to me that Jawaharlal should be the new President. Accordingly on 26 April 1946, I issued a press statement proposing his name for the President. .... I have regretted no action of mine so much as the decision to withdraw from the Presidentship of the Congress at this critical juncture.

The Maulana had been elected to preside over the Ramgarh Congress in 1940. The normal term of the Congress presidency was one year, and in the ordinary course he would have stepped down in 1941. However, it so happened that, under Gandhi's leadership, the Congress launched satyagraha—individual civil disobedience movement in 1940 and the Quit India movement in 1942. The Congress organization was outlawed by the government, and its leaders were in gaol for the next three years. They were released in the summer of 1945, and therefore the election of a new president for the 1946 session of the Congress was in any case due. It is surprising that the Maulana should have forgotten the procedure for the election of the Congress president. Never in the history of the Congress had an outgoing president proposed the name of his successor through a press statement. A definite procedure existed for election to the highest office in the gift of the Congress. Recommendations were submitted by the provincial Congress committees to the office of the All India Congress Committee by a certain date. The final choice was usually made from among the recommended names before the meeting of the A.I.C.C. by informal consultations among senior Congress leaders, and after taking Gandhi's advice. Indeed, so far as the 'crown of thorns' (as Gandhi termed the Congress presidency) was concerned, he had the last word. In September 1929, at the Lucknow meeting of the A.I.C.C., even though his own name had been recommended by an overwhelming majority of provincial Congress committees, Gandhi had inducted Jawaharlal into the presidency.

As for the sequence of events in 1946, we have a first-hand account from J.B. Kripalani (who was the General Secretary of the Congress at that time), which is totally at variance with the Maulana's. According to Kripalani, three names were received from the provincial Congress committees, those of Sardar Patel, Pattabhi Sitaramayya, and Kripalani himself. Nehru's name had not been recommended, but according to Kripalani, 'Gandhiji had expressed a desire that at that juncture Jawaharlal should be the President'.

The last date for receiving recommendations from the provincial Congress committees was already over. However, fifteen members of the A.I.C.C. could propose a name. Kripalani obtained the signatures of the members of the Working Committee, who had assembled for a meeting at Delhi, and of a few local members of the A.I.C.C., and duly proposed Nehru's name. The three candidates proposed by the provincial Congress committees retired from the contest, and Nehru was elected unopposed.

As regards Nehru's press conference at Bombay on 10 July, the Maulana has overrated its significance. The failure of the Cabinet Mission Plan was due to deeper causes which can be understood only in the larger political context of those turbulent years. The negotiations between the Cabinet Mission and the Indian political leaders lasted for several months; it was a triangular battle of wits and wills, in which the British ministers, the Congress, and the Muslim League were engaged, each with its own separate objectives. The record of these negotiations, which took a zigzag course, runs to several hundred pages. To attribute the failure of these efforts to a sentence or two uttered by Nehru at his press conference on 10 July 1946 is to trivialize history. Nehru had made similar remarks at the meting of the All India Congress Committee in response to his Socialist critics three days earlier. He could have been more careful in the choice of his diction, but both on the sovereignty of the Constituent Assembly and on the grouping of provinces he was taking the line, which other Congress leaders, including Azad, had taken in their talks with the Cabinet Mission. According to M.A.H. Ispahani, soon after the Muslim League Council had passed its resolution of 6 June, accepting the Cabinet Mission Plan, Jinnah had second thoughts, 'but it was too late. . . . All that he could do was to hope that the Congress would either reject the proposal or ask for such amendments or put such interpretation on it as would vitiate their acceptance.'

In retrospect, it is clear that the kind of centre the Muslim League was prepared to accept was wholly unworkable in the mid-twentieth century in a subcontinent like India. When a similar proposal was mooted for East and West Pakistan after the elections in 1971, with foreign affairs, defence, and communications as federal subjects, Bhutto declared that the lot of the Central Government would be comparable to that of 'a widow without pension'.

In any case, given the political situation in India in 1946–7, it is doubtful if any consensus could have emerged from a constituent assembly in which both the Congress and the League with their different ideologies, were locked in a duel. It might have taken ten years to draft a constitution, which would not have lasted ten months.

## III

In an account running to nearly 300 pages by a great scholar and an elder statesman, the reader may expect an analysis of the deeper causes of the partition of India, but the Maulana contents himself with dwelling on particular incidents and apportioning blame; he cannot see the wood for the trees. We are asked to believe that a cataclysmic event, such as the division of India, was caused by Jawaharlal Nehru's refusal to concede two seats to the Muslim League in the Congress ministry in UP in 1937, or by his intemperate comments at a press conference on the Cabinet Mission Plan in 1946, or by Vallabhbhai Patel's insistence on the Congress retaining the Home portfolio in the Interim Government.

The reality is that the roots of the confrontation between Indian nationalism and Muslim separatism, of which the partition of the country was the culmination, did not lie in the decade covered by the Maulana's book; they are to be traced back to the 'Muslim leaders' deputation' to Lord Minto, the Viceroy of India, the demand for separate electorates, and the foundation of the Muslim League in 1906, and indeed, even earlier, to the days of Sir Syed Ahmad Khan, who threw his powerful influence in favour of the isolation of his community from the national movement when the latter was in its infancy. Sir Syed raised the great questionmark which was to shadow Indian politics for the next sixty years: what would be the position of the Muslim community in a free India? If British autocracy were to be replaced by an Indian democracy, would it give a permanent advantage to Hindus who heavily outnumbered Muslims? Was it (as Syed Ahmad Khan put it) a game of dice in which one man had four dice and the other only one?

In the years immediately preceding the First World War, the Balkan Wars and the travails of Turkey aroused much anti-British feeling amongst Indian Muslims, and for a few years the Muslim

League came to be controlled by a Lucknow-based faction with nationalist proclivities. Hindu–Muslim *rapprochement* received a boost after the war, when Gandhi lent his support to Indian Muslims' demand for preserving the territorial integrity of Turkey and the preservation of the institution of the Caliphate. In 1919–20 Hindu–Muslim unity reached its zenith. However, it was not so much the nationalist sentiment as the concern for Turkey and the holy places of Islam which had provided the main impulse for Muslim participation in the non-cooperation movement. Deep and sincere as the Muslim feeling on the Khilafat issue may have been, it was harnessed to a romantic cause which was brought to an inglorious end by the Turks themselves when they abolished the institution of the Sultan–Caliph. Thus the one successful experiment in bringing the Muslim community into the mainstream of Indian nationalism failed to break its psychological isolation, and indeed confirmed its tendency to view political problems from a religious angle.[4]

The fabric of Hindu–Muslim unity, at which Gandhi had laboured so hard, went to pieces after the collapse of the non-cooperation and Khilafat movements; his voice, once so powerful, was drowned in a din of communal recrimination by bigots on both sides. A favourite recipe for harmony in the 1920s between the communities was a communal pact through an All Parties Conference. Leaders of a number of political parties and religious organizations tried to allocate jobs under the government and seats in the legislatures—the spoils of Swaraj, as it were—but found it difficult to reconcile their antagonistic claims. Gandhi disliked this pettifogging politics: he would have liked to disarm Muslim fears by generosity on the part of Hindus. His offer of a 'blank cheque' to Muslims was ridiculed by them, and resented by Hindus. Unfortunately, Hindu politicians were as incapable of generosity, as the Muslim politicians were of trust. What was seen as a safeguard against future risks by the Muslim, was seen as a thin end of the wedge by the Hindu.

The same futile pattern of the unity conference was repeated at the Round Table Conference in the early thirties. In 1932 the British Government imposed a solution, in the form of the Communal Award, which laid down the quantum and mode of representation in the legislatures. The perpetuation of separate electorates in the Communal Award was repugnant to the Congress; but it decided not to reject it until an alternative proposal, acceptable to all the communities, emerged.

Even though the Communal Award conceded almost all the political demands of the Muslim League *vis-à-vis* the Hindu community, Muslim politics continued in their time-worn path. Far from being suppressed, the communal controversy raged like a hurricane over the next decade when Muslim separatism culminated in the demand for Pakistan which dominated and changed the course of Indian politics.

Maulana Azad in his book raises the question of responsibility for the tragedy of the partition: he describes Vallabhbhai Patel as its 'author'. This is an extraordinary statement, because no one was more consistently opposed to the two-nation theory and the partition of the country than Patel. It was only after his experience of working with the representatives of the Muslim League in the Interim Government, and the series of communal riots in Bengal, Bihar, and Punjab, that Patel came to the conclusion that the British would not leave India without a settlement with the Muslim League and there was no possibility of the Congress being able to reach a reasonable settlement with the League. A similar conclusion was reached by Nehru after his frustrating experience in the Interim Government. The riots in Bengal, Bihar, and Punjab proved the last straw. By the time Mountbatten replaced Wavell, the Congress leadership, sobered by its experience in the Interim Government and the growing lawlessness in the country, was getting reconciled to the idea of salvaging three-fourths of India from the chaos which threatened the whole.

There is a remarkable document in *India Wins Freedom*: a press statement addressed to Indian Muslims in 1946 by Maulana Azad, giving his critique of the Pakistan scheme. In lucidity, irrefutable logic, and impassioned eloquence, the Maulana's analysis could not have been surpassed, but it was all in vain. His warnings remained unheeded:

The Muslim League [the Maulana wrote] had carried on propaganda to arouse religious fanaticism and communal passions. This clouded the political issue so much so that Muslims who stood on Congress or other ticket had difficulty even in securing a hearing from the people.

The fact that the elections of 1946, which decided the fate of the subcontinent, were based on separate electorates, facilitated the exploitation of religious passions. As the Maulana brooded in the evening of his life on the events of those years, it must have been a galling thought that his words had failed to carry weight with his own community. This could not but add to the sadness and bitterness which are reflected in *India Wins Freedom*.

## Notes and References

1. The 'complete' and 'original' version of Maulana Azad's *India Wins Freedom* was published in 1988, thirty years after his death.
2. A book listing errors in Maulana Azad's book was indeed published. *See* Rajmohan Gandhi, *India Wins Errors* (Delhi, 1989).
3. B.R. Nanda, *Gandhi, Pan Islamism, Imperialism and Nationalism in India* (Delhi, 1989), pp. 330–3.
4. Ibid., pp. 372–95.

# 9

## Nehru and Socialism

### I

No part of Jawaharlal Nehru's political philosophy has evoked sharper controversies than his avowed faith in socialism. When he affirmed in his presidential address to the Lahore Congress in December 1929, that he was 'a socialist and republican and . . . no believer in kings or princes or in the order which produces the modern kings of industry',[1] he was regarded as an *enfant terrible* of Indian politics. Coatman, a former British civilian, in his book *Years of Destiny* published in 1932, credited Jawaharlal with 'one secret ambition which is to rival Lenin, or Stalin in the history of communism'.[2]

Since Nehru's autobiography was not published until 1936, Coatman could be forgiven for his ignorance of his intellectual make-up, the influence upon him of English liberalism and Fabian economics during his formative years in England, and the powerful impact that Gandhi made from 1919 onwards. The non-cooperation movement brought Nehru into contact with what he described, as the 'naked hungry mass' of rural India. The Brussels Congress and a four-day visit to Moscow in 1927 gave a sharp economic edge to Nehru's politics, and stirred his interest in Marxism and in planned economic development. In 1933, in a series of articles entitled, 'Whither India?', Nehru spelt out his socialist faith at some length and argued that the capitalist system had outlived its day and had to give way to a better and saner order of human affairs.[3] He paid a magnificent tribute to Lenin in his *Glimpses of World History.* 'As time passes, he grows greater; he has become one of the chosen company of the world's immortals.'[4] The choice before the world in the 1930s seemed to him 'between some form of communism and some form of Fascism'; so far as he was concerned, he was, he writes, all for the former. In his autobiography written in 1934 he frankly avowed his sympathy with the Labour world of the Second International rather than with that of the Third International.[5]

In 1936 he wrote to Lord Lothian that the transition to socialism would require nationalization of the instruments of production and distribution: 'There may be half-way houses to it, but one can hardly have two contradictory and conflicting processes going on side by side. The choice must be made and for one who aims at socialism there can be only one choice.'[6] One of the most emphatic statements of Nehru's socialist faith was made during the same year in his presidential address to the Lucknow Congress. There was, he said, no way of ending the poverty and subjection of the Indian people except through socialism. He was, he said, speaking of socialism not in a vague, humanitarian way, but in the 'scientific, economic sense', which would entail:

vast and revolutionary changes in political and social structure, the ending of vested interests in land and industry, as well as the feudal and autocratic Indian states system. That means the ending of private property, except in a restricted sense, and the replacement of the present profit system by a higher ideal of cooperative service. It means ultimately a change in our instincts and habits and desires. In short, it means a new civilization, radically different from the present capitalist order.[7]

Nehru's presidential speech thrilled members of the Congress Socialist Party, which had been formed in 1934 when he was in prison. He never became an office-bearer or even a member of the party, but was undoubtedly its hero. Some of its prominent leaders, such as Narendra Deva, Jayaprakash Narayan, and Achyut Patwardhan, were known to be close to him, and to share his outlook on national and international affairs. They were outspoken critics of Gandhi's ideology and methods, and urged Nehru to give a new, militant twist to Congress policies at the Lucknow Congress. On the other hand, the older leaders of the Congress hoped that Jawaharlal—who had received the Congress presidency as a gift from the Mahatma—would be sobered by the responsibility of his office and avoid polarization of views which could threaten the unity of the Congress party.

The socialist creed was anathema to the Congress old guard, but in 1936 their main argument was that it was suicidal for the Congress to raise the social issue while the principal political issue, that of Indian freedom, remained unresolved. Their view was succinctly expressed by J.B. Kripalani in a letter to Nehru:

I believe it is a blunder to try to lower Bapu's prestige and attack his politics. I believe we shall again need him for a fight, if he is alive. . . . That being so, it is politically unwise to try to undermine his influence and ridicule his plans. The Congress Socialists individually and collectively have done and do so.[8]

In 1936 the Congress organization had not fully recovered from the savage oppression it had undergone during the Willingdon regime. Further, a general election was due at the end of the year; the Socialist slogan of class struggle could prove costly to the Congress party, as barely 10 per cent (and largely propertied section) of the population was entitled to vote.

The Congress old guard felt that they were being unfairly attacked and ridiculed in the press, and that Nehru was doing nothing to curb the militancy of his Socialist friends. Seven members of the Congress Working Committee, including Vallabhbhai Patel, C. Rajagopalachari, and Rajendra Prasad sent in their resignations. A grave crisis was in the making, but Gandhi handled it with perspicacity and firmness. A split in the Congress was what the British desired and indeed expected. In May 1935 the Viceroy, Lord Willingdon had envisaged that 'Moderate Congressman' would amalgamate with Liberals, and the extreme Socialists would either capture the Congress or break away to form a separate organization.[9] Two years later, Willingdon's successor, Lord Linlithgow, wrote: 'It would be convenient if the various sections now preserving a somewhat artificial unity in the Congress ranks were to part company and sort themselves out.'[10] Thanks to Gandhi's skill, the crisis in the Congress Working Committee was resolved in a way which strengthened rather than weakened the Congress. A secret appreciation, prepared in the Home Department for the Viceroy in March 1937, perceptively summed up the implications of the compromise:

Socialists and nationalists have agreed to combine in a programme in which a moderate socialism is to be yoked to a nationalist mass movement against British rule, and in which the socialist urge is to be employed to supplement the nationalist urge and not, as might until recently have been expected, to disrupt it. The essence of this combination is a tactical tolerance, a tolerance by the Socialists of a programme which falls far short of their desires; tolerance by the nationalists of a Socialist weapon which may return boomerang-like on their heads. The immediate objective is independence of the British connection and establishment of an Indian democratic government.[11]

The crisis of 1936 was resolved; but it had a chastening effect upon Nehru; he decided to subordinate ideological considerations to his overriding loyalty to Gandhi's leadership and to the Congress party as the chief instrument of the anti-imperalist struggle. This tactical flexibility was facilitated by the fact that Nehru's socialism had never been doctrinaire. In the late thirties and early forties, as India was convulsed with communal tensions released by the Muslim League's campaign for Pakistan, and the Congress itself was riven with dissensions, Nehru realized that even socialism must fit in with the paramount objectives of national freedom and unity.

The advantages of pragmatic approach became clearer to Nehru when he presided over the National Planning Committee of the Congress in 1939–40. 'If we start,' he wrote to K.T. Shah, the economist, in May 1939, 'with the dictum that only under socialism can there be planning, we frighten people and irritate the ignorant. If, on the other hand, we think of planning apart from socialism, that is a logical process which will convert many who are weary of words and slogans. . . . Here in India, a premature conflict on class lines would lead to a break-up and possibly to prolonged inability to build anything. The disruptive forces in the country seem to be growing in strength and it almost seems that we are going the way of China.'[12]

## II

In 1944, in his *Discovery of India*, Nehru advocated economic planning 'in the context of democratic freedom and with a large measure of cooperation of some at least of the groups who were normally opposed to socialist doctrine. . . . If [class] conflict was inevitable, it had to be faced; but if it could be avoided or minimized that was an obvious gain.'[13]

This was a far cry from the call for a full-blooded socialist society Nehru had made from his presidential chair at the Lucknow Congress. The imperative need to maintain a united front against British imperialism was a constraint on his socialist zeal before 1947. After the attainment of independence, this constraint did not apply, but he had to reckon with other, and, in some ways, more serious constraints. The communal fanaticism and violence which followed the partition of the subcontinent, the mass migration of refugees across the new borders with Pakistan, the virtual break-down of an administration whose cadres had been reshuffled on a religious basis, the reorganization of the armed forces, the scarcity of food and necessities of life, the accentuation of inflationary pressures inherited from the war period, the problem of integrating 500-odd princely states in the Indian Union, the crisis in Hyderabad and the armed conflict with Pakistan over Kashmir, together made up a formidable agenda for Nehru's government during the first years of independence. And as if this was not enough, the international situation was bedevilled by the cold war between the United States and the Soviet Union.

In those first critical months of independence, it was a matter of the utmost importance for Nehru and his colleagues to restore the authority of the government and the health of the economy, if only to falsify the prophets of doom like Winston Churchill, who had warned that India was being turned over to 'men of straw'. And, then there was the inevitable transition from a colonial to a demo-cratic polity, the framing of a new constitution, and the setting up of institutions of parliamentary system of government. Nehru knew that neither the political party he had inherited from the freedom struggle nor the civil service bequeathed to him by the British were ideal instruments for a revolutionary programme. The Left parties, which in later years were to accuse him of not living up to his socialist faith, were themselves more of a hindrance than a help to him. The Congress Socialists seceded from the Congress party in 1948 and splintered into several factions, thus weakening the elements committed to social change in the Congress party without themselves becoming a tangible political force in the country. And the Communist Party of India chose to embark on an adventurist policy on the Maoist pattern by taking to subversion, sabotage, and open revolt in Telengana in 1948.

Even if these challenges and dangers had not existed, it is extremely doubtful if Nehru would have resorted to Stalinist methods to build a socialist utopia. Even in the hey-day of his Marxist ideology he had expressed his reservations about the Soviet model. In his autobiography, while acknowledging his inclination towards Communist philosophy, he had avowed that he was very far from being a Communist:

My roots are still perhaps partly in the nineteenth century, and I have been too much influenced by the humanist liberal tradition to get out of it completely.... I dislike dogmatism and the treatment of Karl Marx's writings or any other books as revealed scripture which cannot be challenged, and the regimentation and heresy hunts which seem to be a feature of modern Communism. I dislike also much that has happened in Russia, and especially the excessive use of violence in normal times.[14]

The truth is that Nehru found it difficult to give up any of the three basic tenets of his political creed: secularism, democracy, and socialism. Above all, he was not prepared to jeopardize the stability and unity of India. He persevered in the strategy which had appealed to him during his association with the National Planning Committee. Socialism was to be ushered in not at one blow, nor to be imposed on the country; its introduction was to be graduated to fit in with the needs of the country. Nationalization of key industries was to be undertaken, but a wide field was to be left for private enterprise; both the public and private sectors were to coexist in a system of 'mixed economy'. This was, of course, a compromise. When Jayaprakash Narayan urged a more drastic socialist programme, Nehru told him: 'I cannot by sheer force of circumstances do everything that I would like to do. We are all of us in some measure prisoners of fate and circumstances. But I am as keen as ever to go in a particular [socialist] direction and carry the country with me.'[15] Many years later, Jayaprakash Narayan conceded that Nehru had been right in not imposing a socialist programme, as a forcible imposition would have established totalitarianism in the name of socialism.[16]

III

It is significant that for nearly seven years after independence, even while Nehru was engaged in launching the country on planned economic development, urging rapid agricultural and industrial growth, and talking of a casteless and classless society, he had refrained from holding aloft the banner of socialism. Not until December 1954 did he ask the Parliament to pass a resolution declaring that the object of the country's economic policy was a 'socialist pattern of society'. In January 1955 a similar resolution was adopted by the Indian National Congress at its Avadi session on planning in India 'with a view to the establishment of a socialistic pattern of society when the principal means of production are under social ownership or control, production is progressively speeded up, and there is a equitable distribution of national wealth'. The enunciation of the socialist ideal was evidently designed to mobilize popular enthusiasm for the Five Year Plan, but it was also a shrewd move to steal the thunder of the Left parties.

The declaration of 'socialistic pattern', however, made little difference to the strategy of the Five Year Plans. Though Nehru's initial inspiration for economic planning had been derived from the Soviet example, he never faltered in his commitment to democracy and a polity which guaranteed the rule of law and individual freedom, and ruled out violence and dictatorship. He resisted the temptation of indulging in ideological polemics and populist rhetoric. His emphasis was on the content rather than on the definition of socialism. 'Our problem', he said in March 1949, 'is to raise the standard of the masses, supply them with their needs, give them the wherewithal to lead a decent life. . . . I do not care what 'ism' it is that helps me to set them on that road provided I do it. And if one thing fails, we will try another.'[17] He rejected the notion that the adoption of socialist or communist methods would automatically lead to riches; the way to prosperity lay through hard work, increased productivity, and equitable distribution. A socialist utopia could not be achieved by simply dividing the existing wealth, for in India there was 'no existing wealth for you to divide; there is only poverty to divide'.[18] Socialism was not a magic wand, indeed if introduced in a backward and underdeveloped country, it did not suddenly make it any less backward; in fact, it was possible to have 'a backward and poverty-stricken socialism'. He ruled out measures in the name of ideology which would adversely affect production and employment. And this was why, despite his own strong predilection for state ownership and management, he insisted on a wide field being left to private enterprise.

An eminent economist, and a member of Nehru's cabinet, V.K.R.V. Rao observed that Nehru was reluctant to force the pace, that he was constantly trying to educate his countrymen to create 'the climate for the needed massive social and economic change'.[19] Mahalanobis, Nehru's chief planning adviser, also noted Nehru's preference for agreed solutions; when differences persisted, he would adjourn the meeting to resume discussion on another day.[20] T.T. Krishnamachari, whose opinion on economic matters carried great weight with Nehru, recalled that though nationalization of the Imperial Bank of India and life-insurance companies had been thought of as early as 1952, Nehru waited for three years to bring round his dissenting cabinet colleagues to his point of view.[21] He did not make a fetish of ideology. In the National Planning Committee in 1940 he had taken a strong stand against foreign capital because he feared that it could bring about alien control of economic affairs. However, after Independence, he felt that the objection was no longer valid, and agreed to foreign loans for speeding up economic development.

The 'mixed economy', the coexistence of the private and public sectors, which brought on Nehru's head the wrath of his Leftist critics, seems in retrospect to have been not an act of pusillanimity, but of wisdom in the context of the recent events in the Soviet Union and China. Long before the emergence of Gorbachev, Nehru had questioned some of the Marxist orthodoxies: 'Marx was a great man,' he said in the Parliament, 'and everybody could profit by his teaching. But am I to be told that what he said about England one hundred or one hundred fifty years ago, is to be applied to India or any other country? It is completely unjust to Marx, if to nobody else'. 'The socialism of Marx—not all the ideas of Marx', Nehru added, 'was completely out of date today because the technological aspect had changed in a tremendously rapid way so that the conclusions of Marx did not apply today.'[22]

The most important and urgent task for independent India, as Nehru saw it, was a practical one of combating poverty and raising the standard of living of the Indian people. 'It is not a question', he said,

of the theory of communism or socialism or capitalism. It is a question of hard fact. In India, if we do not ultimately solve the basic problems of our country—the problems of food, clothing, housing, and so on—it will not matter whether we call ourselves capitalists, socialists, communists or anything else. If we fail to solve these problems, we shall be swept away and somebody else will come in and try to solve them.[23]

In Nehru's armoury the chief weapon for the assault on poverty was economic planning.

## REFERENCES

1. *SWJN*, vol. 4 (Delhi, 1973), p. 192.
2. J. Coatman, *Years of Destiny* (London, 1932), p. 95.
3. *SWJN*, vol. 6 (Delhi, 1974), pp. 1–32.
4. J. Nehru, *Glimpses of World History* (Delhi, 1982 rpt), p. 660.
5. J. Nehru, *An Autobiography* (Delhi, 1958 rpt), p. 591.
6. J. Nehru to Lord Lothian, 17 Jan. 1936 (NP) in *A Bunch of Old Letters* (Bombay, 1958), p. 141.
7. *SWJN*, vol. 7 (Delhi, 1975), p. 181.
8. J.B. Kripalani to J. Nehru, 11 July 1936 (NP).
9. Willingdon to Hoare, 5 May 1935 (Templewood Papers).
10. Linlithgow to Zetland, 5 March 1937 (Zetland Papers).
11. Home Pol. & KW File 4/10/36 (NAI).
12. J. Nehru to K.T. Shah, 13 May 1939, *SWJN*, vol. 9 (Delhi, 1976), p. 373.
13. J. Nehru, *Discovery of India* (Calcutta, 1946), p. 480.
14. J. Nehru, *An Autobiography* (Delhi, 1962 rpt), p. 591.
15. J. Nehru to Jayaprakash Narayan, 10 Aug. 1948 (NP).
16. J.P. Narayan, *Jail Life* (Bombay, 1977), p. 35.
17. *Speeches of Jawaharlal Nehru*, vol. I (Delhi, 1949), pp. 190–1.
18. Ibid., vol. III (Delhi, 1958), p. 17.
19. V.K.R.V. Rao, *The Nehru Legacy* (Bombay, 1971), p. 75.
20. R. Zakaria, ed. *A Study of Nehru* (Bombay, 1960), p. 317
21. T.T. Krishnamachari, Oral History Transcript (NMML).
22. Quoted in R.C. Dutt, *The Socialism of Jawaharlal Nehru* (Delhi, 1981), p. 202.
23. V.K.R.V. Rao, 'Planning Without Dogma' in Zakaria, ed. *A Study of Nehru*, p. 307.

# 10

## *Letters to Chief Ministers*

### I

In October 1947 Jawaharlal Nehru started writing a fortnightly letter to the Chief Ministers, or rather to the Prime Ministers, as they were then called, of the provinces in India. 'In times of exceptional stress like the present', he wrote in his first letter, 'it is more than ordinarily incumbent on us to keep in close touch with each other so that we can put forth concerted efforts to overcome the grave dangers facing us'. Even in normal times private correspondence between the heads of the central and provincial governments had been a regular feature of the British administration in India: the Viceroy and the Governors periodically wrote to each other, and the Viceroy exchanged weekly letters with his immediate superior in London, the Secretary of State for India.

Nehru turned his fortnightly letters to provincial premiers into an additional link in the Indian political system, setting in perspective events in India and abroad, and focusing their attention on urgent and important issues.

It is not easy for us to realize the gravity and the complexities of the problems which confronted the government of independent India during the first two years. The terrific explosion of hatred a nd violence, the massacres and mass migrations of the minorities across the newly formed borders between India and Pakistan, which accompanied the partition of India, the disorganization of the transport system, the invasion of Kashmir, the war with Pakistan, the uncertainties in Hyderabad, the border disputes with Pakistan, the scarcity of food and near-famine conditions in Madras, the political terrorism in Bengal and Hyderabad all posed formidable threats with which Nehru and his colleagues had to cope. However, it is significant that even in those dark days, Nehru was not overwhelmed by the immediate issues. 'In spite of the more obvious problems that confront us', he wrote to the Chief Ministers in November 1947, 'the basic problems still continue to be economic'. A month later, he reverted to the problem of poverty, which 'we had temporarily put in the second place in the midst of the preoccupation of communal disorder'. On 1 April 1948, he mentioned the 'Central Planning Commission', which he proposed to set up. In the same month came the 'industrial policy resolution'. 'Our future depends', he wrote, 'upon our production. If our production does not go up, then we can't have progress'. The river valley projects seemed to him 'the most important work in front of us'. The foundation of the Hirakud Dam in April 1948 and the launching of a new ship, 'Jal Usha' of the Scindia Steam Navigation Company, thrilled him. In August 1948 he set up the Atomic Energy Commission with Homi Bhabha as chairman and K.S. Krishnan and S.S. Bhatnagar as members.

Adhering to the style of his days in the nationalist struggle Nehru, even in his years of office, used these letters to inform, educate, exhort, and warn the heads of provincial governments. On 1 April 1948 we find him writing, 'Recently there have been indications of the growth of a narrow provincial outlook in some of the provinces. We have viewed this development with apprehension. If communalism was bad, as it undoubtedly was, provincialism could almost be equally bad'. In another letter he refers to 'a strong opinion in the country with which I sympathize, that no political or religious organization, or rather no organization confined to a particular religious group and aiming at political ends, should be allowed to function'. In May 1948 he draws the attention of the Chief Ministers to complaints from the public 'about our inefficiency, inaccessibility, delays, and above all, of corruption. I fear that many of these complaints are justified. We are perhaps busy, as all of us are, in our respective offices. We are rather apt to grow self-complacent and imagine that all is well in the best of all possible worlds. I suggest that all of us should remember always Lord Acton's famous dictum about power.'

He is refreshingly frank about the use of difficult Hindi words in political and administrative work. 'There is no reason whatever', he writes, 'why we should give up using well-known words even though they might be English and try to coin new and unknown words. Words get their inner content of meaning from use, and a mere artificial coining is not enough.'

He refers to the possibility of the abuse of power by executive and police officers, and reminds the Chief Ministers that civil liberties and the freedom of the individual had been part of the ethos of the national movement. He questions the feasibility of prohibition because of the difficulty of enforcing it and financial stringency. Even if prohibition were to be viewed from the moral plane, he wondered whether some other social reforms were not more urgent:

A large number of people are living in miserable hovels which are a disgrace to our country. . . . We hardly provide them with any amenities of life. Surely, it is far more necessary to progress along these other lines first.

As early as 22 November 1947, we find the Prime Minister urging the Chief Ministers 'to finish the task of liquidating the zamindari system. We cannot take much time over every step, for we have to go far.' Two years later, he is, if anything, more emphatic: 'The abolition of the zamindari system and land reform . . . is of the highest importance as it affects millions of people and has already been delayed too long. It is the basis for further progress.'

## II

The second volume of Jawaharlal Nehru's *Letters to Chief Ministers* covers the 28 months from January 1950 to May 1952, which spanned the inauguration of the Indian Republic, and the first general elections under the new Constitution.

'The two dominating issues at present', Nehru noted on 19 May 1950, 'are Indo–Pakistan relations with all their ramifications and the economic policy to be pursued by the country.' The shadow of Partition still hung heavily over the subcontinent. There were riots in East Pakistan, exodus of the Hindu minority to India, and the inevitable repercussions in West Bengal: 1.7 million non-Muslims crossed over from East Pakistan to India, and seven hundred thousand Muslims from India to Pakistan. Nehru was dismayed by the hysterical tone of the Pakistani press which gave a distorted picture, but he added with a Gandhian touch: 'I regret to say that many newspapers in India are equally hysterical, and give a completely one-sided picture. All of us have a natural tendency to slur over our errors, and look only to the errors of opponents.'

There were several outstanding issues between the two countries: canal waters, evacuee property, exchange ratio and, above all Kashmir, but the immediate task was to stem the tide of mass migration and to prevent war. This Nehru was able to achieve, by concluding a pact with the Pakistan Premier, Liaquat Ali Khan. In April 1950 he refers to the 'odd relationship' that had developed between India and Pakistan: 'We are trying to come to grips with that relationship and to straighten out its curves.' Little did Nehru know that the 'curves' would continue to defy straightening for the next four decades!

On May 1950, Nehru confides in the Chief Ministers that Liaquat Ali Khan had visited the United States, 'disparaged India', and 'asked for more and more arms from America, presumably to be used against India'. Much would depend, he wrote a year later, upon the attitude which the British and United States governments would adopt: 'I do not mean that either of these governments wants war. . . . But I am quite sure that if they make it perfectly clear to Pakistan that it must not indulge in its warlike activities, then there would be no war.'

The Kashmir issue had soured India's relations with the Western Powers, but there were welcome signs of a thaw in the relations with the Soviet Union; Radhakrishnan, the Indian ambassador in Moscow, was granted an audience by Stalin. India tried conciliatory moves to end the Korean War, and backed the admission of China to the United Nations.

These letters leave no doubt that during these turbulent years, whatever his other preoccupations and distractions, Nehru regarded economic development as the most important task before the country. A visit to Bhakra-Nangal, thrills him; he looks forward to the day when 'the life-giving waters of the Sutlej', would flow into Punjab and Rajasthan; he is pleased at the transformation of the Terai district into a granary of Uttar Pradesh; he hopes Chandigarh, the new capital of Punjab, would become a 'model city'. He briefs the chief ministers on the preparation of the First Five Year

Plan, and calls for a 'joint effort', not only of the central and state governments but of the people of India. He considers 'grass-roots cooperation' essential both in the formulation and execution of the plan. This might well be done, he suggests, in a district 'with the help of the village panchayats and the like. They would probably put up schemes for roads, wells, etc. We might tell them that we would gladly help if they help themselves both financially and by voluntary labour.' Planning is, he reminds the chief ministers, not merely a question of statistics and allocation of financial resources, but 'the energy of the nation, the spirit of the people and the crusading ardour which might be put into the task'.

The first general election of 1952 looms large in Nehru's letters. He intensively campaigns for his party. He recognizes that 'by tradition and historic necessity' the Congress stood for India's unity and against disintegrating tendencies, but the party was suffering from a certain breed of 'boss-type' local politicians who alienated the people from it. However, when the elections were over, he pronounced adult franchise a success: 'on the whole, there has been freedom and secrecy of voting. That achievement itself is creditable.'

Even though in these early years, Nehru seems to exude an air of optimism, he is disconcerted by certain trends. In May 1952, we find him deploring the decline in educational standards. 'This is bad for our future', he writes, 'apart from educational standards deteriorating, physical, and if I may say so, cultural and moral standards go down. We become sloppy and lack all discipline in life.' He wonders whether the inclusion of a year's manual work and drill—without arms—in the curriculum would redress the balance. He is saddened by the reluctance of young medical graduates to work in rural areas. An attempt had been made to get some of them to work in the border mountain tracts, but no volunteers were forthcoming, and the work had to be left to foreign missionaries. 'This is not very complimentary to our young men and women of the new generation', Nehru wrote, 'it means that they have no spirit of adventure, no grit, no capacity for hard work. If this is so, how then are we to progress?' What the country needed was, 'men and women with a purpose and a will to achieve and with a capacity to work together without finding too much fault with each other'.

III

The first two volumes of the *Letters to Chief Ministers* cover the years from 1947 to 1952; the next three volumes deal with the period from 1953 to 1964. There are in all 378 letters in these five volumes; they constitute a vivid running commentary on the seventeen years of his administration by India's first Prime Minister. It is doubtful if any comparable record by any other head of government in modern times exists. There was, of course, regular correspondence during the British days between the Viceroy and the Provincial Governors, but its focus was narrower, dealing principally with day-to-day problems. Nehru's letters concentrated on broad issues of policy. He used them, as he once put it, for 'thinking aloud about important developments and possibilities'. He let the Chief Ministers into his confidence, into his very intellectual processes. He sought a common approach to basic problems in the short as well as in the long run. Even on external relations and defence, which were the exclusive domain of the Central Government, Nehru took pains to brief the Chief Ministers in great detail so as to promote a national consensus on India's foreign policy.

Such a consensus was not difficult to achieve, as the same party, the Indian National Congress, was in power at the Centre as well as in most of the States. Most of the Chief Ministers had in fact been the Prime Minister's colleagues in the national movement. Indeed, from Nehru's standpoint, the task of nation-building was a continuation of the freedom struggle. He had always envisaged that struggle as a prelude to a massive reconstruction of the polity and economy of India.

The first seven years of his premiership seem to have been on the whole years of light and hope for Nehru. His optimism was at its peak in 1954–5. 'There is no doubt', he wrote, 'that the country is in a mood of hope and expectation. It is looking forward to . . . big achievements. . . . We have all the basic elements for rapid progress.' The First Five Year Plan was in operation; large hydroelectric projects were under construction; fertilizer and locomotive factories were coming up; the public and private sectors were both expanding. In rural India a beginning had been made with agricultural extension and community development. Abroad, there were signs of a better understanding of India's policy of non-alignment between the two power blocs, whose rivalry dominated the international scene. India's unobtrusive but constructive role in ending the Korean war and negotiating the Geneva Pact was being lauded. 'India's voice', Nehru proudly told the Chief Ministers, 'was a thin, small one, criticized, derided, laughed at and disliked. It was one of the turning points of history for that voice suddenly to assume a certain importance in the world.' So buoyant was Nehru's mood that he looked forward to 'getting some leisure to read and think'.

There was hardly any aspect of national life on which the Prime Minister did not have something eminently sensible and practical to tell the Chief Ministers. He advised them to attend to the problems of housing and town-planning, and to prepare master-plans of the metropolitan cities before it was too late. He emphasized the importance and urgency of launching land reforms, village *panchayats*, and village cooperatives. He commended Rajasthan and Andhra Pradesh for acting on the recommendations of the Balwantray Committee for 'decentralizing and democratizing' local administrations:

Thus the Panchayat and the village co-operatives become the foundations as well as the strong pillars of our democratic structure both in administration and in economic matters. No one imagines that these changes can take place easily or quickly, but the foundations have been clearly laid. It is for us to bring them about. Such an effort should not be a party effort but an all-India effort.

## IV

While it was Nehru's strategy to encourage and even inspire the Chief Ministers to promote economic development, he did not hide from them his doubts and misgivings. 'Somehow we have got entangled in mighty or expensive schemes,' he wrote in September 1958, 'which no doubt are good in themselves, but which take a long time to yield results.' The smaller projects were often more economical and gave quicker results. 'All this leads me to the conclusion', Nehru added, 'that the basis of all our work must be intimate contact with our people in almost every phase of our activity'. As for the 'mixed economy', while he wanted the public sector to be the dominant partner, he warned that excessive restrictions on the functioning of the private sector would mean that it would cease to have the advantages of the public as well as the private sector.

The decline in educational standards worried the Prime Minister. 'If this process goes on', he wrote in September 1955, 'it simply means we shall become a third-rate nation, in spite of our efforts in other directions.' Even the universities that used to take pride in their high standards were going downhill:

Many of our teachers [Nehru wrote] do not impress at all. Research is almost non-existent among the teachers. Some of them indeed are much too busy in manoeuvring and canvassing for some position in the universities . . . we can hardly blame the students when the teachers act in this way.

It seemed to Nehru that many of the students who went to the universities were incapable of understanding lectures or writing correctly in any language. The change-over from English to the Indian languages had, 'resulted in the ignorance of all languages'. The standard of English was lamentable: indeed it was no English at all. The result was the rearing of an 'ignorant generation with just a smattering of knowledge'. There were few books in Indian languages on science, economics, technology, engineering, medicine, and a number of other subjects; it was obviously impossible to translate hundreds of technical books. In Europe an educated person was supposed to be well versed in two or three languages; it was, therefore, odd that in India there was a tendency to neglect or even discard English. As if this was not enough, student indiscipline had become endemic; this could however be remedied, in Nehru's view, by a gentleman's agreement among political parties not to meddle with educational institutions.

A network of national laboratories was being set up in the country with the Prime Minister's enthusiastic support, but as early as April 1950 he was warning against the dangers of separating scientific research from teaching in the universities.

## V

In his correspondence with the Chief Ministers, Nehru shows awareness of the critical role of clean, constructive, and cooperative politics in a federal and democratic system. He calls for 'a cooperative approach', between the Government of India and the State Governments. He himself consulted leaders of opposition parties in Parliament on food and other problems. He admitted that the administrative machine was slack and slow-moving:

In the lower grades there is a fair amount of corruption. This leads me to the conclusion that centralization is more likely to lead to delays and corrupt practices than a decentralized administrative system. It is easy to criticize such decentralization and devolution of powers, but there appears to me to be no other demonstrative way to deal with the multitude of problems that arise.

In September 1958. we find the Prime Minster urging the injection of a 'vital spark' into the administrative system. 'That vital spark can only be injected' he wrote, 'if it is present in the top leadership which includes the leadership of all grades, including the village grade. This spirit of dedication is not very evident today.' He feared his own partymen were losing contact with the people. 'We live apart, he wrote, 'in a world of offices, telephones and jeeps.' When even voluntary agencies started demanding funds and vehicles to move about, Nehru nostalgically recalled the days of his youth when, inspired by Gandhi, he and his colleagues had cycled or even walked through the villages and 'still shaken the country'. What disturbed him more than anything else was the unscrupulous exploitation of caste, language, and religion for political ends. He noted that, even some of the leftist politicians, the professed champions of a classless society, had been afflicted with the extreme spirit of caste, which struck Nehru as 'worse than class: it was petrified class'. Again, regionalism, based on language, had introduced a new disruptive factor, which had 'something of the bigotry of religion'. 'Each person', Nehru wrote, 'thinks that his doxy is orthodoxy; other doxies are heterodoxies.' Religious fanaticism and communalism, which had been somewhat muted in the first few years of independence, were again rearing their heads. In 1956, several towns in Uttar Pradesh, Madhya Pradesh, and West Bengal were rocked by demonstrations and riots provoked by the reprinting of a book entitled *Living Biographies of Religious Leaders* by two American authors which carried a preface by K.M. Munshi. Muslim communalism seemed to fuel Hindu communalism, and vice versa: it was obvious that the freedom of speech and press granted by the democratic constitution of India was being abused by communal organizations.

## VI

The question then is why, even though Nehru had been able to identify some of the critical problems facing the country so clearly and so early in his long tenure as Prime Minister, they remained intractable. Was it because in a federal system he lacked the power—or the will—to enforce the policies of the Central Government on the States? Or, was it the lack of strong support from his colleagues and party?

For seventeen years the flow of information, advice, and admonition from the Prime Minister to the heads of the State governments had gone on on every aspect of politics and administration—land reforms, village *panchayats*, village cooperatives, elementary and higher education, vocational training, slum clearance, religious strife, caste conflicts, linguistic divisions, nepotism and inefficiency, and so on. Nehru kept himself abreast of problems, analysed them, and suggested solutions. He was pragmatic and persuasive. With the Congress party in an absolute majority in Parliament, and his unrivalled charisma in the country, he enjoyed an unassailable position. He did not adopt a superior or hectoring attitude to the heads of State administrations.

You would forgive me [Nehru wrote] for thinking aloud in these matters, but I have to bear a heavy burden and my mind gropes to find the light. I realize too well my own failings and imperfections and I know that the demands cannot be fulfilled by a few individuals. We have to draw the whole nation, including ourselves of course, on the right path.

Nehru's having to revert to the same themes again and again in his letters was proof enough that the policies he was commending were not being speedily implemented. This may have been due partly to lack of effective leadership in the States. Perhaps something more than advice was necessary even within a federal and democratic constitution. If he had set up a small secretariat to monitor the action in the field, the results may have been better. We know, however, that the elaborate secretariats which his successors set up did not much improve matters. The truth is that Nehru failed to draw able young men into the party and the government to build a second line of leadership. He was not a good judge of men, and was perhaps too indulgent to old comrades and friends. K.N. Katju as Home Minister and Syed Mahmud as Minister of State for Foreign Affairs were obviously questionable choices. Of his older colleagues, Krishna Menon was incorrigibly controversial and an erratic defence minister; Maulana Azad was a great scholar but had little aptitude for administration, and lacked the experience or the energy to impart to the educational system the radical reorientation it needed in independent India.

As for the State governments, it is obvious that Nehru's exhortations and warnings fell on deaf ears. It is easy to say that he was not ruthless enough as a ruler, but the Indian Constitution left to the States a wide field including agriculture, forests, irrigation, industry, education, health, law and order. The record varied from State to State, but most of the Chief Ministers failed to live up to the expectations of the Prime Minister: They had themselves become prisoners of the electoral process and the exigencies of power politics in their parties and States. With adult franchise and large constituencies making elections expensive, a nexus grew between local politicians and vested interests. For example, domination of the State legislatures by affluent farmers weighted the scales against small farmers and the landless labourers. Agrarian legislation in most provinces was riddled with loopholes which hindered the transfer of land to the tillers of the soil.

It seems in retrospect that Nehru should have trusted his own instinct and resigned office after ten years to devote himself to the revitalization of the Congress party. As the older leaders of the Congress party in the States died or faded out, the field was left clear for a new breed of power-brokers without scruple who flouted the rules of the political game and pandered to caste, religion, and linguistic prejudices. Nehru was distressed by

the gap between what we proclaim and what we do. . . . We used to be criticized in days gone by and called a nation of talkers and not men of action. That criticism faded away when Gandhi came on the scene. And we now are reverting to our previous habits and justifying that criticism.

Meanwhile, with the passage of years and growing burdens and anxieties, Nehru had less and less time to write to the Chief Ministers. In the first five years he had written 142 letters; in the last five years he wrote only 91. The war with China was a severe blow, but after the first few weeks, with remarkable resilience, Nehru regained his bearings and steered India back to an independent posture between the two power blocs.

In his last fortnightly letter to the Chief Minsters in May 1963 Nehru referred to the conflict with China, the relations with Pakistan, the problems of economic development, and the inefficiency and corruption in the administration. 'It is true', he said, 'that even countries that have fought each other may become friends later. . . . We should not, therefore, think in terms of permanent enemies and we should always leave the door open for friendship.' The tragedy was that just when India was able to make a tremendous effort to push her economy forward, the external dangers had compelled her to divert her resources to defence. He was glad that the people of India had demonstrated their solidarity during the Chinese invasion but he feared that as the actual military conflict became a thing of the past, 'many people would revert to their party squabbles and to their normal industry of running down and blaming Government for everything that happens'. What the country needed was strength, unity, and hard work:

We have too many weaknesses and disruptive forces at work [Nehru told the Chief Ministers] Caste still plays an unhealthy role. Caste also helps in bringing about inefficiency, nepotism and corruption. One leads to the other. . . . Our government apparatus is still slow-moving and full of brakes which comes in the way of all the brave schemes that we have in mind. Our law, good as it is, is slow-moving also in regard to the punishment of the guilty. I am writing about this to you because I feel strongly that we must clean up our public life and make it worthy and efficient for the objectives we have in view.

What are these objectives? There must be a life worthwhile for all the hundreds of millions who live here so that all of us can lead a purposeful existence and rid ourselves of the curses of poverty, unemployment, disease and ignorance. . . .

In the final analysis, right education open to all is perhaps the basic remedy for most of our ills.

After the death of Maulana Azad and Govind Ballabh Pant, Nehru had begun to feel lonely, but if he felt a sense of fatigue or despair, he did not betray it in these letters. As he told the Chief

Ministers: 'I do not despair. Although sometimes I feel a little angry at our failings and weaknesses, I have faith in our people and in the future of India, and also in a better ordered world. It is because of this faith I carry on.'

Even the letters written in his last days testify to Nehru's clarity of thought and tenacity of purpose. Despite failing health, he bravely soldiered on, holding cabinet meetings, facing Parliament, plodding through protocol, touring, addressing party and public meetings, granting interviews, and working away at the memoranda and files which came to him for orders. Almost the last words he spoke on the midnight of 26 May to his secretary were, 'I have cleared all the papers'.

# 11

## *Economic Planning*

I

By the time he became the Prime Minister of independent India, Nehru's ideas on a socialist reconstruction of India had considerably mellowed, but the poverty and backwardness of the country continued to weigh heavily on his mind. Like Gandhi, he had always thought of the political liberation of the country as a prelude to its economic development. More than any other Congress leader, he was conscious that the Industrial Revolution, which had transformed the economies of Europe and America in the eighteenth and nineteenth centuries, had bypassed India, and she had to make up for the lost centuries. Rapid economic growth required a colossal effort; massive additions had to be made to the economic infrastructure, irrigation, road and rail transport, postal and telecommunication network, steel mills, power plants, heavy engineering, chemical, drug and fertilizer factories. Such a magnitude of investment was obviously beyond the horizon and even the means of India's private sector in the early 1950s.

It was also clear to Nehru that a poor country had to put its scarce material and managerial resources to the best use. Seven years before Independence, he had presided over the meetings of the National Planning Committee of the Indian National Congress which had defined planning under a democratic system 'as the technical coordination by disinterested experts of consumption, production, investment, trade, and income distribution in accordance with the social objectives set by representative bodies of the nation.' This was broadly the role which Nehru envisaged for the Planning Commission he set up in March 1950. It was designed, *inter alia,* to coordinate economic development in the states, prescribe priorities for investment, promote modernization of industries and fix targets for production in agriculture and manufacture.

The First Five Year Plan (1951–6) provided for a total investment of Rs 2378 crores. A series of good harvests and the sterling balances which the country had accumulated during the war years enabled the targets of the First Five Year Plan to be easily met, and without any inflationary pressures. The First Plan constituted a modest beginning, largely based as it was on the collation of existing schemes, some of which were already under execution.

Planning in India really started with the Second Five Year Plan (1956–61). It was the first systematic attempt at economic planning, and set the direction for priorities and policies of the government for the next thirty-five years. Its chief architect was Professor P.C. Mahalanobis. 'The Professor', as he was called, was a brilliant mathematician and the founder of the Indian Statistical Institute. He consulted the Soviet economist M.I. Rubinstein and the Polish economist Oscar Lange, and produced a model which was a variant of that constructed by Feldman for the Soviet Union's First Five Year Plan. Its basic assumption was that the greater the proportion of investment in the metal-producing and machine-building sectors, the higher the long-run rate of growth. Savings were to be stepped up for investment, and foreign exchange was to be conserved by import substitution. The shortage of consumer goods was to be made good in the cottage industries sector. A short-run restraint on present consumption was postulated as a *sine qua non* for the creation of basic industries and the infrastructure for sustainable growth in future.

Mahalanobis' scheme met with strong opposition in the Planning Commission, but after he won over Nehru, the Commission waived its objections. A few economists, such as B.R. Shenoy, C.N. Vakil, and P.R. Brahmananda, suggested alternative wage-goods models, but most Indian economists were brought round to endorse the Mahalanobis–Nehru approach to planning. Indian industrialists were at first sceptical, but soon realized that they would be the chief beneficiaries of the infrastructure which the public sector was designed to create.

The basic philosophy of the Second and Third Five Year Plans—

which were launched in Nehru's lifetime—was the development of the Indian economy along socialist lines to achieve rapid economic growth, expansion of employment, reduction in disparities of income and wealth, and promotion of values and attitudes of a free and egalitarian society. Nehru himself provided the vision and the drive for the preparation and execution of the plans; as the Chairman of the Planning Commission, he endowed it with great prestige and authority, and insulated it from the vicissitudes and short-run political pressures of India's democratic system.

Nehru looked upon the five-year plans as levers for the transformation of a poor, agrarian economy of continental dimensions into a self-generating modern economy within two or three decades. The plans were to build up the country's resources, thereby relieving the masses from extreme poverty and establishing a just society based not on individual greed and private profit, but on cooperative effort. For Nehru, the plans were not merely a method of economic management, but a means of promoting the integrity, continuity, and stability of India's democratic system. While commending the First Five Year Plan to Parliament, he described it as an attempt to bring the whole picture of India, agricultural, industrial, social and economic, 'into one framework of thinking'. The plan, was, he said, a challenge to the people of India to think in terms of the good of the nation as a whole, apart from the particular problems which faced villages, districts, and provinces.[1] Nehru thus wanted the Planning Commission and the National Development Council to serve as additional links in the federal structure of the Indian Republic.

The gains of the first decade of planning—1951–61—were not inconsiderable. There was a sizable increase in public investment in major and medium irrigation projects, power, transport, basic industries, and higher education. Agricultural production rose by 41 per cent and industrial production by 94 per cent; steel production increased from 1.4 to 3.5 million tons. Domestic savings as a proportion of the gross domestic product (at 1960–1 prices) rose from 10 per cent in 1954–5 to 15 per cent in 1964–5. Life expectancy went up from 40 years in 1951 to 50 years in 1966. These gains were, however, partly offset by a serious miscalculation on the part of the planners in assuming an annual growth of 1.25 per cent in population; the actual increase turned out to be 2.5 per cent. The net result was only a modest increase in per capita income from Rs 284 in 1951 to Rs 331 (at 1961 prices). The plans thus failed to make—what Nehru had intensely desired—a significant impact on the fundamental problem of poverty.

The Third Five Year Plan (1961–6) was a logical extension of the philosophy of the Second Five Year Plan. Nehru did not live to see its completion, but he wrote part of its first chapter on 'Objectives of Planned Development', and to the last never took his eyes off it. The implementation of the Third Plan was unfortunately dogged by misfortunes such as the border war with China in 1962, a series of failures of the monsoon and, finally, the war with Pakistan in 1965.

## II

Nehru's economic policies were assailed both from the Right and the Left even in his lifetime. His Socialist and Communist critics charged him with over-indulgence to the private sector. They urged him to live up to the socialist faith of his youth, and objected to the very concept of a 'mixed economy'. They demanded wholesale nationalization of the means of production. The right-wing critics charged Nehru with blindly following the Soviet model, sinking scarce resources in heavy industries with long gestation periods, and enlarging the public sector, with its inevitable concomitants of bureaucratization, delays, and corruption. C. Rajagopalachari, one of the veterans of the freedom struggle, and the first Indian head of State after independence, denounced the whole planning regime as 'a licence-permit raj', and argued that free enterprise was the only way to root out corruption, prevent authoritarianism, and preserve individual liberty and democracy. Charan Singh, a UP Congress leader, who was to enjoy a brief stint in national politics during the late 1970s, in his book *India's Economic Policy* (1977) attributed all India's economic ills to the 'Nehru Model' of development, and went on to make the fantastic suggestion that all large-scale industrial enterprises in India, except those exporting their entire output, should be wound up.

After the collapse of the collectivist economies in the former Soviet Union, eastern Europe, and some of the African states, there has been a tendency to pronounce Nehruvian economics as intrinsically flawed, and to argue that Nehru's socialist orientation had put the Indian economy on the wrong track.

Nehru's affair with socialism had begun early in his youth when he read books by Bernard Shaw, the Webbs, R.H. Tawney, and other socialist writers. This may seem an illustration of Keynes' dictum that 'in the field of economic and political philosophy there are not many who are influenced by new theories after they are twenty-five or thirty'.[2] Nehru's interest in socialism was, however, sharpened by his visit to Soviet Russia in 1927 and the study of the writings of Karl Marx and Lenin in the 1930s. He conceived great admiration for economic planning in the Soviet Union and for the massive and seemingly successful assault it seemed to have made on poverty and economic backwardness. Nevertheless, as we have already seen, Nehru's social and economic ideas were never frozen in an ideological mould; on the contrary, with the passing of years, they grew increasingly eclectic and pragmatic.[3]

It is important to remember that the centralized economic planning initiated in India in 1950 was not the brain-child of Mahalanobis and Nehru alone. In the years immediately following the Second World War, there was a wide, almost universal belief, that in countries, which were emerging from colonial rule, the state was the ideal instrument for restructuring the economy and ensuring rapid growth and development. Since, under the colonial regime, the free operation of the global markets had usually worked to the disadvantage of the subject countries, it followed that the governments of the newly-liberated countries should want to redress the balance. This was something on which most perceptive observers seemed to agree in the early 1950s. Mahalanobis was of course an ardent admirer of Soviet planning and consulted Russian and Polish experts, but the final model, which bore his name, took account of the views and won the appreciation of western experts and institutions. Among the distinguished economists of Europe and America, who visited India during these years and commended the Indian experiment were Paul Rosenstein, Rodan, Wilfred Malenbaum, Paul Baran, J.K. Galbraith, Nicholas Kaldor, Paul Streeten, W.S. Reddaway, Donald McDougall, and Trevor Swan.

Indian development strategy during the Nehru period, 'thus represented a fairly widespread intellectual consensus of the time',[4] and it must be conceded that, for some time, this strategy was remarkably successful in mobilizing resources and accelerating growth. Indeed, India's economic development was being held forth as a model for other developing countries. In those early years Nehru himself exuded optimism. 'There is the air of hope in this country, a faith in our future. . . . There is the break of the dawn, the feeling of the beginning of a new era in the long and chequered history of India', he wrote in June 1955.[5] He was almost lyrical over the possibilities of the five year plans in transforming Indian economy and society. Before long he was to discover that the planning process was going to be neither as rapid nor as painless as he had hoped.

### III

There were some flaws in the Mahalanobis model which became more visible with the passage of years. D.R. Gadgil, who became Deputy Chairman of the Planning Commission under Indira Gandhi, wrote in 1959, that 'planning as such does not operate in India today. There are only schemes of public expenditure or of aid to private or cooperative enterprises.'[6] Gunnar Myrdal, the Nobel-Laureate Swedish economist, detected the same lacunae in Indian planning:

The core of all the Plans was the programme and in some respects a forecast of public and private investment. The plans were not operational in the sense that they avoided giving even broad directions for various levels of government policy, as for instance, interest rates and exchange controls.[7]

The planners themselves were probably handicapped by the lack of dependable data on unemployment and poverty. Every plan recognized that it was a critical problem, but it was only in 1971 that V.M. Dandekar and R. Rath revealed that in the last year of Nehru's prime ministership, 40 per cent of the population was below, what they described as 'the poverty line'.

In retrospect it seems that the centralized system of planning did not provide enough scope for popular participation. Nehru's own speeches and writings certainly helped in creating a consensus amongst the political élite, but something more than exhortation was needed. Walter Lippman, the eminent American columnist, after a visit to India in 1959, suggested that the 'revolutionary objectives of the Third Five Year Plan require the organized pressures of a popular movement under government leadership, so dynamic and purposeful that it can inspire people to do voluntarily the kind of things that in Communist China are done by compulsion.' Unlike the Chinese Communist Party, the Congress party in India was not cadre-based. In January 1958 Nehru acknowledged that his party was suffering from a 'deep malaise'.[8] He might have been able to revive it had he followed his own instinct, retired even temporarily from the office of Prime Minister, and devoted himself to party work. Unfortunately, Nehru had neither the time nor the aptitude for party management. There was hardly anyone else who could evoke mass enthusiasm for a concerted and constructive effort. The hopes raised by the Bhoodan movement were not realized; Vinoba Bhave's message of a non-violent transformation momentarily focussed the attention of the country, but he lacked both Gandhi's charisma and his organizational and political skills.

It is not surprising that the centralization of decision-making occasionally resulted in faulty allocation of investment and poor utilization. The plethora of controls devised by the central and state governments bred delays and corruption. Import substitution was carried to absurd lengths in the name of self-reliance, and resulted in the production of shoddy and costly goods which crippled the ability of Indian exporters to compete in world markets. The prevention of practically all foreign firms from entering India provided a protected market for both the public and private sectors which produced sub-standard manufactures and did not bother about costs, or about research and innovation. Miscalculations on the availability of foodgrains and over-optimistic licensing of imports, especially of capital goods, drained precious reserves of foreign exchange, and upset the country's balance of payments. The powerful farmers' lobby in almost all political parties successfully resisted the imposition of any central tax on agricultural income. The high rate of income tax—perhaps the highest in the world—resulted not in an equitable distribution of wealth, but in the creation of an extensive black market. 'Everybody is agreed', remarked B.K. Nehru in 1970, 'that they [the Indian rates of taxation] have converted, what used to be by and large a reasonably honest community of tax-payers, into dishonest tax evaders on a very large scale, thereby leading to the evils of black money and the black market.'⁹

It has been suggested that driven by his enthusiasm for industrialization, Nehru did not realize the importance of agriculture and neglected it. This charge does not seem to be tenable. Nehru was acutely aware of the pivotal importance of agriculture in the Indian economy. 'If our agricultural foundation is not strong,' he told the Indian Parliament in December 1952, 'then the industry we seek to build will not have a strong basis either. Apart from that, if our food front cracks up, everything else will crack up too.' A few months before his death, he said: 'Agriculture is more important than anything else, not excluding the big plants; because agricultural produce sets the tone to all economic progress.' The importance he attached to agricultural development is indicated by his suggestion to State Chief Ministers that they personally take charge of their respective agricultural portfolios.

The investment in agriculture during the years 1950–65 was Rs 3446 crores, 22.7 per cent of the total plan outlay, as against 17.2 per cent for industry and 37.7 per cent for transport and power, and 18.1 per cent for social services. It would be relevant here to recall that the growth rate of agriculture in India, which was less than .25 per cent per annum during the years 1904–5 to 1944–5 under the British regime, went up to 3.1 per cent for the period 1949–50 to 1964–5. This growth was achieved largely by increasing irrigation, electric power, research, and extension. It is, of course, true that in the Nehru years the food situation seemed grim: Nehru himself was worried about the imports of food which shot up from 12 million tons in the First Plan to 17 million tons in Second, and to 26 million tons in the Third Plan. However, the foundation for the great technological transformation—the Green Revolution—which brought about self-sufficiency in foodgrains in the mid-seventies was also laid during the Nehru regime.

If more was not achieved in the agricultural sector, the explanation is to be sought not in the degree of importance which Nehru attached to agriculture, but on the practical plane of resources and inputs, efficiency in implementation, and action to bring about institutional changes.

The most important institutional change, which was urgently

needed but was botched up was land reforms. After independence the *zamindari* and old feudal structures had been dismantled by the Congress Governments, but there were heavy delays and much laxity in implementation of the reforms by the State administrations, dominated as they were by the powerful landed interests. Large areas continued to be cultivated through informal crop-sharing arrangements. Ceilings on holdings were circumvented by fictitious transfers and partitions, and scarcely any land was left for distribution to landless cultivators.[10] According to Dr K.N. Raj, in 1971–2, seven years after Nehru's death, over 50 per cent of the rural households in India, with holdings of less than 2.25 acres, accounted for less than 10 per cent of all agricultural land, while 10 per cent of the rural households with holdings of 10 acres or more owned nearly 55 per cent of the total land under cultivation; and finally, no more than 2 per cent of the agricultural land was being cultivated by 40 per cent of the households including landless labour.[11]

Nehru had cherished the hope that land reforms would break up the 'old and stagnant class structure' of Indian society, that the countryside would revive with an intensive programme of community development, that the village *panchayat*, school, and cooperative would become the true foundation of the new rural India. In May 1956 he told the Indian Parliament that the community development programme was creating a 'revolutionary atmosphere in our countryside'. Unfortunately, the community projects, more official than popular in character, were sustained more by hope than by achievement. Nehru's choice of the man for this challenging assignment was not a happy one. S.K. Dey, the Minister for Community Development, 'an engineer by training and salesman by profession', was a poor administrator. The programme was neither fully thought out, nor well-funded, nor vigorously executed. Community development and schemes of cooperative planning never got a fair chance of success because of the realities of the power structure in the Indian countryside.

## IV

Nehru's belief that public ownership of the means of production would promote a high degree of social responsibility and work-ethic stemmed from his socialist creed, but it proved illusory. There were unconscionable delays in the execution of several public sector projects, and even after they were completed, their utilization often fell short of their capacity because their managements tended to be bureaucratized and the workers' unions were more intent on extracting their pound of flesh than on raising productivity. Despite its huge size and massive investment, the public sector failed to generate enough surplus for further investment. The long gestation period of some of the large projects and the poor returns from them reduced the availability of resources for other sectors of the economy. The government had to resort to deficit financing to balance the budget despite high levels of taxation. The private sector too was subjected, in the name of socialism, to a jungle of controls by the state, which left enormous scope for obstruction in the hands of dishonest officials and politicians.

These deficiencies and lapses in economic management were to become more glaring in the post-Nehru period, but Nehru was conscious of them and gave anxious thought to their correction. Day in, day out, he pondered over the problems referred to him by the Planning Commission, the central ministries, and the state governments. For him development was more than the attainment of certain statistical targets: he viewed it in human terms, in the difference it would make to the quality of life of the common people. It was all very well, he said, for planners to talk of investing thousands of crores in river valley schemes and steel plants, but were they touching the life of the people? Why not, he asked, invest in a large number of smaller schemes for irrigation and industry requiring less capital and yielding quicker results?[12] Why not provide adequate resources to the village *panchayat*s and make them responsible for implementation of the plans?[13] Was it not shameful that even in 1963 there were areas in India where it was difficult to get proper water to drink and 'people had to go miles and miles to fetch a pot of water'? What was the difficulty in replacing the traditional plough, which could barely scratch the surface of the earth, with the modern plough costing as little as Rs 25 to 75? The lackadaisical attitude of most politicians and bureaucrats distressed him. Soon after the approval of the Third Five Year Plan by Parliament he wrote to the Chief Ministers in October 1960:

Is there anything in India which is more important than this mighty task? . . . And yet I wonder how many of our politicians, how many of our Members of Parliament and Assemblies or those who aspire to become Members of Parliament and Assemblies have given much thought to the Plan. They are too busy with party squabbles, not realizing that a government or party success may have no meaning at all if we lose the major battle.[14]

Alva Myrdal, the Swedish Ambassador in New Delhi, recalled a visit to Rajasthan with the Prime Minister for the opening of a public library. Nehru was garlanded on arrival and everything was ready for him to cut the ribbon, when he said: 'I would like to have a look at the books first. Show me the premises.' He went into the building and found there were no books. 'I am not going to inaugurate the library like that, he said; it is nonsense', and walked away.[15]

Implementation was a problem which continually exercised Nehru, but a satisfactory solution eluded him. He sought help from the Planning Commission, his ministers and advisers like T.T. Krishnamachari, whom he had specially inducted into his Cabinet for economic coordination. Vishnu Sahai, who served as Cabinet Secretary under Nehru, has testified to the Prime Minister's burning desire to discover some personal or organizational device to oversee implementation and achieve coordination. 'I think it is only fair to say', writes Sahay, 'that he failed to discover a practical way of institutionalizing a system of watching implementation. For that matter, none of his professional advisers, including myself, made any really useful suggestions to him on this.'[16]

There was hardly a subject of economic development to which Nehru did not apply his mind; in his letters to Chief Ministers, he reeled off instructions on cooperative farming, consolidation of holdings, water-management, educational reforms, town planning, slum-clearance, and so on. He warned against the forces of disintegration, which exploited, caste, language and religion, and diverted national energies into wrong channels. He called for a crusading spirit from his colleagues and subordinates, but he called in vain. As Gunnar Myrdal noted in his *Asian Drama*, while there was in Nehru's time 'a discernible trend in all the ideological activity towards explicit radical commitments, practical politics moved in a pragmatic and conservative direction'.[17]

Effective implementation was what Nehru sought, but there were several factors which militated against it. Few of his colleagues could muster the zeal which he himself brought to bear on social and economic issues. Then there was the diffusion of power inherent in India's parliamentary and federal system, aggravated by the factional and populist politics in which all parties, including the Congress, indulged.

In the last years of his life Nehru's desperate search for effective plan implementation manifested itself in the appointment of Asoka Mehta, the Socialist leader, as Deputy Chairman of the Planning Commission. Mehta had been critical of the Government's handling of economic planning. In the early months of 1964, even while Nehru's health was failing, the uppermost thought in his mind was how to make the Third Plan work better so as to improve the lot of the masses, especially of the rural poor. A few days before Nehru's death, S.K. Dey, Minister for Community Development was summoned to meet the Prime Minister at his house. It was already past midnight. Dey found Nehru at his desk, looking 'uncharacteristically sad and melancholy'. 'Tell me', he asked Dey, 'what is happening to your Panchayati Raj institutions? Do you think they can withstand an organized pressure on them, if the system were to be reversed?' Dey replied that the system had spread out to the majority of the states, but had not received the requisite support except in Gujarat and Maharashtra, where the system had been firmly established. As for the other states, the process, Dey said, might take longer. 'You have no time', Nehru replied with a sense of urgency, 'you have no time, dear friend, take it from me, you will have no time.'[18]

## V

After the eclipse of the collectivist economies in the Soviet Union and eastern Europe, China, and other countries, and the recent 'liberalization' of the Indian economy, there is an understandable temptation to decry Nehru's socialist proclivities and economic planning. He has been accused of an obsession with the public sector and an antipathy to private enterprise. T. Thomas, a former chairman of Hindustan Lever and director of the multinational Unilever, who had the opportunity of watching the Indian industrial scene at close quarters both in the Nehru and post-Nehru eras, has effectively refuted this charge against Nehru:

Many people have forgotten and the young people have never experienced the period following our independence when the government actually encouraged and facilitated the entry of private sector businessmen into several manufacturing industries. That is when the Tatas, Birlas, Escorts, Thapars, MRF and many others began to spread their wings.[19]

According to Thomas, the Indian Government fell into 'the trap of the Russian model' after Nehru's death from the mid-1960s and became obsessed with state ownership and control during the 1970s. The fifteen year period 1966–80 was, according to another critic, 'the dark period for Indian industry'.[20] Unfortunately, these were the very years when a spurt in world trade and tremendous technological changes fundamentally altered the traditional pattern of comparative advantage and organization of productive capacity among nations. The processes of production became global; the old distinction between exporters of manufactures and exporters of primary products was blurred, and some developing countries were able to demonstrate their ability to export manufactures. It also became evident that state control tended to make economic organization costly and inefficient, that investment decisions must be made by entrepreneurs on the merits of each case and not on the basis of preconceived notions of planners alone as to what is desirable in the social interest. Even before the disintegration of the Soviet Union, there were clear indications that state-controlled socialism could not deliver the goods. In Britain, under the premiership of Margaret Thatcher, several government-controlled organizations, such as British Airways, British Telecom, British Gas, British Petroleum, Royal Ordnance factories were privatized. Indeed, Margaret Thatcher boasted that she had sent socialism back to the library of the British Museum where it had originally been picked up by Karl Marx. The British Government shut down some of its coalmines and compensated workers at £30,000 per head, counselled and retrained them for other occupations. Japan privatized several organizations such as Nippon Telegraph and Telephones, France and Italy denationalized a number of state enterprises; so did West Germany, Spain, Italy, Malaysia, Korea, Poland, Brazil, and Turkey as a means of divesting themselves of companies which were over-staffed, inefficient, and propped up with government subsidies.

The eclipse of the public sector has thus been a worldwide phenomenon of the last quarter of this century. Nehru could hardly have foreseen this denouement, though it must be said to his credit that he was conscious of the pivotal role of technology in economic development. As early as December 1952, he warned that 'many of our methods of production will become completely out of date'.[21] Two years later, he spoke of 'this new world of science and technology and engineering. . . . Old slogans have ceased to have much meaning today. . . . The new world requires new minds and new thinking and new training.'[22]

J.K. Galbraith, distinguished American economist, US ambassador in Nehru's last years, and a sympathetic observer of the Indian economic scene, has attributed India's economic difficulties in recent years to the failure to keep abreast of changes and to recognize that 'public action must always be related to the particular stage that a country has reached in that process'.[23]

India's economic crisis in the early 1990s could have been avoided or at least considerably moderated if Nehru's successors had modified his policies to suit the changed economic realities in 1970s and 1980s. There was nothing inherently wrong in using the state as a catalyst for economic development and social justice. What was wrong was not state intervention, but the kind of state intervention practised under the Indian planning regime. In some countries, such as France and Japan, the state has played and continues to play a positive and effective role in promoting economic development.

As for Nehru's socialist vision, it may continue to be valid, to some extent, even after the idea of public sector as a key to socialism has been discredited. The Indian State can hardly abdicate its role completely: market forces by themselves will not be able to cope with all the complex and intractable problems of a country in which 70 per cent of the people still live in villages, with little or no public infrastructure, and 30 per cent of the population lives below the poverty line. The gods of communism may be dead, but the poor are still with us.

Notes and References

1. H.K. Paranjpe, 'Jawaharlal Nehru and Planning', in *Indian Journal of Public Administration*, vol. X, no. 2.
2. J.M. Keynes, *The General Theory of Employment, Interest and Money*, pp. 383–4.
3. *See* Chapter 9, 'Nehru and Socialism', pp. 185–93.
4. Bimal Jalan (ed.), *The Indian Economy: Problems and Prospects* (Delhi, 1992), pp. XII–XIII.
5. J. Nehru, *Letters to Chief Ministers* (New Delhi, 1988), vol. 4, p. 188.
6. D.R. Gadgil, *The Approach to the Third Five Year Plan*.
7. Foreword to Tarlok Singh, *India's Development Experiences* (Delhi, 1974), p. IX.
8. Quoted in R.C. Dutt, *Socialism of Jawaharlal Nehru* (Delhi, 1981), pp. 230–1.
9. B.K. Nehru, *Thoughts on the Fundamentals of Indian Polity* (Jorhat, 1970), p. 25.
10. 'In the course of the last four decades no more than 2 per cent of the total cultivated area in the country could be acquired as surplus for distribution among the landless.' C.H. Hanumantha Rao in Bimal Jalan (ed.), op. cit., p. 118.
11. *India International Centre Quarterly*, vol. 4, no. 3, 1977.
12. J. Nehru, *Letters to Chief Ministers* (Delhi, 1989), vol. 5, p. 138.
13. Ibid., p. 7.
14. Ibid., p. 416.
15. Interview with Alva Myrdal by the author, Oral History Transcript (NMML).
16. Vishnu Sahai, 'Nehru's Impact on Public Administration', in *Jawaharlal Nehru Centenary Volume* (Delhi, 1989), p. 557.
17. Gunnar Myrdal, *Asian Drama*, vol. I (New York, 1968), p. 297.
18. S.K. Dey, *Destination Man, Towards A New World* (Delhi, 1982), p. 88.
19. *The Economic Times*, 9 May 1992.
20. Rakesh Mohan, 'Industrial Policy and Controls', in Bimal Jalan (ed.), *The Indian Economy* (Delhi, 1992), pp. 96–100.
21. Nehru's speech in the Lok Sabha on 15 Dec. 1952.
22. J. Nehru, *Letters to Chief Ministers*, 1955, vol. 4 (Delhi, 1988), p. 440.
23. J.K. Galbraith, *Nehru Centenary Volume* (Delhi, 1989), p. 234.

# 12

## *Nehru and Non-Alignment*

### I

'It is completely incorrect,' Jawaharlal Nehru told the Indian Parliament in 1958, 'to call our [foreign] policy Nehru's policy . . . I have not originated it. It is a policy inherent in the circumstances of India, inherent in the past thinking of India . . . inherent in the conditioning of the Indian mind.' He went on to assert that any other party in power, or any other foreign minister in his place could not have deviated very much from the policy he had pursued.[1] Nehru's disclaimer, besides being an exercise in conscious humility, was probably designed to promote a national consensus on foreign policy within the country. In reality, Indian foreign policy could hardly have taken the course it did had Nehru not been at the helm in the early years of Indian independence.

It is true that some Indian leaders and publicists in the nineteenth and early twentieth centuries took interest in international affairs, but this interest was generally confined to the problems of Indians living in British colonies and to the vicissitudes of British politics in so far as they affected the administration of India. The Irish national movement and the rise of Jàpan stirred Indian public opinion, and during the First World War some ardent patriots like Lajpat Rai and revolutionaries like M.N. Roy travelled to Europe and the United States to seek support for the cause of Indian freedom, but their efforts made little impact on the course of events.

The Khilafat movement in India before and after the war revealed the colossal ignorance of Indian leaders, including Gandhi, of the realities of Turkish and European politics.[2] Not until Jawaharlal Nehru's visit to the Brussels Congress in 1927 did the Indian National Congress begin to acquire the rudiments of, what might be called, a foreign policy. Nehru organized a Foreign Affairs Department in the office of the All India Congress Committee at Allahabad; the anti-imperialist and anti-Fascist planks in the Congress policy during the late 1930s were largely Nehru's handiwork. Most of his colleagues regarded his preoccupation with foreign affairs as a bee in his bonnet; but they did not question his expertise in this area. No one seemed to be surprised when Nehru took charge of Commonwealth and Foreign Affairs Department in the Interim Government formed by Lord Wavell in September 1946. Sardar Patel and other Congress leaders had little interest in foreign affairs and allowed Nehru virtually a free hand in framing the foreign policy of the country.

In his first broadcast on the All India Radio on 7 September 1946, Nehru spelt out his approach to foreign affairs. He offered India's hand of friendship to Britain, the United States, the Soviet Union, and China. India would, he said, 'keep away from the power politics of groups, aligned against one another, which have led in the past to world wars and which may again lead to disaster on an even vaster scale'.[3]

To most knowledgeable observers of the international scene in 1938–9, the idea of any country avoiding all alliances would have seemed totally unrealistic; this option was open only to a few countries like Switzerland and Sweden. Historically, military alliances were a device to ensure a balance of power to prevent war and, if that became impossible, to win the war. During the critical days of the Munich Pact and its aftermath, Britain and France were acting together. And so were Germany and Italy. If the Soviet Union had joined Anglo–French alliance in 1938–9, no one would have been happier than Nehru himself. Nehru's opposition to military alliances seems to have been derived from his study of the origins of the First World War for his *Glimpses of World History*; it was strengthened by two critical developments at the end of the war: the global polarization between USA and the Soviet Union, which came to be known as cold war, and the invention of the atom bomb.[4]

## II

It is not easy to visualize today the world scene after the defeat of Germany and Japan in 1945–6. The wartime alliance of the United States, Britain, France, and the Soviet Union had broken down.

The Soviet thrust into Europe had aroused the deepest suspicions of the United States and her West European allies. The fear of Communism and a misreading of the Munich Pact of 1938 led to a widespread impression in the United States that any compromise with the Soviet Union would amount to appeasement of a potential aggressor. In the words of an American writer, the Truman Administration 'allowed their fears to distort their perceptions and their ideology to blur reality'.[5] American trade, the American economic system, and even American political freedom—which was supposed to rest on capitalism—were supposed to be in danger. In this heated political climate, North Korea's attack on South Korea in 1950 seemed the first move in a grand, sinister design of international Communism to extend its power to other parts of the world. The Korean war thus contributed to the militarization of the thinking about the cold war. An entry dated 14 August 1950 in the diary of George Kennan, the veteran American diplomat–historian, graphically mirrored the exaggerated fears and suspicions of Russian motives and aims which were current in the United States:

Never before had there been such utter confusion in the public mind with respect to foreign policy. The President does not understand it, the Congress does not understand it, nor does the public, nor does the press. They all wander around in a labyrinth of ignorance and error and conjecture in which truth is intermingled with fiction at a hundred points.[6]

It was against this background that the Truman Administration evolved its policy of the 'containment' of Soviet Russia and international Communism. Nehru's refusal to join this crusade puzzled even the pro-Indian American liberals. Louis Fischer, the American journalist, who had met Gandhi and Nehru during the Second World War and supported the cause of Indian nationalism, appealed to India to join the democracies because 'there could be no neutrality in favour of dictatorship, aggression and totalitarianism'.[7] 'The feeling in American diplomatic circles', the *New York Times* wrote on 23 October 1948, was 'that eventually India will arrive at a point when she cannot stay on the fence in the East–West conflict and that at that point she will choose to stand with the Western democracies.'[8] In August 1950, the same newspaper described Nehru as a 'a counter-weight on the democratic side to Mao

Tse-tung', and added: 'To have Pandit Nehru as an ally in the struggle for Asiatic support is worth many divisions.' A year earlier, at a meeting in the State Department on 30 August 1949, Secretary of State Acheson had told Mrs Pandit, the Ambassador for India:[9] 'The Ambassador's brother, the Prime Minister has emerged as a world figure of great influence and that we look to him to assume the leadership in the rehabilitation of Asia . . . in this role the entire world now has a claim upon him as one of its great statesmen.'

Neither American persuasion nor American blandishments could wean Nehru from his neutral stance. Not surprisingly, he drew upon himself the wrath of American officials and the American press. 'Nehru and I were not destined to have a pleasant personal relationship,' Acheson wrote in his memoirs;[10] 'he was one of the most difficult men with whom I have ever had to deal.' Loy Henderson, the US Ambassador in Delhi, called on Girja Shanker Bajpai, Secretary-General, External Affairs Ministry in October 1950, and protested against Prime Minister Nehru's 'systematic undermining of US prestige and character' by his public statements on the Korean war.[11] A year later, the *New York Times* in an article entitled 'The Lost Leader', wrote:

Jawaharlal Nehru is fast becoming one of the great disappointments of the post-war era . . . To the West he seemed (a few years ago) a logical champion of a free, democratic anti-Communist Asia, and the India he directed was the obvious candidate for the leadership of Asia. Instead of seizing the leadership of Asia for its good, Nehru turned aside from his responsibilities, proclaimed India's disinterestedness, and tried to set up an independent third force India, suspended in mid-air between the two decisive movements of our time—the Communism that Russia heads and the democracy of which the United States is the champion.[12]

### III

The high priest of the policy of containment of Soviet Russia and China in the 1950s was John Foster Dulles, Secretary of State from 1953 to 1959. A British ambassador to the United States compared him to the leaders of Europe during the wars of religion, who 'saw the world as an arena in which the forces of good and evil were continuously at war'.[13] In 1956 Dulles proposed his 'peace insurance plan' which included $36 billion for the cost of the US military establishment at home and abroad and approximately $5 billion in the mutual security programme. He was proud of the fact that the United States had in the previous decade become a signatory to 40 treaties in South America, Central America, Europe, and Asia. Non-alignment between the western and eastern blocs championed by Nehru struck Dulles as 'an obsolete conception, and, except under very exceptional circumstances . . . an immoral and short-sighted conception'. This crusader of the cold war saw in neutrality 'a serious threat to a world order of free nations'.[14]

The containment of Soviet Russia was the aim not only of the Americans but also of the British. In 1946–7 Attlee and Bevin, Mountbatten and Auchinleck had all hoped that, after the transfer of power, 'military links between Britain and the successor states would remain'.[15] Noel Baker in a report to the Labour Cabinet in 1949 pointed out that in the event of a threat from the Soviet Union, India and Pakistan as members of the Commonwealth could 'put reasonably equipped and trained forces into the field at short notice'.[16] Nehru did not, however, view the Commonwealth connection in this light. Indeed, he distinguished associations like the Commonwealth, which were based upon mutual equality and freedom of action, from military alliances that divided the world.[17]

Strange as it may appear, Nehru's refusal to ally India with the West did not endear him to the Soviet Union. For several years after the attainment of independence, the Soviet leaders insisted that India was still a part of the British Empire. Indian diplomats were subjected to the same nagging restrictions as the diplomats of other countries in Moscow. India's first ambassador, Prime Minister Nehru's sister, Vijaya Lakshmi Pandit did not receive an audience with Stalin. Dr Radhakrishnan, who succeeded her, was more fortunate, but when he was leaving, the best he could get in the way of a friendly comment from Stalin was: 'We know, Mr Ambassador, that you and Prime Minister Nehru are not our enemies.'[18]

K.P.S. Menon, who served both as Foreign Secretary and as Indian ambassador in Moscow, compared the relations between India and the Soviet Union in these early years to 'two embarrassed acquaintances who had to be polite but could not be friendly'.[19] There were occasions when Nehru was driven to despair by the captiousness of the Soviet government and the press. In January 1948 he asked Vijaya Lakshmi Pandit 'to speak frankly to Molotov, Vyshinsky and other important functionaries in the Soviet Foreign Office, and tell them that it is quite absurd for anyone to think that we are tied to the apron-strings of England or that we attach ourselves to the USA'.[20] Five months later, Nehru confided in Krishna Menon that

There has been a progressive deterioration in [Indo-Russian relations] . . . the Russian attitude towards India has become progressively one of condemning and running down the Government of India and all its works. Further, the Communist Party of India [which presumably will never go against the main trends of Russia's foreign policy] has been adopting not only a hostile but practically rebellious attitude.[21]

Nehru was referring to the Communist inspired revolt in Telengana in Hyderabad State. Indeed, the Communist policy at that time was one of inciting insurgency in Asian countries. In April 1948, the Burmese Communist Party revolted against the government headed by Thakin Nu. In June 1948, the Malaysian Communists took up arms against the British Government, and three months later a coup was attempted in Java.

Nehru realized the difficulty of conducting a diplomatic discourse with Stalinist Russia. 'Russian policy', he wrote in September 1948, 'usually swings between two extremes, and it is a little difficult to become really friendly with a country which adopts a hostile attitude, or which expects you to become just a camp-follower.'[22] Despite his own socialist predilections and admiration for the Soviet experiments in planned economic development, Nehru had long since shed his illusions about the Soviet political system. His view of the Stalinist regime had changed after he learnt about its mass purges in the late 1930s. When Chester Bowles, the American ambassador in New Delhi, remarked that Stalin had a kindly face, Nehru told him: 'You have not seen him and I have. Stalin had the cruellest face I had seen on any man.'[23] As for Russia's economic development, Nehru knew the heavy price which had been paid by the people of Russia. 'I am certain,' Nehru told the Indian Parliament, 'that no country in any kind of parliamentary democracy can possibly pay it.[24]

As if Russian hostility was not enough, from 1949 onward Nehru had to face antagonism from the new Communist regime in China. In October 1949 Mao Tse-tung sent a telegram to the Communist Party of India, expressing the hope that, under its leadership India would certainly not long remain 'under the yoke of imperialism and its collaborators'.[25] In Chinese Communist jargon, India, Burma, Philippines, and Indonesia continued to be semi-colonies, which had to be freed from the stranglehold of western imperialism. In the Chinese press, Nehru figured as 'a running dog of imperialism', and 'a stooge of the Anglo-Saxon bloc'.

## IV

Despite rebuffs from both the power-blocs, Nehru persevered in the policy he had proclaimed in 1946: while seeking cooperation with the Great Powers, India would keep clear of entanglements in 'power politics'. This was not 'neutralism', a refusal to take a definite line on disputed issues, the kind of stance, associated with Switzerland and Sweden during world wars. India was only claiming the right to make up her own mind according to the merits of every international issue and the requirements of her own national interests, regardless of what other nations or groups of nations might say or do. Nehru had adopted this policy at a time when he was under pressure from both the East and the West, and from the Right and the Left in his own country. Nehru acknowledged that India possessed neither military might nor economic strength. 'Nor do I delude myself', he said, 'about what can happen to us if a great power in a military sense goes against us.' Nevertheless, India would not, he declared, become a camp-follower of any great power in 'the hope that some crumbs might fall from their tables'.

Some of Nehru's colleagues in the Congress party and Cabinet doubted the wisdom of his policy. 'We have no friends left in the world,' bewailed Acharya J.B. Kripalani.[26] Professor N.G. Ranga, a Congress legislator from Andhra, considered Nehru's approach to Chinese encroachments on the autonomy of Tibet as too passive.[27] Shyama Prasad Mookerjee characterized Nehru's foreign policy as unrealistic, especially in regard to China. He doubted whether India could defend her territories 'against big aggression'; she had to strengthen her military position, and if she could not do it alone, she had to do it in collaboration with those with whom the people of India could stand on a common platform and ideology.[28] It was not Mookerjee alone who was inclined towards an alliance with the Western bloc. After the outbreak of war in Korea, the conservative wing in the Congress party wanted India to side with the USA. On 25 February 1950, Philip C. Jessup, the American 'Ambassador at Large', who was visiting Delhi and was staying with Loy Henderson, the American ambassador, cabled to Washington:

Mr Masani, former Ambassador to Brazil, called at the [American] Embassy Residence late Saturday afternoon. He is . . . a member of the Congress Party, but not an active politician. He is strongly pro-American and is very close to Patel. Henderson thought he might have been sent by Patel.

His general theme was that there was a good deal of dissatisfaction in the party with Nehru's foreign policy. He thought Nehru respected strength, and that it was very important that the United States showed strength particularly in Indo–China.[29]

Jessup's report also quoted a dinner conversation with G.D. Birla, who had expressed the view that Nehru 'had antagonized a great many countries without making any friends',[30] and that a large number of members of the Congress party were critical of Nehru's foreign policy.

Perhaps the sharpest criticism of Nehru's foreign policy came from Sardar Patel, the Deputy Prime Minister who, five weeks before his death, wrote to Nehru to review the policy towards Communist powers, and especially towards China. A careful reading of Patel's letter of 7 November 1950 indicates that he saw India confronted with Communist threats within as well as outside India, and favoured a tilt towards the USA.[31] Three days after Patel wrote to Nehru, Henderson, the US Ambassador, informed his superiors in Washington, that there was a crisis in the Nehru Cabinet because of events in Tibet and Nepal, that Nehru was the only member of the Cabinet who still hoped for friendship between India and China.

Even those members of the Cabinet [Henderson cabled] who are Nehru's adherents appear to be convinced that time has come for India to recognize that international communism is country's chief danger

& to make corresponding shifts in policy . . . Patel and others advocating change in India's policies are arguing that India must strengthen its military establishment if it is to effectively face its communist neighbour & that it cannot properly strengthen its military establishment without aid from West, particularly US & that it cannot expect aid from US unless it makes it clear before the whole world that it stands with the West against international communism.[32]

It is difficult to say how the differences between Nehru and Patel would have been resolved if Patel had not died in December 1950. But it is significant that while recognizing the gravity of the crisis in the Cabinet, Henderson expressed the view that 'Nehru and Patel will be able to work out some kind of formula which will enable India gradually to shift in direction towards West, without too much publicity being given to this change'.

Fear of Communism was not confined to politicians in and outside the Congress party and government. The top echelons of the Indian bureaucracy were manned by members of the Indian Civil Service whose education as well as experience predisposed them towards the Western bloc. Gundevia, an officer of the Indian Foreign Service, tells us in his memoirs, that on his posting to the Indian Embassy in Moscow, he went to see C.C. Desai, the Commerce Secretary, to talk about trade between India and Russia. Desai was very peremptory: he did not want, he said, any business relations with 'these damned Communists'.[33] It need hardly be added that during these early years India was wholly dependent on the western countries for the import of essential capital goods, and for weapons for her armed forces which had been trained and equipped on the British model.

## V

The question then is why, despite strong pressures from within and without the country, Nehru persisted in spurning the western alliance. It has been suggested that by keeping his distance from both power blocs, Nehru may have been serving 'practical self-interest'[34] and seeking economic aid from both sides. Actually, Nehru raised the banner of non-alignment in 1946 before even the Marshall Plan for economic aid for Europe was announced by the United States (June 1947). With the other superpower, Soviet

Russia, India's economic relations did not really develop until after Stalin's death in 1953. Nor did India's political relations with Soviet Union take a significant turn for the better until Khrushchev came to power. Nehru's policy could not have, therefore, stemmed from calculations of economic or political gains. Nor did he suffer, as some of his critics may have imagined, from megalomania and a desire to strut on the international stage. In 1947 he had refused to entertain the suggestion that he should visit China to mediate between the Kuomintang and the Communists. 'My job remains in India,' he wrote, 'and it is a difficult enough job.'[35] He reacted similarly to the proposal of Brailsford, the British Labour leader, that he should make an attempt to bring the USA and the USSR together by taking advantage of the universal feeling aroused by Gandhi's death. 'It amazes me,' Nehru wrote to B. Rama Rau, 'how some intelligent people are led by frustration to make fantastic suggestions. Here I am having to deal with groups and people in my own country who are pulling in all manner of directions . . . if we cannot put our own country in right shape, how are we to address others?'[36]

Nehru was aware of the criticism by some of his compatriots, that he gave disproportionate time to foreign affairs to the detriment of domestic problems. In a recent review of Indian foreign policy it has been suggested that Nehru's 'globalism' and 'utopianism' prevented him from doing justice to important issues of national security and regional relations.[37]

Nehru certainly had a strong streak of idealism which found expression in his involvement in international relations. He had a rare gift for articulating the aspirations and anxieties of millions of thinking men and women all over the world. 'Peace has been said to be indivisible,' he said in his first speech to the Parliament of independent India on the midnight of 14 August 1947, 'so is freedom, so is prosperity now, and so also is disaster in this one world that can no longer be split into isolated fragments.'[38] While addressing the UN General Assembly he harked back to Gandhi, and hoped that the human spirit would prevail over the atom bomb. The basic problem was that of comprehending the tremendous potentialities for prosperity and destruction of the industrial and military revolutions of the nuclear age. He pleaded for right means of attaining even right ends. 'That was the lesson,' he said, 'which our great leader Gandhi taught us, and though we in India have failed in many ways in following his advice, something of his message still clings to our minds and hearts.'[39] If Nehru persevered against heavy odds in his policy of non-alignment between the two superpowers, it was because of his conviction that he was strengthening the forces for peace in the world. That this policy was not an end in itself, but only a part of a coherent and well-thought out world-view is clear from a 2500 word note he wrote in September 1948 for the guidance of the Indian delegation to the United Nations.[40]

Indian foreign policy, Nehru wrote, was in the process of being formulated, and there could be no finality about it. While it had to be based on certain fundamental principles, it was also to be evolved in the light of experience, and adjusted to changing circumstances. Foreign policy had thus a long-distance objective as well as short-distance objectives; but the latter had to be in keeping with the former.

'What is our long-distance objective?' Nehru asked, and replied: 'Apart from maintaining the independence of India and her rapid economic and social progress, India by virtue of her position and resources is bound to play an increasing part in world affairs.' India's part in world affairs was to be divided up into 'Asian affairs' and 'general world affairs'. Asian affairs related to South-East Asia, China, and the Far East, the Middle East and Western Asia, and the Soviet part of Asia. India was to seek political and economic cooperation, 'and ultimately in defence' with countries of South-East Asia, including Australia and New Zealand. With regard to China, Nehru wrote, nothing much could be done while China was in a state of civil war. As regards Japan, India's policy was to welcome the growth of the Japanese economy. With regard to Communist revolts in countries of South-East Asia, while acts of terrorism were to be condemned, India would not be party to any measures to suppress them, because these revolts were also tied up with the movements for independence from colonial rule.

From the Middle Eastern countries, owing to the growth of the Islamic sentiment, Nehru anticipated some difficulties after the emergence of Pakistan, but apart from Islamic sentiment, there were some other factors which could incline these countries towards India.

In world affairs [Nehru wrote] generally we should stand for everything that promotes peace and avoids war, and everything that puts an end to any imperialist domination of one country over another. At the same time, we should work for close cooperation between nations with a view to ultimately help in the establishment of some world order.

We have repeatedly stated that India should not ally herself with any of the power blocs. This policy fits in with our basic principles, and is at the same time beneficial even from the narrow opportunist point of view . . . The idea that we can gain some immediate end by alignment with one of the power blocs is essentially wrong. If once we do so, we will even lose our bargaining power, even though we may gain some petty temporary advantage. If India ceases to have a neutral policy in regard to these power conflicts, many other countries would also be forced to line up with this or that power bloc. There would be no neutral countries left, and no lead in any direction away from war. Indeed, India's lining up might bring the world war nearer.

Nehru admitted that India's proclaimed neutrality had had little effect on the cleavage among nations, had actually isolated India, and brought her brickbats from both the parties to the cold war. 'That perhaps is to some extent inevitable,' Nehru wrote,

and need not alarm us. If we adhere honestly and consistently to the policy we have laid down, we shall certainly gain the respect of most countries. During recent months we have had evidence of certain coolness towards India both in the USA and USSR. This was regrettable, but we need not get alarmed or excited about it.

He was all for the maintenance and encouragement of economic and cultural contacts with the Western world, but such contacts were not to lead to any political or military subservience or development of any economic vested interests of foreign countries in India.

With the USSR, India was to try to develop such trade or cultural relations as were possible, but India was to keep clear of 'political entanglement'. 'Russia's policy', Nehru wrote,

usually swings between two extremes, and it is a little difficult to become really friends with a country which adopts a hostile attitude, or which expects you to become just a camp-follower. That we are not prepared to do on any account. It is probable, however, that the USSR might realize that the policy they have recently pursued towards India does not pay, and they might change that policy somewhat . . . In any event our attitude to the USSR should be as friendly as possible subject to all this. We are not getting tied up in any way with its [Russia's] world policies some of which we disapprove. We are too busy with our own country to desire any entanglements elsewhere. We want peace and avoidance of world war. (The fact that we are carrying on little wars in India, or roundabout obviously weakens our position.)

Nehru concluded his note with a warning to Indian diplomats and delegates to the United Nations against striking a 'self-righteous pose and making remarks and aspersions which might wound the self-respect of nations or individuals'. India's representatives were on no account to speak in terms of India being the leader in any part of Asia or forming an Asian bloc.

## VI

Nehru's enunciation of the fundamentals of his foreign policy in February 1948 shows that 'non-alignment' was not only the assertion of the right of newly liberated countries to pursue an independent foreign policy; it was also his response to the grave threat to peace in the world inherent in two antagonistic ideological-cum-military blocs in the post-Hiroshima age. Chester Bowles, US Ambassador to India in the early fifties, recounts in his memoirs his first long conversation with the Indian Prime Minister in 1951. This conversation reveals Nehru's remarkable grasp of the realities of the post-war international scene and uncanny insight into the drastic adjustments and realignments of the major powers which were to take place in the next forty years. Nehru told Bowles that American foreign policy was based on a series of assumptions which 'were at best questionable and at worst dangerously wrong'.[41] The argument that American security faced a threat from a worldwide Communist conspiracy in which the Soviet Union and China were cooperating seemed fallacious to Nehru. Nehru was convinced that Communism could not be contained by military means alone. The primary worldwide political force, he argued, was not communism but nationalism. He predicted a rift between Russia and China:

The Chinese–Soviet association was unlikely to last for more than a few years. Not only did the Chinese traditionally look down on Russians as semi-barbarians, but the Russians were the only imperial power that had retained control over what for centuries had been Chinese territory. In dealing with China, he said, the Soviets . . . are concerned about the vast and rapidly expanding population of China pressing against their eastern or southern borders. It was only a matter of time, he said, before a confrontation of some kind would occur.[42]

Nehru felt that Stalinist Russia was faced with an 'impossible dilemma' in regard to its domestic policies. If Russia was to become an advanced nation with the benefits of modern technology it had to promote education at all levels and on an intensive scale. But an educational effort of that magnitude could not but affect over a period the attitudes of the Soviet people and lead to a liberalization which Stalin did not anticipate.[43]

Nehru's policy of non-alignment was put to its first severe test with the outbreak of the Korean war in June 1950. India supported the resolution sponsored by the United States in the General Assembly of the United Nations branding North Korea as an aggressor. But it soon became clear that India had not lined up with the United States against the Communist bloc. Indian delegates to the UN, by voting on each issue on its merits, incurred the displeasure of both the power blocs, and especially of the USA. Nehru strove hard for a negotiated settlement of the Korean conflict, and despite recurrent difficulties and setbacks, a settlement was at last achieved in 1954 through the Geneva Agreement. India was not invited to the Geneva Conference, but her role behind the scenes was known and appreciated. The French Premier, Mendès-France wittily described the Geneva Conference as 'this ten-power conference—nine at the table—and India'.

Nehru's labours to localize and finally to end the conflict in Korea met with a large measure of success. At the end of the war, his credentials as an advocate of non-alignment in a bipolar world were established. The Soviet Government was impressed by India's independent stand on a highly contentious issue, and the result was a thaw in Indo–Soviet relations, a significant indication of which came in the Soviet veto on the Kashmir issue in India's favour from 1952 onwards.[44]

The Korean war showed how deep the suspicions and hatreds between the protagonists of the cold war were. Nehru had played a significant role in the protracted negotiations that led to the conclusion of the Geneva Agreement of 1954, and had offered India's services in chairing the International Control Commission.

His hopes of consolidating the peace and security of South-East Asia, however, remained unrealized. The success of the Geneva Agreement, which ended the first Indo–China war (1946–54), depended upon elections throughout Vietnam in July 1956, which were expected to lead to the reunification of the country. The United States, which supported South Vietnamese government, and believed in the doctrine of containment of Communism, was determined to wreck the Geneva Agreement. Within two months of the Geneva Agreement, the Southeast Asia Treaty Organization (SEATO) had come into existence. Thus while the Soviet Union, China, and non-aligned countries like India, Indonesia, and Kampuchea put their faith in the Geneva Settlement to maintain peace in the former French Indo–China, the SEATO powers, especially the United States, trusted to military strength to forestall any attempt by the Communists to change the political map of the region.[45] By mid-1958 the International Control Commission had outlasted its utility and was asked to quit Laos; the Commission itself became the arena of a bitter struggle between the East and the West, with India receiving brickbats from both sides. The possibility of peace in South-East Asia was undermined, partly by US preoccupation with containment of Communism and partly by the unpredictable behaviour of the Chinese.

Later in the 1960s, when the second Indo–China war (1964–75) broke out, US involvement in it was based on the relevant articles of the SEATO Pact as well as of bilateral agreements between the United States and government of South Vietnam.[46] Nehru did not agree with the American assessment of the situation in Vietnam and told Galbraith, the American Ambassador, in 1961 that 'there might be more trouble between the Vietnamese and the Chinese than appeared on the surface or was consistent with the cold war vision of monolithic Communist unity'.[47] When President Kennedy was going to the 'summit meeting' with Khrushchev in Vienna, Nehru asked Galbraith to warn him of Khrushchev's 'tendency to unguarded and violent responses' which 'would be disturbing to the President, but less so if he realized that it would also be disturbing to Khrushchev when he later had occasion to reflect on them'.[48] Nehru foresaw the rift between the Soviet Union and China and between China and Vietnam, but his pleas for restraint were not heeded by the United States. The result was that Vietnam had to go through a terrible ordeal for more than a decade. Thousands of American and hundreds of thousands of Vietnamese lives were lost, and over a hundred billion dollars wasted before the policies which Nehru had suggested for bringing peace and freedom to Vietnam and for peace in South-East Asia were accepted.

India's relations with the United States did not follow a steady course, influenced as they were by the relative intensity of the cold war. As Pakistan was increasingly drawn into the orbit of US global strategy against the Soviet Union, the US attitude to the Kashmir issue at the UN tended to tilt in favour of Pakistan. Nehru protested that the United States had brought the cold war to the borders of India by concluding the Baghdad and SEATO Pacts. Indo–Pakistan disputes, and especially the Kashmir issue, loomed large in Indo–American relations. Nehru had told President Truman in October 1949 that the Kashmir problem had to be resolved on a basis other than that of adherence to one religion or the other, as its determination on a religious basis was likely to have 'a deeply unsettling effect upon the Muslims living in India and upon the Hindus living in Pakistan'.[49] When Nehru explained the Indian concept of the secular state, Truman said that it was in accord with American institutions and ideas. Nehru argued that while Kashmir was certainly a cause of tension between India and Pakistan, there were other causes too, 'the root cause being the emotional climate of Pakistan' whose people were being constantly encouraged by the government and leaders to pursue a policy inspired by fear of and hatred towards India in the false belief that India sought to destroy the new State. Kashmir was thus not so much a cause of the passions in Pakistan, but an illustration of them.

Nehru's protests against the Baghdad and SEATO pacts had little effect, as these military alliances were an essential part of American global strategy for the containment of Soviet Union and China. In this strategy Pakistan had a definite role. A high level intelligence estimate of the political situation in Pakistan in March 1955, prepared for the State Department, expressed satisfaction that, after more than two years of recurrent crises, political power in Pakistan had been 'openly assumed' by a small group of British-trained administrators and military leaders, centring around Governor-General Ghulam Mohammed and his two principal assistants, General Iskander Mirza and General Ayub Khan:

The regime favours a strong central government, economic development through austerity measures and foreign aid, and close alignment
with the US . . . Its firm control on the armed forces will almost
certainly enable it to discourage, or if need be, defeat any attempt to
challenge it, and it is unlikely to allow itself to be ousted by political
manoeuvres or legal challenges to its authority.[50]

Three months later, the US Ambassador to Pakistan informed the
State Department that this group was publicly identified with the
policy of cooperation with the United States in the international
sphere, and their position in Pakistan 'depended in considerable
measure on its success. . . .'[51]

Pakistan, like Greece, Turkey, and Iran, thus became an ally of
the US; it became important not only as a base for the US intelligence network, but as a possible moderating influence on some of
the Islamic countries of the Middle East.

When Nehru protested that US military aid to Pakistan would
heighten tension in the subcontinent and start an arms race,
President Eisenhower offered military aid 'of a type contemplated
by our mutual security legislation' to India as well. 'In making this
suggestion', Nehru replied, 'the President has done less than justice
to us or to himself; if we object to military aid being given to
Pakistan, we would be hypocrites and unprincipled opportunists to
accept such aid ourselves.'[52]

The US administration had foreseen the resentment which
military aid to Pakistan would cause in India. However, it knew that
whatever the provocation, India, because of her avowed policy of
non-alignment, was unlikely to draw any nearer to the Communist
bloc. In a top secret State Department note on the probable
repercussions of US military aid to Pakistan, it was pointed out that
it was extremely improbable that Indian protests would result in
any significant political concessions to the Communist bloc, because so long as India continued to pursue its 'basic policy of
independence and non-alignment in the cold war, it has little
additional room for a manoeuvre'.[53]

If India's basic policy left her little room for manoeuvre in the
cold war, it also limited the scope for US pressure on India. A report
of the Operations Coordinating Board of the State Department in
July 1957, acknowledged that the USA had 'little leverage on
India', apart from India's need for greater foreign assistance. But the

level of US assistance was so small in comparison with total economic development expenditure that it could 'exert little, if any influence on its policy outlook. The same applies to the present level of Communist bloc economic assistance to India.'[54]

There was a stage in the late fifties when, within the highest echelons of the US administration, doubts began to be privately aired on the wisdom of US policies in the Indian subcontinent. President Eisenhower told a meeting of the National Security Council in Washington on 3 January 1957 that military aid to Pakistan was proving too costly, and needed to be scaled down.

The decision to give military aid to Pakistan was perhaps the worst kind of a plan and the decision we could have made. It was a terrible error. . . .

Our tendency [Eisenhower said] to rush out and seek allies was not very sensible. Suppose, for example, we undertook to make India a positive ally of United States. In such a circumstance . . . there wouldn't be enough money in the United States to provide the support that India would need as an ally of the United States.[55]

The President reiterated his belief that in some instances the neutrality of a foreign nation was to the direct advantage of the United States.

President Eisenhower spoke to Bunker, the American Ambassador to India in the same terms: 'We are better off with India following its policy of non-alignment than were she to join up actively on our side with consequent burden on the American taxpayer and 2000 miles more of active frontier.'[56]

In December 1957 Langley, the US Ambassador to Pakistan, wrote that 'it was not too difficult to make a rather convincing case, that the present military programme [of US aid to Pakistan] is based on a hoax, the hoax being that it is related to the Soviet threat.' He pleaded with the State Department not to promote an arms race in the subcontinent because all the military strength built in Pakistan would be of little use if India went Communist. He considered the Pakistan forces 'unnecessarily large' for their primal purpose of assuring 'internal security and dealing with any Afghan or Pushtoon threat'. Such was the concentration of Pakistani forces on India that 'a considerably larger Pakistan arms programme would not yield a division for use to the West within the Baghdad Pact area'.[57] President Eisenhower's own criticism of the decade-old prejudices and suspicions of the Pentagon and the State Department. The prejudice against 'neutralist India' is well illustrated by the record of a meeting held by President Eisenhower in the White House on 12 November 1957, which was attended by Vice President Nixon, Secretary of State Dulles, and Secretary of Treasury Anderson to discuss the question of a loan to India. 'India is talking about a 1.4 billion dollars loan to cover trade deficit over the next three years,' Anderson said; 'if we were to provide that kind of money we would have to go to Congress for a specific loan. Aid to India will be hard proposition to sell because their behaviour has been very offensive on the Communist issue, and because they have gone out of their way to insult us on many occasions.' Dulles opposed the loan on the ground that it would have a 'bad impact on Turkey, Iran, and Pakistan, who were supporting the US while India has been working against us'. It required all the tact and skill of the President to secure some palliatives for the Indian economy in the form of assistance from West Germany and loans from the Development Fund and Import and Export Banks in the United States.[58]

## VIII

The occasional misunderstandings and tensions between India and the Western bloc were compounded by the choice of Krishna Menon to represent India at the United Nations. Menon was an incisive debater, adept in constructing arguments in a fine legal structure, and had a flair for evolving formulae, such as the one he devised for repatriation of prisoners at the end of the Korean War. But he did not measure his words when speaking in public, and tended to introduce unnecessary bitterness in criticizing the United States. Nehru knew that Menon was extremely unpopular in the United States, but he insisted on sending him as India's representative to the United Nations. His argument was that Menon was not India's ambassador to Washington for which approval of the US administration was necessary. Krishna Menon's unpopularity, however, inevitably reflected on the Prime Minister himself. This was particularly so when in 1956, during the Suez and Hungarian crises, Nehru came under fire for his failure to denounce the Soviet action in Hungary with the same urgency and vigour with which he had denounced Anglo–French aggression against Egypt. The truth is that, to Nehru, the use of violence in Hungary was as abhorrent as it was in Egypt, but it took him some time to make sure of the facts about the situation in Hungary. India had no senior resident diplomatic representative in Budapest. K.P.S. Menon, the Indian ambassador in Moscow, was concurrently accredited to Hungary, but in the critical days of October–November, Menon was not only unwell, but because of the disruption of communications, could not rush to Hungary. K.A. Rahman, the First Secretary, a relatively junior officer, was the seniormost Indian diplomat in Budapest, but he was unable to communicate with the External Affairs Ministry in Delhi until the first week of November, when his reports started coming in via Vienna. During the crucial days of the turmoil in Hungary, the Government of India had to depend almost entirely on press reports, mostly of western origin, which it did not consider 'entirely dependable'.[59]

After the receipt of Rahman's reports, which candidly described the peoples' resistance and its ruthless repression by the Soviet forces, Nehru took the earliest occasion to publicly condemn the suppression of the Hungarian people. In his speech to the General Conference of UNESCO in New Delhi on 5 November 1956, he said: 'We see today in Egypt as well as in Hungary both human dignity outraged, and the forces of modern arms used to suppress peoples and to gain political objectives.'[60]

Two weeks later, speaking in the Indian Parliament, Nehru left no doubt as to where his sympathies lay. He described the Hungarian revolution as a 'national and widespread revolution'. When Imre Nagy was executed, he expressed deep shock. But this denunciation of Soviet action in Hungary came too late to save Nehru from the charge that he had one scale of values for the West and another for Soviet Union. It is true that Nehru's reaction to the Soviet action in Hungary was not as swift and forthright as was his condemnation of Anglo–French invasion of Egypt. Nehru knew that he could best influence the Western powers by criticizing them publicly, for in democratic countries such criticism could set the corrective process in motion by arousing public opinion. But in a 'closed society' like the Soviet Union, it was a more fruitful strategy to convey Indian doubts and criticisms and pleas for restraint privately through diplomatic channels, because private criticism from friendly countries could influence Communist leadership more than public denunciation.

'The world is a hard place', Nehru wrote, 'for an idealist.' This was certainly true of his experience of conducting Indian foreign policy in the first decade after independence. It was not easy to remain neutral between conflicting ideologies and hostile power-blocs, and to act as a buffer between them. It was a hard and thankless task, calling for endless patience and persistence. Accused in the Western bloc of 'being non-aligned with the USA and aligned to the Soviet Union', Nehru was labelled a hanger-on of the Anglo–Saxon bloc by the Communist bloc. Not until the advent of Khruschev did the Soviet Union learn to recognize non-alignment as a constructive policy. It was the Twentieth Congress of the Communist Party of the Soviet Union in 1956, which pronounced 'that in the context of the general contradiction between the camps of socialism and capitalism, particularly under the shadow of the imperialist war preparations, the position of neutrality of some countries is a positive contribution for peace'. This change in the Soviet attitude became possible because of Moscow's revision of two basic Leninist doctrines: the inevitability of war between capitalism and socialism and the necessity of violent revolution as a midwife of socialism.

So far as the United States was concerned, as we have already seen, a few American leaders and diplomats saw rational and constructive elements in non-alignment, but during the cold war it was difficult for American statesmen and Pentagon to reconcile themselves to India's independent stance. Nehru had to do a lot of tightrope walking in the diplomatic field; he had not only to remain neutral but to seem so. K.P.S. Menon, who served as India's ambassador in Moscow, relates that during the Indian Prime Minister's visit to the Soviet Union in June 1955, the Soviet side suggested an addition to the joint communiqué to the effect that both governments condemned the policy of creating military blocs, and that neither would participate in any coalitions or actions directed against the other. The Indian side did not agree to this, on the grounds that such a guarantee 'would have amounted to a negative military alliance'.[61] Four years earlier, Nehru had turned down the proposal of S. Radhakrishnan, the then India's ambassador to Russia, for a treaty of friendship between India and the Soviet

Union, even though this treaty would have been perhaps no more than a cultural exchange agreement. Nehru felt that it was likely to be misunderstood by the West.[62]

## IX

The greatest challenge to Nehru's foreign policy was to come neither from the USA nor from USSR, but from China which culminated in the Sino–Indian conflict of 1962. Nehru has been blamed for indulging in a romantic vision of a pan-Asian comity of nations, for underrating the threat from Communist China, and for not making adequate preparations to meet this threat which resulted in a military defeat for India in 1962 and damaged Nehru's own prestige as well as his policy of non-alignment.

There is no doubt that Nehru, with his sense of history had long cherished a vision of 'a thousand million strong cooperative of Chinese and Indian peoples', to form a base of Asian cooperation, and ultimately a new cooperative world order. There is ample evidence, however, to show that, after the emergence of Communist China, Nehru was conscious of the long-term threat it posed to India. In his conversation with the American ambassador, Chester Bowles, in 1951, Nehru had referred to this concern, but he felt confident that the 'non-aligned bridge-building role', which he was playing in Asia, was not only in India's interest but in the interest of Asian and world peace. 'He staked his hopes', Chester Bowles wrote, 'for a peaceful relationship, not on the Chinese goodwill, but on the assumption that the Chinese leaders needed a period of peace in which to consolidate their revolution and to build a solid economic base', just as the Soviet Union had done in the 1930s.[63] B.N. Mullik, who headed the Intelligence Department of the Government of India, has recorded in his book *The Chinese Betrayal*, how acutely aware Nehru was of the threat from China.[64]

The problem, as Nehru understood it, was one of giving to China assurances of normal peaceful growth and removing 'the bitter complexes and frustrations of a giant that had been suppressed and oppressed for centuries'. He was prepared to make every possible concession to Chinese fears and complexes. In 1948 he had instantly turned down the suggestion by Thakin Nu, the Burmese Prime Minister, for a defence treaty against China.[65] In 1949 he lost no time in recognizing the Communist Chinese regime; in the following year he showed extraordinary restraint when the Chinese asserted their authority in Tibet, and encroached on the age-old autonomy of the Tibetan people; he pleaded for Communist China's admission to the UN. His strategy was to expose China to the winds of international politics and blunt the edge of her isolation and militancy. He wanted to convince China that India had no territorial or ideological ambitions against her, and the two countries had everything to gain from a cooperative relationship.

Unfortunately, while we know a great deal about Indian Government's and Nehru's attitude to China, we know very little about the undercurrents of Chinese politics and diplomacy. It is possible that in 1962 the ideologues in Peking became the victims of their own theoretical formulation when they asserted that the national bourgeoisie government in India, headed by Jawaharlal Nehru, was swerving to the right, and 'deliberately manufacturing border disputes' with China to divert the attention of the Indian people from the deepening political and economic crises in India. It is also possible that the growing Soviet–Chinese rift had repercussions on Sino–Indian relations. Soviet economic aid to India and the agreement on the production of MIGs seem to have been taken amiss in Peking. Finally, it is possible that the hawks in the Chinese leadership, especially the military leadership, got the upper-hand for a while in 1962.[66] The attack on India may thus have been partly a fallout of the intra-party tussles in Peking.

We know now that Nehru had ruled out a full-scale Chinese invasion of India from across the Himalaya. This judgement was not as irrational as it seemed later. The global power alignment was such that neither the United States nor the Soviet Union could let India be overrun by the Chinese military machine. The attitude of the two Superpowers would have at once become clearer and might even have acted as a brake on the Chinese war-machine, if in 1962 the Chinese had not astutely timed their attack to coincide with the Cuban crisis, the effect of which was to temporarily immobilize both the Superpowers.

We can only speculate on the motive of the Chinese attack. It might have been a desire to humble India, the chief protagonist of non-alignment or an attempt to compel her to divert her resources from economic development to defence, and thus to weaken the appeal to the new nations of Asia and Africa of Indian democracy and the mode of development, which were often cited as alternatives to the Chinese way. Finally, China may have been simply trying to score a point against the Soviet Union in the bitter doctrinal controversies on coexistence and non-alignment which were raging in the Communist camp.

Whatever the Chinese motives, Nehru's own policy towards China can be faulted on two counts. In 1950 he did not protest when China marched her troops into Tibet. When a resolution was moved in the UN condemning Chinese action, India opposed it on the ground that China had given assurances of its intention to settle the matter peacefully. By keeping the Tibetan question alive at the UN, Nehru could have linked it with the question of Chinese representation at the UN. Four years later, the recognition by India of complete Chinese sovereignty over the 'Tibet region of China', without any *quid pro quo*, aggravated the earlier blunder. The argument that India's opposition to China's encroachment in Tibet in 1950–4 would have hastened the border conflict with India is unconvincing because, in the early years, China herself was caught up in its own problems and in the Korean war, and was in no position to provoke a crisis with India. It is true that the Chinese reacted very sharply to the grant by India of asylum to the Dalai Lama in 1959, but by this time they had consolidated their position in Tibet, and were able to pose a much greater challenge to India than they could have done in 1950 or even in 1954.

It has been suggested that a flexible attitude on India's part to the rectification of the western border on the issue of Aksai Chin would have mollified the Chinese. Nehru, however, feared that any concessions might lead to further Chinese demands, and that India could hardly make a gift of the Himalaya to China. Among the causes of the Indian debacle in 1962, in the border war with China, were those at the administrative and local command levels. However, the defence strategy adopted by the Government of India in the fifties and early sixties left much to be desired. It is true that the Indian army was only one-fifth the size of the Chinese army, but not enough had been done to equip the Indian troops for mountain warfare. Since the Chinese combined general war with guerilla warfare, it was necessary for India also to raise mountains troops, capable of adopting guerilla tactics. As it was, even the programme for the construction of roads on the border was not really put into operation until 1961. When the Chinese attack came, poorly equipped troops were hurriedly sent up to the high mountains to fight against Chinese forces which were vastly superior to them in numbers and equipment. The Indian troops had to negotiate extremely difficult terrain without any roads; they suffered from acute shortage of essential provisions and ammunition, and lacked in many instances even adequate winter clothing. Obviously, there was a lack of communication and coordination between the political leadership, the bureaucracy, and the military leadership in India. The Defence Minister, Krishna Menon, was impulsive, abrasive, and erratic, and his known proximity to Nehru prevented the evolution of more rational policies for the defence of the border with China.

It had been India's policy before 1962 not to accept arms aid from foreign countries, even though some other non-aligned countries, such as Egypt, had accepted it. After the Chinese attack Nehru was prepared to accept foreign arms, but not foreign troops. When he asked for American help in 1962, it seemed to some observers that he had abandoned the policy of non-alignment and joined the Western camp. For a while there was even some arm-twisting by the Western powers over the Kashmir issue, but Nehru quickly swung India back to a neutral position. By early 1963 it became evident that neither the Soviet Union nor the United States was happy about the Chinese aggression against India. And even in the hour of India's discomfiture at the hands of China, no attempt was made by the United States to draw India within the American orbit. B.K. Nehru, India's ambassador in Washington, told President Kennedy that Nehru 'being all those years in the neutralist camp' found it difficult to make a direct request for armaments from the United States, and hoped instead that the President, in his reply to Nehru's letter, would offer support in the shape of military assistance on the basis of sympathy, rather than alliance. Kennedy appreciated Nehru's position, and said that he would not take advantage of India's misfortune to coerce her into a pact. Indeed, the President discouraged the idea among his advisers that the Indian Himalaya might be the place to stand against Chinese expansion in Asia, 'with the Soviets caught in the middle and world opinion sympathetic to Nehru'. Theodore Sorensen tells us that Kennedy 'saw no gains for India, for the United States or for the free world in making this fight our [American] fight in the Himalayas'.[67]

In March 1964 Robert MacNamara, the US Secretary of State for Defence, described Iran, Pakistan, and India as nations forming 'the front line of the free world defence against Communist encroachment in the Near East and South Asia'.[68] He was soon to discover that he had misunderstood the Indian position, and that India had not really abandoned non-alignment. Within a few months Nehru had swiftly and firmly disengaged India from the Western bloc and veered back to a neutral position. Curiously enough, after the 1962 debacle, India was able to simultaneously improve her relations both with the USA and the Soviet Union. With the latter country, the process was assisted by the widening of the Sino–Soviet rift.

## X

The concept of non-alignment, as conceived and practised by Nehru was neither narrow nor static. Originally, it was an assertion of India's right, after attainment of independence, to conduct her foreign policy without being tied to the apron-strings of Great Britain or any other great power. But it also became a calculated and sophisticated response by Nehru to the post-war scene, dominated as it was by antagonism between two ideological-cum-military power blocs. Nehru, who besides his lifelong association with Gandhi, had been trained as a scientist, and was a self-taught historian, was quick to perceive that the two 'super powers' were poised for mutual destruction which, in the post-Hiroshima era, posed a serious threat to the future of civilization. In his foreword to a report on *Nuclear Explosions and their Effects*, edited by the Indian physicist, D.S. Kothari, Nehru expressed the hope that the book would 'help to bring a clearer realization to people of the perils and dangers that humanity has to face'.[69] India's refusal to be stampeded into either bloc provided an example which most of the newly liberated countries of Asia and Africa were to emulate during the 1950s and 1960s. Nehru was able to enlist the support of Tito of Yugoslavia, Nasser of Egypt, and other leaders of the Third World who helped to provide a semblance of organization to the non-aligned movement at Bandung in 1956, and at Belgrade in 1961. The non-aligned movement remained somewhat amorphous and loosely knit, but it, nevertheless, became a force to reckon with in and outside the United Nations, and acted as a powerful pressure group against imperialism, neo-colonialism, and racialism.

Nehru lived long enough to see the growing recognition on the part of both the power blocs of the constructive aspects of non-alignment. He also sensed the dynamic potentialities of the movement. By the early 1960s, when the process of decolonization was well under way, Nehru felt that it was time that non-aligned countries, instead of flogging the dead horse of imperialism, turned their energies to important issues such as disarmament and economic cooperation. If the great powers had to compete with each other, Nehru argued, they could do so in underdeveloped countries, treating them as 'a kind of workshop for peace', where Russians, Americans, Britons, and others could help build oil refineries, steel plants, and undertake other major projects.[70] There was indeed a time in the 1950s when this did actually seem to be happening in India. Ludwig Erhard, the West German economic wizard, told me in 1971: 'In those years three countries were at the same time constructing steel plants in India. I think it was the United Kingdom, the Soviet Union and the Federal Republic of Germany, and each of these countries tried to leave, let me put it that way, a very good visiting card in India.'[71]

Nehru has been criticized for giving greater attention to global than to regional issues of direct concern to India. He was sensitive to India's security interests, but he realized that even the regional issues in Asia were entangled with global politics, and could not be resolved in isolation. In any case, given the geopolitical, ideological and psychological fixations of the regimes in India's two important neighbours, China and Pakistan in the 1950s and early 1960s, there was hardly much room for manoeuvre for Indian diplomacy. The wider role, which Nehru assumed in organizing non-aligned countries to act as a moral buffer between the rival power blocs, seems in retrospect to have been a significant contribution to the causes nearest to his heart, those of decolonization, disarmament, and *détente*. His influence in defusing some of the serious international crises of his time was often exercised behind the scenes. According to Willy Brandt, the Chancellor of the Federal Republic of Germany, during the Berlin wall crisis, Nehru 'used his influence with the Soviet Union to calm down the crisis'.[72] Similarly, Chancellor Kreisky of Austria bore testimony to Nehru's 'tremendous contribution' to the settlement of the Austrian question. 'Nehru had', Kreisky recalled, 'already before 1955 begun to mediate between Austria and the Soviet Union, and it was at a time when I was under-secretary and Mr Gruber was the Foreign Minister, and we asked Nehru to tell the Soviets that if the Soviets were to sign a treaty, Austria would become a neutral country.'[73]

It is to Nehru's credit that whenever peace was threatened, whether in Korea, the Suez, the Middle East or the Congo, he offered India's good offices for conciliation and even for the thankless task of international policing. In a period of suspicion, fear, and hatred among nations, he sought to create a climate for peace. 'In this critical moment of human history', Bertrand Russell wrote in 1959, 'it would be Nehru who would lead us from the dark night of fear into a happier day.'[74] President Nasser described Nehru as 'the expression of the human conscience itself'.[75] Even Winston Churchill, who had bitterly opposed the Indian national movement and its leaders, paid a unique compliment to Nehru's crusade for peace when he told him: 'You have conquered two of man's greatest enemies, hate and fear.'[76] During a decade of great tension, when nations were arming themselves to the teeth, and the shadow of a thermonuclear war was lengthening over the world, Nehru became a symbol of the yearning of the common people of all countries for peace. This is illustrated by an incident recalled by Subimal Dutt, Foreign Secretary under Nehru, in his memoirs; while he was on his way to the UN building in New York in 1960, he was asked by the American driver of his car whether Nehru had been able to find a solution to the difficult problems facing the world. 'He is our only hope', the old man said, 'I fought in the first world war, my son fought in the second, and I do not want my grandson to fight in the third.'[77]

## NOTES AND REFERENCES

1. J. Nehru, *Indian Foreign Policy: Selected Speeches, 1946–61* (New Delhi, 1961), p. 80.
2. B.R. Nanda, *Gandhi, Pan-Islamism, Imperialism and Nationalism in India* (Delhi, 1989), Chs 19 & 20.
3. J. Nehru, *Speeches, 1946–9* (Delhi, 1949), vol. 1, p. 2.
4. *See* J. Nehru's article 'The Death Dealer' on the atom bomb in *National Herald*, 1 July 1946.

5. Barton J. Bernstein, *Politics and Policies of the Truman Administration* (Chicago, 1970), p. 70.
6. George Kennan, *Memoirs* (Boston, 1967), p. 70.
7. S. Gopal (ed.), *SWJN*, 2nd srs., vol. 7 (Delhi, 1988), p. 671.
8. Quoted in K.P. Karunakaran, *India in World Affairs February 1950— December 1953* (Delhi, 1958), p. 238.
9. *Foreign Relations of the United States*, 1949, vol. VI, p. 1735.
10. Dean Acheson, *Present at the Creation: My Years in the State Department* (New York, 1969), p. 336.
11. Loy Henderson to Secy of State, 5 Oct. 1950, National Archives, State Department, Washington. 791–13/10–550.
12. *New York Times*, 28 Aug. 1951.
13. Townsend Hoopes, *The Devil and John Foster Dulles* (Boston, 1973), p. 491.
14. Michael A. Guhin, *John Foster Dulles, A Statesman and His Times* (New York, 1972), p. 257.
15. Partha Gupta, 'Imperial Strategy and The Transfer of Power, 1939–51', *in* Amit Kumar Gupta (ed.), *Myth and Reality* (Delhi, 1987), p. 42.
16. Ibid., p. 38.
17. R.K. Karanjia, *The Philosophy of Mr Nehru* (London, 1966), p. 63.
18. Y.D. Gundevia, *Outside the Archives* (Hyderabad, 1984), p. 109.
19. K.P.S. Menon, *Many Worlds: An Autobiography* (London, 1965), p. 268.
20. S. Gopal (ed.), *SWJN*, 2nd srs, vol. 5 (Delhi, 1987), p. 541.
21. J. Nehru to Krishna Menon, 26 June 1948, in Gopal, op. cit., 2nd srs, vol. 6, pp. 463–4.
22. Gopal, op. cit., 2nd Srs, vol. 7, p. 613.
23. Chester Bowles, *Promises to Keep* (Bombay, 1972), p. 542.
24. J. Nehru, *Speeches 1953–7* (Delhi, 1958), p. 11.
25. V.B. Karnik (ed.), *Indian Communist Party Documents, 1930–56* (Bombay, 1957), p. 48.
26. *Parliamentary Debates*, pt II, vol. VI, 1950, p. 1290.
27. Ibid., p. 1277.
28. Ibid., p. 1282. Also see *Statesman*, 7 Dec. 1950.
29. State Dept File 611–91/2 1750 (National Archives of the United States).
30. State Dept File 611–91/2.650 (National Archives of the United States).
31. 'It is possible', Patel wrote, 'that a consideration of these matters may lead us into wider questions of our relationship with China, Russia, America, Britain and Burma.' Durga Das, *Sardar Patel's Correspondence*, vol. 10 (Ahmedabad, 1974), p. 340.
32. *Foreign Relations of the United States*, 1950, vol. 5, pp. 1474–5.
33. Gundevia, op. cit., p. 80.

34. Neville Maxwell, *Foreign Affairs*, April 1974, p. 635.
35. Letter to B. Rama Rau, 7 Feb. 1948, in *SWJN*, 2nd Srs, vol. 5, p. 543.
36. Ibid.
37. Ashok Kapur, 'The Indian Sub-Continent', in *Asian Survey*, July 1988, pp. 693–4.
38. J. Nehru, *Speeches, Volume I, 1946–9* (Delhi, 1949), p. 26.
39. Ibid., vol. IV, p. 324.
40. Note dated 12 Sept. 1948, reproduced in *SWJN*, 2nd srs, vol. 7, pp. 609–14.
41. Bowles, op. cit., p. 489.
42. Ibid.
43. Ibid.
44. Gundevia, op. cit., p. 98.
45. D.R. Sar Desai, *South East Asia* (Boulder, San Francisco, 1989), p. 266.
46. Ibid.
47. J.K. Galbraith, *A Life in Our Times Memoirs* (Boston, 1981), p. 467.
48. Ibid., p. 409.
49. *Foreign Relations of the United States*, vol. VI, 1946, p. 1751.
50. Ibid., vol. VIII, 1955–7, p. 423.
51. Ibid., pp. 430–1.
52. *Keesing's Contemporary Archives*, vol. IX, 1952–4, p. 13462.
53. *Foreign Relations of the United States*, vol. XI, p. 1843.
54. *Foreign Relations of the United States, 1955–7, South Asia*, vol. VIII, pp. 354–6.
55. Ibid., pp. 26–7.
56. Ambassador Bunker to Frederick P. Bartlett, 27 June 1957, *Foreign Relations of the United States*, vol. VIII, p. 348.
57. Letter from Ambassador Langley in Pakistan to Asst Secy of State Rountree, 27 Dec. 1957, *Foreign Relations of the United States, 1955–7*, vol. VIII, p. 488.
58. *Foreign Relations of the United States, South Asia, 1955–7*, vol. VIII, pp. 404–6.
59. Subimal Dutt, *With Nehru in the Foreign Office* (Calcutta, 1977), p. 175.
60. Ibid., p. 178.
61. K.P.S. Menon, *The Flying Troika* (Bombay, 1963), p. 31.
62. Gundevia, op. cit., pp. 92–3.
63. Bowles, op. cit., p. 490.
64. B.N. Mullik, *My Years with Nehru, The Chinese Betrayal* (Delhi, 1971), pp. 84–5.
65. Gundevia, op. cit., p. 17.
66. Author's interview with R.K. Nehru, former Ambassador of India to China, Oral History Transcript (NMML).
67. Theodore Sorensen, *Kennedy* (New York, 1965), p. 663.

68. Z.A. Bhutto, *The Myth of Independence* (London, 1969), p. 69.
69. D.S. Kothari, *Nuclear Explosions and their Effects* (Delhi, 1958), Foreword by Jawaharlal Nehru.
70. Karanjia, op. cit., p. 73.
71. Interview with the author, Oct. 1971, Oral History Transcript (NMML).
72. Interview with the author, Oct. 1971, Oral History Transcript (NMML).
73. Interview with the author, Nov. 1971, Oral History Transcript (NMML).
74. Rafiq Zakaria (ed.), *A Study of Nehru* (Bombay, 1959), p. 243.
75. Ibid., p. 84.
76. Vijayalakshmi Pandit, *The Scope of Happiness* (New Delhi, 1979), p. 283.
77. Dutt, op. cit., p. 259.

# 13

## *Nehru and the British*

### I

'Communist, revolutionary, most capable and most implacable of the enemies of the British connection with India', was Winston Churchill's description of Jawaharlal Nehru in 1937.[1] Most British politicians, and the 'guardians' of the Empire would have concurred.

Ironically, the arch rebel against the Raj belonged to one of the most anglicized families in India at the turn of the century. His father, Motilal Nehru, had built up a fabulous practice at the bar of the Allahabad High Court. He had clashed head-on with Hindu orthodoxy, defied the caste taboo on foreign travel, dressed, lived, and even looked an Englishman. The process of 'modernization' in the Nehru household involved not only adoption of western furnishings and use of knives and forks at the dining table, but employment of European governesses and resident tutors for the children. High British officials enjoyed Motilal's company and were recipients of his hospitality; one of them, Sir Harcourt Butler, who rose to be Lieutenant-Governor of the United provinces, claimed in 1920 'a friendship of thirty years' standing' with him. In the evening of his life, Motilal was asked by Aldous Huxley, the English novelist, whether it was true that Sir Harcourt Butler had provided him with maple furniture and champagne in gaol. Motilal laughed and responded, 'No, it is not true. But in the good old days rivers of champagne must have flowed between us.'[2]

It is not surprising that Motilal with all his admiration for everything British should have decided to send his only son to Harrow and Cambridge. He even envisaged for Jawaharlal a career in the Indian Civil Service, the 'steel frame' of the British Empire.

Jawaharlal had little difficulty in making the transition from a resident British tutor in Anand Bhawan in Allahabad to an English public school. He earned good reports from his teachers, and seemed at home in Harrow School. His letters to his father, however, show that though he was barely sixteen, he was already feeling the stirrings of an ardent patriotism. The news of the crushing defeat inflicted on the Russian fleet by the navy of Japan, an Asiatic power, thrilled him. He eagerly pored over Indian newspapers which his father occasionally mailed to him from India, scouring them for political news. He made no secret of his sympathy with the Extremists in the Indian National Congress. He made it a point to attend the meetings of the Majlis, an association of Indian students at Cambridge, when they were addressed by visiting nationalist leaders such as Lajpat Rai and B.C. Pal. These were the years when a scheme for constitutional reforms in India was on the parliamentary anvil. Young Nehru doubted the bona fides of the Liberal Government headed by Campbell-Bannerman and even sensed ulterior motives in the delay in formulating the reforms measure. He regarded Secretary of State Morley's stance on the reforms halting and half-hearted. When a writer in the *Saturday Review* argued that self-government required long training, Jawaharlal wrote to his father:

Indians were bound to have self-government but—and herein lies the difficulty—not before a few aeons of geological time! This may mean anything between a few million years and wholly incomprehensible period. The chief difficulty was the want of education and some million generations will be required to educate them [Indians] up to the Colonial standard.[3]

Jawaharlal was attracted by the Sinn Fein movement in Ireland, which questioned the right of the English to rule that country. He was attracted by Fabian socialism and other radical ideas of pre-1914 England. The aesthetic side of life appealed to him, as did the idea of going through life 'worthily, not indulging in it in the vulgar way, but rather making the most of it and living a full and many-sided life'. He frequented theatres and bookshops, bought a 20-volume edition of Thackeray, was fascinated by a 40-volume edition of Dickens, and suggested that his father open an account with The Times Book Club.

It is, however, important to remember that it was not uncommon for Indian students in England to pass through a phase of intellectual and political ferment. However, when they returned home to coveted posts in the Indian Civil Service or joined in the frantic race for professional success, the fireside chats at Cambridge or Oxford became dim memories of an exuberant youth. This was the experience of the majority of Jawaharlal's contemporaries; it could have been his as well. Indeed, in his statement at his trial in 1922 he acknowledged that:

less than ten years ago, I returned from England after a long stay there. . . . I had imbibed most of the prejudices of Harrow and Cambridge, and in my likes and dislikes I was perhaps more an Englishman than an Indian. I looked upon the world almost from an Englishman's standpoint . . . as much prejudiced in favour of England and the English as it was possible for an Indian to be.[4]

## II

It was Gandhi's advent on the Indian scene early in 1919 which changed the course of Jawaharlal's life. His decision to throw in his lot with the Mahatma also drew his father into the political vortex. Motilal had a meteoric rise in the hierarchy of nationalist leadership, and in the 1920s came to occupy a position in the Congress which was second only to that of Gandhi. The elder Nehru's defection to the Gandhian fold shocked his numerous English friends whose feelings, in the words of an Anglo-Indian journal, 'resembled those of a fond Edwardian father whose delightful daughter became a suffragette and broke his windows'.

Strangely enough, Motilal had friendly relations with senior British officials and members of the Executive Council of the Viceroy even when he was the Leader of the Opposition in the Central Legislative Assembly. This was a phenomenon which intrigued M.R. Jayakar, eminent lawyer, politician, and contemporary of Motilal. What was it, Jayakar asked, that drew Motilal to the representatives of the Empire, which he was openly trying to subvert? Jayakar wondered whether 'some secret affinity' existed between them, 'born perhaps of the power to rule and govern men'.

In 1926 difficulties arose over the issue of passports to Jawaharlal to enable him to take his wife for medical treatment to Europe as he refused to give an undertaking that during his stay in Europe he would not take part in politics. Motilal spoke to Sir Alexander Muddiman, the Home Member, and the Government of India directed the UP Government to waive the condition.[5]

Jawaharlal began his political career as an ardent disciple of the Mahatma. Because of his father's means and generosity, he was not obliged to work for a living and could give undivided attention to the work of the Congress. The visit to Europe in 1926–7 imparted a sharp political and economic edge to his policies. On his return to India, he engaged himself in organizing students and industrial workers, and became the champion of a passionate and defiant nationalism. He seemed to have outgrown the ideological framework of the Indian National Congress. He rejected Dominion Status as the goal of the nationalist struggle, and advocated complete independence. His presidential speech at the Lahore session of the Congress in December 1929 was at once an assault on feudalism, capitalism, and imperialism. He was, he said, no believer in kings or princes or 'in the order which produces the modern kings of industry'. He called for the total withdrawal of the foreign 'army of occupation' and the British economic stranglehold on India. He demanded the democratization of the princely states. Above all, he questioned the right of the British Parliament to determine the measure and manner of India's advance towards self-government. 'India is a nation on the march', he declared, 'which no one can thwart . . . if we fail today, and tomorrow brings no success, the day after tomorrow will bring success.'

The uncompromising anti-imperialist and socialist tone of Jawaharlal Nehru's speech at the Lahore Congress could not but disconcert the British. The *Statesman* wrote that Jawaharlal Nehru's speech was 'not nationalism, but revolutionary republican socialism', that it threatened to abolish the maharajas and rajas, *zamindars* and industrialists, and, if all this was realized, it would mean bloodshed and chaos.[6]

Seven years before the Lahore Congress, Lord Reading, the then Viceroy, had told the Secretary of State for India that Jawaharlal Nehru was 'fanatical in his hostility to Government'.[7] In October 1928 Lord Reading's successor, Lord Irwin, directed that 'the utterances of Jawaharlal Nehru should be watched carefully'.[8] What worried British policy-makers was that Jawaharlal had come to occupy a key position in the Congress, and seemed to be pushing senior Congress leaders, including his father and Gandhi, into collision with the Raj. Jawaharlal's position was no longer on the radical fringe of the Congress organization, but in its vanguard and at Gandhi's side.

Henceforth, Jawaharlal was a thorn in the side of the British bureaucracy in India. Lord Irwin's private secretary, Emerson, who had met Nehru in 1931 during the uneasy truce in the wake of the Gandhi–Irwin pact, recalled six years later that he had found Nehru 'intractable, uncompromising and determined to work for complete independence. He hopes for mass revolution and will not shirk from violence, if necessary . . . I regard Nehru as more dangerous than Gandhi ever was.'[9] Another senior civil servant, Sir Henry Craik, Home Member in Lord Willingdon's Executive Council, characterized him 'as an active and dangerous revolutionary'.[10] Willingdon fully agreed with this view and indeed confided to his immediate superior in London that 'jail is really the safest place for a person with his [Nehru's] political views'.[11]

Paradoxically, while some British officials disliked and feared Nehru, they also tended to underrate him. One of them, J. Coatman, in his *Years of Destiny*, described Jawaharlal Nehru 'as a fisher wherever the waters are troubled . . . whose secret ambition was to rival Lenin or Stalin in the history of communism'. Coatman, however, considered it unlikely that Nehru was destined to have a long and successful political career, and indeed predicted that history would write him down as 'a pinchbeck Lenin'.[12]

To most British observers of the Indian scene, Nehru's political views seemed not only extreme, but highly impractical. Lord Linlithgow, who met Nehru in September 1938, found him 'a doctrinaire to a degree',[13] and told Gandhi a few days later that Nehru had 'soared above the mundane matters with which I was trying to wrestle and lifted us all with him into the airy height of his brilliant imagination'.[14] 'It is a tragedy in many ways', the Viceroy wrote soon after the outbreak of the war in 1939, that 'we should have in so important a position a doctrinaire like Nehru with his amateur knowledge of foreign policies and of the international stage.'[15] After the 'Quit India' challenge from the Indian National

Congress, British propagandists with the Viceroy's cordial approval revelled in portraying Nehru as 'a Hamlet of Indian politics'.

It was easy enough to underrate or ridicule Nehru, but he was too influential a figure in Indian politics to be ignored. Sir Evan Cotton, in the officially sponsored book *Political India*, conceded that Nehru had captured the ear of 'young India' and 'as matters stand, has been proving a formidable rival to Mr Gandhi'.[16] The relationship between Gandhi and Nehru intrigued and baffled the British. Nehru was a favourite disciple of Gandhi, but he was not a blind disciple, and their differences occasionally spilled over into party meetings and even the press. The British policy-makers hoped against hope that Nehru would push Gandhi off the political stage. In February 1938 Frances Gunther, the wife of John Gunther, the author of *Inside Asia*, relayed to Nehru a talk she had with the Viceroy, Lord Linlithgow: 'He said that you were very brilliant etc. but Gandhi was a great man. . . . He wanted to know how far you would go and how far the people will follow you; his feeling [was] Nehru has the brains, but Gandhi has the people; if they can be separated, we are safe.'[17]

## III

It was in the mid-thirties, in the shadow of the savage repression of the Congress under the Willingdon regime, that Nehru's alienation from the Raj seemed to have reached its highest pitch. He was more often in jail than out of it. His disillusionment with the British rulers was reflected in his autobiography as well as in his letters. Indian freedom and British imperialism were, he wrote, 'two incompatibles and neither martial law nor all the sugar coating in the world can make them compatible'. Real Indo–British cooperation was simply unthinkable until British rule came to an end. In a letter to Agatha Harrison of the India Conciliation Group in London, Jawaharlal recalled his father's description of the British Government in India as 'the greatest terrorist organization'.[18] Harsh words, but they mirrored Jawaharlal Nehru's mood at that time; but even in such a mood he had the capacity for introspection, and could describe his predicament in his autobiography in a Gandhian perspective:

It would be natural enough if there was bad blood between India and England after what has happened . . . I write this sitting in a British prison, and for months past my mind has been full of anxiety . . . Anger and resentment have often filled my mind at various happenings and yet as I sit here, and look deep into my mind and heart, I do not find any anger against England or the English people as a whole responsible for this. . . . They are as much the victims of circumstances as we are.[19]

Nehru went on to acknowledge how much Harrow and Cambridge had influenced him and how much he owed to England; all his predilections, he wrote, apart from the political plane, were in favour of England and the English people, and if he had become an uncompromising opponent of British rule in India, it was almost in spite of himself.

Curiously, just when Nehru's alienation from the Raj was the deepest, circumstances were propelling his party and the British Government towards a *rapprochement*. The Reforms Act of 1935 had been passed, and both the British Government in London and the new Viceroy, Lord Linlithgow, were anxious to see the new constitution launched under as favourable conditions as possible.

It was at this time in the summer of 1936 that Nehru's auto-biography was published. It provided discerning British readers not only with insights into Nehru's mind, but also into the struggle led by Gandhi. The book became a best seller in Britain, and earned highly favourable reviews in the British press. In the *BBC Listener*, Lord Lothian referred to Nehru's 'astonishing philosophic detach-ment and unflinching honesty', and noted that his quarrel was 'with systems, with imperialism, capitalism and religious and social obscurantism'.[20] The Calcutta *Statesman*, usually a sharp critic of Nehru's policies, exhorted all government officials at least to read Nehru's autobiography.[21]

The *Autobiography* helped to reveal something of the 'Nehru charm', which political prejudice had prevented Englishmen from noticing earlier. In July 1936, a British I.C.S. Officer, who was District Magistrate of Multan in the Punjab, heard Nehru at a public meeting and noted that the 'Pandit is by far the most attractive public speaker whom I have heard in India . . . there is no doubt that his manliness, frankness and reputation for sacri-fice attracts a large public.'[22] At about the same time Hallett, the

Secretary of the Home Department, strongly opposed the banning of Nehru's autobiography, and described him as 'a clean and honest fighter',[23] and commended his freedom from bitterness.

The breach between the Congress and the Government, especially after the Congress call to the British to quit India in 1942, again made Nehru a *bête noire* of the British Establishment. But from 1945, after the return of the Labour Party to power, and the imminence of the devolution of power to Indian hands, British politicians and administrators began to see the Congress and its leaders in less lurid colours. After his meetings with Nehru, Lord Wavell described him in his journal as 'honest and sincere', 'friendly and pleasant', 'attractive and interesting'. 'I have seen much of Nehru', Wavell wrote to King George VI, 'and cannot help liking him. He is sincere, intelligent and personally courageous . . . lacks the political courage to stand up to Gandhi when he knows he is in the wrong.'

It was not difficult for Nehru to forget and forgive past bitterness after it became clear that the British had decided to part with power. 'This is not a conflict between India and England,' he wrote to a British M.P. in 1933, 'much less is it one between the Indian people and the British people. The conflict is with a certain system called imperialism which the British Government represents today in India and elsewhere. If England changed her form and methods of government, and dropped all taint of imperialism from it there would be little difficulty in the two countries cooperating for a common purpose.'[24] Ten years later, the British did exactly what Nehru had suggested. All the ambivalence that had characterized his attitude towards the British vanished with the liquidation of the Empire. In the Indian Constituent Assembly he threw his weight in favour of parliamentary democracy on the British model and, as Prime Minister, did all he could to evolve traditions conforming to the established practices in Britain in such matters as the position of the head of the State, the relationship between the executive and the legislature, the cabinet system, and the relationship between the political leadership and the civil service.

For nearly twenty years Nehru had been the champion of complete independence for India, but it is significant that—with the rest of the Congress leadership—he accepted Dominion Status as part of Mountbatten's package plan for the transfer of power in 1947. The decision to remain in the Commonwealth had certain immediate advantages during the period of transition: it softened the Tory Opposition in the British Parliament, it seemed a useful link with Pakistan even after the transfer of power; it could help retain the loyalty of the senior British officers who had chosen to serve independent India in the defence services, and it could help to disarm the suspicions of the rulers of princely states and thus facilitate their integration into the Indian Union.

Two years later, even when the process of framing the new constitution by the Constituent Assembly was well advanced, and India had decided to become a republic, Nehru began to see the advantages of continuing the Commonwealth link with Britain. The membership of the Commonwealth did not entail any diminution of Indian sovereignty or freedom; on the contrary it was, as Peter Fraser, the Prime Minister of New Zealand once put it, 'independence with something added and not independence with something taken away'.[25] Once Nehru was convinced of this, the problem was reduced to that of finding a constitutional formula which could permit India to remain in the Commonwealth even after becoming a republic. The search for this formula called for much hard work and patience, and among those whose optimism and ingenuity contributed to success were Krishna Menon, Indian High Commissioner in London, B.N. Rau, the Constitutional Adviser to the Indian Government, Gordon Walker, the Secretary of State in the Labour Government, and Clement Attlee, the British Prime Minister.

Despite his past denunciation of the British Empire and Commonwealth, Nehru unreservedly commended the new formula to his countrymen. He described the Commonwealth as a 'unique and constructive synthesis', and said that it was a good thing that the old conflict between India and Britain had been resolved in a friendly way. 'The better mind of the world', Gandhi had said as far back as 1924, 'desires not absolutely independent states working against one another, but a federation of friendly independent states'.[26] Seven years later, the Mahatma told the Round Table Conference in London that the Congress did contemplate a connection with the British people, but the connection had to be such as could exist between two absolute equals.[27]

Nehru justified the decision for India's adherence to the Commonwealth almost in a Gandhian idiom. 'There were', he said, 'too many disruptive forces in the world for India to throw her weight in favour of further disruption', and any opportunity that offered itself to heal old wounds and further the cause of cooperation was to be welcomed. He never regretted the choice he had made in 1949. Many years later, as he looked back, Nehru felt that India's membership of the Commonwealth had been a catalytic factor in expediting the freedom of other British colonies and in setting a constructive pattern for transition from colonialism to independence. The Indian example was followed by most Asian and African countries under British rule when they became free. No wonder then that Professor Mansergh, the distinguished historian of the Commonwealth, described Nehru as the real architect of the new Commonwealth, which had grown out of an Empire and was the beginning of a great new experiment in international cooperation, a bridge between various continents, races, and cultures.[28]

We know now that during the months when the negotiations for India's entry into the Commonwealth were under way, Nehru had sharp differences of opinion with the Attlee Government on its approach to the independence of Indonesia and to the Kashmir issue. But he did not allow such differences to cloud the larger issue of India's association with the Commonwealth.

It was during the meetings of the Commonwealth Prime Ministers that Nehru had opportunities of meeting Churchill. Churchill's lifelong hostility to Indian nationalism made him extremely unhappy when the Labour Government decided to wind up the Indian Empire. Speaking in the House of Commons in March 1947, he warned against handing over power to 'men of straw, of whom, in a few years, no trace will remain'. Professor Mansergh later described this comment 'as one of the more memorable miscalculations of great men'.[29] It is to Churchill's credit that he acknowledged his error of judgement and made ample amends when he wrote in 1955 that one of the most 'agreeable memories' of his last years in office had been his association with Nehru.[30] What was more, Churchill paid a unique compliment to Nehru: 'This man has overcome two of the greatest failings in human nature; he knows neither fear nor hatred.'[31]

As for Nehru's own attitude to England, John Gunther had noted in the 1930s that Nehru's Indian critics complained that he was 'too decent, too honourable to be a good politician. He is a gentleman. Worse, he is an English gentleman.'[32] Galbraith, the US

Ambassador to India in the last years of Nehru's life, says that 'in the nostalgia of age', Nehru loved to reminisce about the world of R.H. Tawney, the Webbs, and of Trinity College and Cambridge in the early years of the twentieth century which he had known in his youth. 'It did not especially surprise me', Galbraith adds, 'when once in a relaxed moment, he said, 'Well, you know that I am the last Englishman to rule in India.''[33]

Nehru, with his sense of history, was conscious and proud of the happy ending of the long struggle between Indian nationalism led by Gandhi and the British Empire. Harold Macmillan, the British Prime Minister, who visited India in 1958, tells us in his memoirs that at a banquet given in his honour in Rashtrapati Bhawan, Nehru turned to him and said, 'I wonder if the Romans ever went back to Britain'.

## REFERENCES

1. Winston Churchill, *Step by Step 1936–9* (London, 1942), p. 116.
2. B.R. Nanda, *The Nehrus* (London, 1962), p. 199.
3. Ibid., p. 97.
4. Ibid., pp. 209–10.
5. Ibid., p. 252.
6. *Statesman*, 31 Dec. 1929.
7. Reading to Montagu, 6 July 1922 (Montagu Papers).
8. Home Pol., File 179/29 (NAI).
9. Emerson to Linlithgow, 19 Feb. 1937 (Linlithgow Papers).
10. Home Pol. File 1/2/36.
11. Willingdon to Samuel Hoare, 29 Sept. 1933 (Templewood Papers).
12. J. Coatman, *Years of Destiny, India 1926–32* (London, 1932), pp. 95–6.
13. John Glendevon, *The Viceroy at Bay* (London, 1971), p. 148.
14. Ibid., p. 149.
15. Linlithgow to Zetland, 18 Sept. 1939 (Zetland Papers).
16. Evan Cotton, 'Some Outstanding Political Leaders' in Sir John Cumming (ed.), *Political India* (London, 1932), p. 193.
17. Frances Gunther to Nehru, 13 Feb. 1938 (NP).
18. J. Nehru to Agatha Harrison, 25 Sept. 1935 (NP)
19. J. Nehru, *An Autobiography* (London, 1936), pp. 418–19.
20. *Listener*, 27 May 1936.
21. *Statesman*, 9 May 1936.

22. Quoted in S. Gopal, *Jawaharlal Nehru: A Biography* (Delhi, 1985), vol. I, p. 216.
23. Home Dept, Pol. Confdl File 121/36.
24. J. Nehru to H.K. Hales, 9 Nov. 1933 (NP).
25. Nicholas Mansergh, *Documents and Speeches on Commonwealth Affairs*, vol. II (London, 1963), p. 734.
26. Report of the Thirty-ninth Indian National Congress, 1924, p. 26.
27. S.R. Mehrotra, *India and the Commonwealth 1885–1929*, pp. 144–5.
28. N. Mansergh, *The Commonwealth Experience* (London, 1969), pp. 394–6.
29. Quoted by Henry Pelling, *Winston Churchill* (New York and London, 1974), p. 571.
30. Winston Churchill to Nehru, 30 June 1955, quoted in *Nehru Centenary Volume* (Delhi, 1989).
31. R. Chaudhary, *From Nehru in His Own Words* (Delhi, 1989), p. 95. Also see Vijaya Lakshmi Pandit, *The Scope of Happiness* (New Delhi, 1979), p. 283.
32. John Gunther, *Inside Asia* (London, 1942), p. 441.
33. J.K. Galbraith, *A Life in Our Times: Memoirs* (Boston, 1981), p. 408.

# 14

## Nehru as a Man of Letters

### I

'At the present moment I can imagine nothing more terrifying', Jawaharlal wrote to his father from London in 1911, 'than having to speak in public.'[1] The sensitive, shy, young scientist-cum-barrister could have imagined himself no more in the role of an author than that of a speaker. It is curious but significant that Nehru, one of the most distinguished and successful writers of our time, made his debut into the world of letters not only comparatively late in life, but unwittingly, almost unconsciously.

Young Jawaharlal had early imbibed a love of reading, and his letters from Harrow to Allahabad were marked by a fluency, elegance and (in political matters) a maturity beyond his years. After having decided against taking the ICS examination, his reading did not have to take a predetermined course. He read widely, browsing happily and discursively on science and law, fiction and poetry, politics and economics. His intellectual zest does not, however, seem to have spilled into a magazine article, or even a letter to the editor of a newspaper.

The years which followed his return from England were taken up by professional and domestic preoccupations, and the little leisure that was available was devoted to local and provincial politics. His intellectual curiosity remained, but his reading lagged. 1917 saw the internment of Mrs Besant and the crisis of the Home Rule agitation. Two years later came the Mahatma and the intoxication of the struggle against the British Raj, when Jawaharlal 'gave up all my other associations and contacts, old friends, books, even newspapers, except in so far as they dealt with the work in hand. . . . I almost forgot my family, my wife, my daughter. . . .'[2] It was during these ecstatic years that he had his first taste of journalism. Early in 1919, he helped his father to start the *Independent*, to offset the influence of the *Leader*, the local Moderate paper. The *Independent* soon ran into difficulties, and became a great drain on Motilal's bank balance, but it provided a useful outlet for Jawaharlal's political and literary enthusiasms. Of one article, Motilal wrote that it was excellent: 'I smelt Jawahar in every word and sentence.'[3] Newspaper articles are notoriously ephemeral; almost every politician in those days was a journalist, and every journalist a politician.

1922 was a year of ecstasy as well as agony for Jawaharlal. The Chauri Chaura tragedy and the withdrawal of civil disobedience dashed his hopes of an immediate, massive and successful blow to imperialism. It was a critical test for Jawaharlal; he had to keep up his faith and courage while his world—his political world—crashed around him. Unlike many of his colleagues in gaol, he did not delve into the scriptures, or seek solace in metaphysical speculation. He confided his plans to his father in a letter:

My mind is full of books I ought to read and it is with great difficulty that I refrain from sending you even longer lists than I have done so far. . . .

Many years ago Colonel Haksar told me that, after he had finished his academic career, he gave a year or two to reading and thinking and did nothing else during that period. I envied him that year or two. And now the chance has been given to me. Shall I not rejoice? . . .[4]

The British Government was generous enough to give Jawaharlal enforced leisure of not one but nine years—suitably spaced—in prison. He put it to good use, embarking on one of the longest and most fruitful courses of adult self-education that a prisoner has ever undertaken. Obviously, prison is not an ideal place for such a venture. The Naini gaol library in 1922 could boast of little besides prison manuals, and the prison Superintendent, an English Colonel of the Indian Medical Service, who confessed to Jawaharlal that he had finished his reading at the age of twelve, was not untypical of his class. The library in Anand Bhawan was well stocked, but gaol regulations prescribed that a prisoner could not keep more than six books at a time, even if they included copies of the Gita and a couple of dictionaries.

Jawaharlal's studies were abruptly interrupted by his release from prison in early 1923. They were not to be resumed in full vigour until 1926, when he accompanied his ailing wife to Europe for treatment, and could take some time off for reading and reflection. In November 1927, he paid a four-day visit to Moscow, and on his return to India summed up his impressions in a few articles in the *Hindu* and *Young India*. In 1928 he issued them in a volume entitled *Soviet Russia* 'with considerable hesitation', describing them as 'disjointed and sketchy'. It required, he wrote, 'a person of considerable knowledge and some courage to write about the complex and everchanging conditions of Soviet Russia. I claim no such knowledge . . . though I may possess the habit of rushing in where wiser people fear to tread.'[5]

Jawaharlal was no less apologetic about his second book. The *Letters from a Father to His Daughter*, were addressed to the ten-year-old Indira in the summer of 1928 when she was in Mussoorie and her father in Allahabad. They dealt with rocks, plants, and the first living things, of the struggle of early man against the forces of nature and of the races, religions, and languages of mankind. The letters were meant only for his daughter, but when he was persuaded to publish them, he expressed the hope, 'though with diffidence', that other boys and girls would find in the reading of them 'a fraction of the pleasure that I had in the writing of them'.[6]

In April 1930, the Salt Satyagraha brought Jawaharlal back to gaol. He was released in October, rearrested after a week, and convicted for sedition. This was his fifth term. As he braced himself to face another two and a half years in prison, he thought of occupying himself by writing a new series of letters to his daughter. She was nearly thirteen and needed more solid fare than he had given her two years before in his *Letters from a Father to His Daughter*. The new series of letters, which was intended to be a broad survey of world history, began on 26 October 1930, but was interrupted by Jawaharlal's sudden release in January 1931 in that unexpected chain of events which culminated in the Gandhi–Irwin Pact.

Jawaharlal did not resume his *Letters to Indu* (as he tentatively entitled them), until after the resumption of civil disobedience and his return to gaol a year later. Between 26 March and 9 August 1933, he wrote 176 letters, running to no less than 1,000 pages. It was an enterprise which might well have daunted a professional historian. Jawaharlal, who had studied natural sciences at Cambridge, had never had any training as a historian. True, he had been a voracious reader, especially in prison, and had enjoyed reading historical works. His reading was eclectic but random. If he read Rene Grousset's *Civilisation of the East*, Spengler's *Decline of the West*, Motley's *Rise of the Dutch Republic*, Trotsky's *History of the Russian Revolution*, R.H. Tawney's *Religion and the Rise of Capitalism*, K.T. Shah's *The Splendour that was 'Ind'*, Babar's *Memoirs*, and Émil Ludwig's *Napoleon*, he also read Bertrand Russell's *The ABC of Relativity*, Tolstoy's *War and Peace*, Swinburne's poems and *How to Keep Fit at Forty*. Since the prison regulations did not permit him—even as a Class A prisoner—to retain more than six books at a time, he made copious notes as he read—usually fifteen to twenty books a month. He did not have ready access to archives and libraries, and most of the books he could lay his hands on were secondary works. The epistolary form was not ideally suited to the writing of history. These were formidable handicaps, and it is doubtful if Jawaharlal would have been able to overcome them if it had not been for a powerful dual impulse: to seek an antidote to the monotony and solitude of gaol life, and to feel closer to his only child from whom the prison walls had cut him off.

Academic historians, who have struggled with masses of source materials and experienced the excitement as well as the frustrations of painstaking research, are suspicious of universal histories, and the theoretical pegs on which they are usually hung. Oswald Spengler's *Decline of the West*, published in 1915, affirming that there were seasonal phases in the historical cycle, and that Western civilization was entering the long winter of decay, had been useful to Hitler in creating the mythology of Nazism. Similarly, Vilfredo Pareto's *Mind and Society*, by distinguishing between rational and non-rational elements in history, and suggesting a recurrent alternation of liberty with authority came to be exploited as an intellectual justification by the theoreticians of Italian Fascism. H.G. Wells's *Outline of History*, which became a best seller in western Europe, was permeated by the author's faith in reason, science, and the educability of mankind. Jawaharlal Nehru shared this faith, but as an Indian nationalist, he saw what Wells, and indeed most European writers, had failed to see clearly: that their image of the past was excessively centred on Europe and America, that it did less than justice to Asia and Africa, and that Western domination of these latter continents was not going to be a permanent phenomenon. Such was Nehru's passionate commitment to India's struggle for freedom that his preoccupation with her present and future could not but intrude into his survey of the past. He did not deprecate the achievements of Europe or the heritage of Greece and Rome, but he gave equal emphasis to the contributions made by Persia, Arabia, India, and China, and by the great non-Christian religions, Hinduism, Buddhism, and Islam. With his deep humanism, nourished by his contact with Gandhi, he made no secret of his hatred of violence, racial discrimination, religious fanaticism, and authoritarian rule. As one reads his account of the French Revolution, the American War of Independence, or the Russian Revolution, one has little doubt about where his own sympathies lie. It is significant that more than a third of his history of mankind is taken up by the twentieth century—a period he had himself intensely lived through. Some of the most interesting chapters in the book concern the political and economic cross-currents in the world as it was moving to the brink of the Armageddon in the 1930s.

'These letters of mine', Jawaharlal told his daughter in his last letter (9 August 1933), 'are but superficial sketches joined together by a thin thread.' He had written, not history but 'fleeting glimpses of our long past'.[7] This was disarming but excessive modesty. When such a wide-ranging work as *Glimpses of World History*, running to nearly half a million words, is subjected to critical scrutiny under the microscope of historical scholarship, it is not difficult to pick out errors of fact and argument. But such errors are to be found in the *Outline of History* by H.G. Wells, even though he had successive drafts of his chapters revised by specialists, and in the *History of the English Speaking Peoples* by Churchill, even though he had the proofs vetted by a small army of historians under the guidance of Alan Hodge, the editor of *History Today*. Nehru of course had no such facilities in prison.

Nevertheless, *Glimpses of World History* remains even today, sixty years after it was written, a good, if somewhat discursive introduction to world history—and not only for children. J.F. Horrabin, who read it in December 1935, and agreed to illustrate the English edition with maps, found it 'absolutely exciting reading'.[8] The book requires scarcely more effort from the reader than a good novel. Doubtless, there are other surveys of world history which are more compact and scholarly than *Glimpses*, but there is scarcely any which is more direct, vivid, and humane, better portrays the creative thrust of mankind, and more effectively constitutes, in the words of Norman Cousins, 'a liberal university education'.[9]

Not until June 1934, when in his mid-forties, did Jawaharlal embark on his first real literary venture, his autobiography. 'The primary object in writing these pages', he explained in the preface, 'was to occupy myself with a definite task, so necessary in the long solitudes of gaol life, as well as to review past events in India, with which I had been connected, to enable myself to think clearly about them.' He felt that if he could take a critical look at his own past, he might be able to see the future in clearer perspective. The book was less a chronicle of his life than of the national movement. There are fascinating glimpses of his childhood, of his father whom he admired, loved, and feared, of his delicate and doting mother, and of Ferdinand T. Brooks the resident tutor in Anand Bhawan who introduced him to the joys of reading and the thrills of science. But the bulk of the book is devoted to the story of the national struggle: the coming of Gandhi, the course of satyagraha, the changing national and international scene. We see Nehru in varying moods, as he reacts to the vicissitudes of politics. We see the blend of admiration, affection, and bewilderment with which he follows Gandhi, and the anger and sorrow he feels at the obscurantism, the divisions and narrowness rampant in his country. He confesses he is 'lonely, homeless, unable to enter into the spirit and ways of thinking of my countrymen'. The black moods do not last. He reasons his way out of his dilemmas; his spirits are buoyed up by the sight of a floating monsoon cloud, a flowering tree, a flitting squirrel, and most of all, by the discipline of reading and writing of which the *Autobiography* was itself a product.

The book ran through ten printings in 1936, and proved to be the most influential of Nehru's books. It was translated into thirty-one languages. It made the first dent in the psychological barrier between the British intelligentsia and Indian nationalists since Gandhi's entry into Indian politics in 1920. Nehru had written in an idiom which the British could begin to understand. A few months before the book was published, C.F. Andrews, a friend of

Gandhi, Tagore, and the Nehrus wrote to Jawaharlal: 'You are the only one outstanding person who seems instinctively to know what the West can understand and follow easily. Bapu's [Gandhi's] writings had to be condensed and explained over and over again. Even Gurdev [Tagore] is very difficult when he gets away from poetry to prose.'[10]

The *Autobiography* thrilled the Indian intelligentsia, who wanted something more than the Gandhian programme, as expounded in the *Harijan*, and hungered for a more coherent and forward-looking ideology which took account of the challenges of nationalism, science, technology, and industrialization confronting India in the twentieth century.

The sensational success of the *Autobiography* established Nehru's reputation as a writer. Allen & Unwin, with whom Horace Alexander had negotiated a contract for reprinting some of Nehru's articles,[11] expressed a wish to commission Nehru to write another book on India. But once out of gaol, Nehru could not find time to revise what he had written, or even to read the proofs. During the next five years, he occasionally contributed articles to newspapers and journals. Some of them were collected and published in India and England.[12] These occasional writings were the utterances of a journalist and politician. 'They are', in the words of a competent critic, 'the little berries plucked hastily from the thorny and tangled bushes of an extraordinarily strenuous public life. But they are not for all that carelessly plucked and they taste uncommonly fresh.'[13]

If we do not take into account the slim volume *India Today and Tomorrow*, which was hastily dictated for the first Azad Memorial Lectures in 1959, Nehru's last book, *Discovery of India*, was written in 1944 in the Ahmednagar Fort prison. Once again he had felt an irresistible urge to explore the past—the past of his own country. 'What is my inheritance?,' he asked himself, 'To what am I heir?' He did not set out to slice up India's past and present it as ancient, medieval, and modern periods, with dates and dynasties, and causes and consequences of wars. We get something more exciting in *Discovery of India*: a pageant of India's past unfolds itself on a screen, as it were. *Discovery* did not provide new facts, but it gave valuable new insights and perspectives: it was a useful corrective to the pride and prejudice of those Hindu, Muslim, and British historians who had been grinding their own sectarian or radical axes.

Jawaharlal's interest in the past of his country, was not for its own sake, but 'in relation to the present'. Indeed, it seemed to him that the nationalist movement in India was a culmination of a historical process, which had been working itself out over the centuries. The political, social, and economic issues facing India in the 1940s were very much on his mind, as also were the potentialities' and the limitations of his own people. *Discovery of India* gives an intimate insight into its author's mind, which had considerably mellowed since he wrote the *Autobiography*. When Nehru wrote *Discovery of India* in Ahmadnagar Fort Prison, he could hardly have imagined that within a couple of years he would be heading the government of independent India. The subjective blend of the past and the present, the personal and the political in his book, while it might detract from its 'architectural' proportion as a historical work, illuminates the personality and philosophy of one of the leading statesmen of the twentieth century on the eve of his assumption of office. Only in rare cases (such as Churchill's) do we have such an intimate account. That we should have a history of India by Jawaharlal Nehru is something to be thankful for. 'What would we not give', J.H. Plumb asks, 'for Roosevelt's *History of America*. Stalin's *History of Russia*, and Mao's *History of China*?[14]

It is dangerous for a writer, says W. Somerset Maugham, 'to let the public behind the scenes'. The danger is the greater if the writer happens to be politician. For Nehru, with his natural reserve and innate loneliness, it must have been a tremendous effort of will to lay bare his intellectual processes and the conflicting pulls on his mind and soul. His candour made his books deeply human documents, but it also helped to foster the myth that he was a man of thought and not a man of action. When Lord Lothian, the British Liberal leader, confided to Sir Thomas Jones in 1936 that Jawaharlal Nehru 'has probably given up action for philosophic meditation for the rest of his life',[15] the wish may have been the father to the thought. A number of Nehru's critics have called him a starry-eyed idealist, a poet, a professor who had strayed into the political arena. Some of his admirers even lamented that he should have given to politics what was meant for literature. This was a complete misreading of the man and his motives. Without his passionate commitment to politics it is doubtful if Jawaharlal would ever have become an author. It is true he had great gifts: a penetrating mind, a tenacious memory, a fertile imagination, and a facile pen. Nevertheless, it is true that he wrote hardly anything before his involvement with politics. Once he had cast in his lot with Gandhi, he felt an irresistible urge to act. He travelled from one end of the country to the other, dividing his time between railway trains and public meetings, reeling off speeches and press statements, organizing, exhorting, admonishing, inspiring. He needed all this ceaseless action to calm the fever in his brain; in gaol, his action took the form of writing about the struggle which raged outside. Jawaharlal's books were thus not only personal, but political testaments: an indictment of imperialism and an outline of the new order he envisaged for India and the world.

*Discovery of India*, published in 1946, was Jawaharlal's last important book. In 1947, he became the Prime Minister of independent India. He continued to write and dictate interminably: letters, press statements, memoranda. He knew the excruciating delights of creative writing, but personal predilections had to give way to the claims of office. A few minutes' reading before retiring at night, or an occasional hour in an aeroplane journey was all he could snatch from his relentless schedule. He was 'condemned', to use his own words, 'to hard labour'. One wonders if the thought ever occurred to him that the spacious Teen Murti House in New Delhi was in some ways a worse prison than the barracks of Naini, Almora, and Dehra Dun gaols. Till the last day of his life he continued to toil at his desk, to plod through protocol, to suffer bores and self-seekers who proverbially hang about in the corridors of power, to do his duty to the party and parliament, and to manfully cope with the never-ending crises in India and abroad. Meanwhile, the world waited in vain for that unwritten masterpiece: *Memoirs of Prime Minister Nehru.*

REFERENCES

1. Jawaharlal to Motilal, 18 Aug. 1911 (NP).
2. J. Nehru, *An Autobiography* (London, 1958 rpt), p. 77.
3. Motilal to Jawaharlal, 26 Feb. 1920 (NP)
4. Jawaharlal to Motilal, 1 Sept. 1922 (NP).
5. J. Nehru, *Soviet Russia* (Allahabad, 1928), p. VII.

6. J. Nehru, Foreword to *Letters from a Father to His Daughter* (Allahabad, 1931), first published in 1929 (Allahabad).
7. J. Nehru, *Glimpses of World History* (Allahabad, 1935), vol. 2, p. 1499.
8. J.F. Horrabin to J. Nehru, 29 Dec. 1955 (NP).
9. *Saturday Review,* 20 June 1964.
10. C.F. Andrews to J. Nehru, 6 Nov. 1935 (NP).
11. J. Nehru, *India and the World* (London, 1936).
12. J. Nehru, *Recent Essays and Writings* (Allahabad, 1934); *Eighteen Months in India* (Allahabad, 1938); *China, Spain and War* (Allahabad, 1940); *The Unity of India* (London, 1941).
13. P.E. Dustoor's article in P.D. Tandon (ed.), *Nehru Your Neighbour* (Calcutta, 1946), p. 62.
14. A.J.P. Taylor et al. (eds.), *Churchill: Four Faces and the Man* (London, 1969), p. 137.
15. Thomas Jones, *A Diary with Letters, 1930–50* (Oxford, 1954), p. 177.

# 15

## The Autobiography

### I

'The primary object in writing these pages'. Nehru wrote in the preface to his autobiography, 'was to occupy myself with a definite task, so necessary in the long solitudes of gaol life.' A few months earlier, he had been struck by the remark attributed to Benjamin Disraeli, the English statesman of the nineteenth century: 'Other men condemned to exile and captivity, if they survive, despair; the man of letters may reckon those days as the sweetest of his life.' Nehru also recalled the achievement of two famous literary gaol-birds, Cervantes, the author of *Don Quixote*, and John Bunyan, who wrote his great classic, *The Pilgrim's Progress*, in prison.[1]

After he had completed the manuscript of *Letters to Indu*, which was published as *Glimpses of World History*, Nehru wondered what he should write about next. He ruled out the suggestion that he should write a life of his father, because he felt that attractive though the project was, 'it was an extraordinarily difficult task to write a biography well'.[2] Instead, he decided to trace his own mental development, and to review events in India with which he had been connected for the preceding fifteen years. He remembered the words of Rousseau, the French writer: 'Man thinks when you prevent him from acting'. In the summer of 1934 Nehru was in jail, unable to act, and there were reasons enough for him to think, and to think hard. The civil disobedience movement started with high hopes in 1930, had languished. Public enthusiasm had ebbed. The leadership of the Congress was unsure and divided; the rank and file was confused or apathetic. Nehru himself felt stale and dispirited; it occurred to him that a critical look at his own past, might enable him to recover his bearings.

The book, which Nehru began on 4 June 1934, and completed on 14 February 1935, took shape as he wrote it. Its structure proved to be quite lopsided. To his ancestry and childhood, covering the period from 1857 to 1905, he gave no more than 16 pages. The next 24 disposed of his seven years in Harrow and Cambridge, return to India, his initiation into the legal profession, his marriage and his early forays into nationalist politics during the First World War. Then came Gandhi: Nehru devoted 350 pages to the story of the national movement under the Mahatma's leadership from 1919 to 1932; the remaining 200 pages of the book brought the story up to 1934. The personal element in the narrative was thus disproportionately small, which became more a chronicle of the struggle against the Raj than an autobiography, as it is commonly understood. However, even as a chronicle of the national movement, the book has its limitations; in 1934 when Nehru completed it, the national movement under Gandhi's leadership had only half run its course. It is not surprising that Nehru's original choice of the title of the book was a modest one: 'In and Out of Prison'.

## II

'All autobiographies', Bernard Shaw once wrote,[3]

are lies. I do not mean unconscious, unintentional lies—I mean deliberate lies. No man is bad enough to tell the truth about himself during his lifetime, involving, as it must, the truth about his family and friends and colleagues, and no man is good enough to tell the truth in a document which he suppresses until there is nobody left alive to contradict him.

If autobiography is 'fiction written by a man who knows the facts', Nehru's account is an exception to the rule. He resists the temptation to write himself up; he does not exaggerate; nor does he pat himself on the back. Indeed, he shows an uncommon capacity for introspection and self-criticism. Of his Cambridge days, he says, that his academic record was mediocre. 'I was superficial', he writes, 'and did not go down deeply into anything.' He recalls the discussions with his friends, the loud voices and heated arguments, but 'it was all make-believe'.[4] He does not brag about his radical ideas on sex. 'As a matter of fact,' he writes, 'in spite of our brave talk most of us were rather timid where sex was concerned. At any rate I was so, and my knowledge for many years, till after I left Cambridge, remained confined to theory.'[5] Vague fancies floated in his mind, but work, games, and amusements kept him busy. He admits that by the time he came to London to be called to the Bar, his intellectual zest was at an ebb, and the only thing that seemed to go up was his conceit. When he landed in Bombay in 1911, he was, he tells us, 'a bit of a prig with little to commend me'.[6]

Throughout the book Nehru is unsparing in his criticism of British rule. He accuses the British of deliberately promoting sectarianism and of setting up formidable obstacles to India's progress. However, he does not slur over the shortcomings of his own countrymen. 'What has been the record of British rule in India?' he asks, 'but who are we to complain of its deficiencies, when they are but the consequences of our own failings?' He is generous enough to give credit to the British for 'one splendid gift' of which they had been the bearers: the gift of science.[7]

It was not easy, perhaps it was not possible, for Nehru to be a wholly objective historian of the struggle in which he himself was deeply involved. The book contains scathing denunciation of the British Government, but there is not the slightest trace of hatred of the British people. The communal leaders, both Hindu and Muslim, and the 'Liberal' politicians also come in for his criticism, but Nehru's judgements as a rule are measured and balanced. Notwithstanding his detestation of the *zamindari* system, he takes pains to explain that the term *zamindar* could be misleading. Of the one and a half million *zamindar*s in the United Provinces, 90 per cent were on the same level as the poorest tenants, and 9 per cent were only moderately off; the 'biggish landowners' did not number more than five thousand, and of these no more than 10 per cent could be considered to be really big landlords.[8]

A good memory and the fact that he was writing from his own personal experience enabled Nehru to produce a narrative which was on the whole factually correct.

Writing about the national movement from a personal angle could have been a serious limitation; but it proved to be an asset. Nehru's chronicle, infused with modesty and gentle irony gained in vividness and credibility. We get some interesting vignettes of crime and punishment in India. In 1930, while in Naini Jail, he met a middle-aged prisoner who had been sentenced on a number of charges to a total of 95 years' imprisonment.[9] In his account of the visit of the Simon Commission to Lucknow in 1928, when he was beaten up by the British mounted police, he admits that he had felt a strong impulse to pull down the police officer who was attacking him, but desisted only after remembering the Gandhian principle of non-violence.[10] In his account of the Nabha episode, Nehru recalls how he and his colleagues were chained and paraded like animals in the streets of the town; the entire episode of his arrest and farcical trial illuminates, as if in a flash of lightning, the lawless and autocratic rule in Princely India. Nehru could laugh at himself. In 1929 he was elected president of the Indian National Congress due to Gandhi's eleventh-hour intervention at the Lucknow meeting of the All India Congress Committee. 'I was sensible of the honour', Nehru writes, 'but I did not come to it by the main entrance or even by a side entrance. I appeared suddenly by a trap door, and bewildered the audience into acceptance.'[11] Of his resignation from the Congress committees and its withdrawal in the 1920s, he tells us, 'it was surprising how easy it was to win me over to a withdrawal of my resignation.'

## III

The *Autobiography* contains some striking portraits of Nehru's eminent contemporaries. About his father, Motilal Nehru, he writes: 'He had no wish to join any movement or organization where he would have to play second fiddle . . . He had a feeling that his countrymen had fallen low, and almost deserved what they got.' Hakim Ajmal Khan was a representative of Indo–Persian culture, 'a link between the old order and new'.[12] Mohamed Ali, the Khilafat leader, had 'a nimble wit but sometimes his devastating sarcasm hurt, and he lost many a friend thereby. It was quite impossible for him to keep a clever remark to himself whatever the consequences might be.'[13] About old Pandit Madan Mohan Malaviya, Nehru says: 'He looks upon this dynamic, revolutionary, post-war world of the twentieth century with the spectacles of a semi-static nineteenth century of T.H. Green and John Stuart Mill and Gladstone and Morley.'[14] There is a magnificent tribute to the British missionary, C.F. Andrews, the friend of Tagore and Gandhi, who had advocated complete independence for India in 1920: 'It was wonderful that a foreigner, and one belonging to the dominant race in India, should echo that cry of our inmost being.'[15]

During his visit to Europe in 1926–7, Nehru encountered Indian revolutionaries who had been living in self-imposed exile. Most of them struck him as eccentric characters who had outlived their day. Raja Mahendra Pratap was, we are told, 'a delightful optimist, living completely in the air, and refusing to have anything to do with realities . . . a Don Quixote, who had strayed into the twentieth century.'[16] Shyamaji Krishnavarma, in his musty and suffocating flat, was 'a relic of the past'.[17] The legendary Madame Cama looked 'rather fierce and terrifying as she came up to you and peered into your face, and pointing at you, asked abruptly who you were'.[18]

The most eloquent sketch in the book is, of course, of Gandhi:

This little man of poor physique had something of steel in him, something rock-like which did not yield to physical powers, however great they might be. And in spite of his unimpressive features, his loin cloth and bare body, there was a royalty and a kingliness in him which compelled a willing obeisance from others. Consciously and deliberately meek and humble, yet he was full of power and authority, and he knew it, and at times he was imperious enough, issuing commands which had to be obeyed. His calm deep eyes would hold one and gently probe into the depths; his voice, clear and limpid, would purr its way into the heart and evoke an emotional response. Whether his audience consisted of one person or a thousand, the charm and magnetism of the man passed on to it. . . .[19]

Nehru is frankly critical of Gandhi's asceticism, his sense of sin, his fear of sex, and his belief in the possibility of changing the hearts of landlords and capitalists and foreign rulers. He pooh-poohs Gandhi's theory of trusteeship. A discerning reader can, however, see that even though the author differs with the Mahatma, every difference is a distress, and adds to his own loneliness in prison. We can see the blend of admiration, affection, and bewilderment with which Nehru was following Gandhi. In June 1933, after Gandhi had survived one of his numerous fasts, Nehru deplored in his jail diary the 'emotional upheaval' in the country:

His continual references to God irritate me exceedingly. His political actions are often enough guided by an unerring instinct, but he does not encourage others to think. And even he, has he thought out what the objective, the ideal should be? Very probably not. The next step seems to absorb him.[20]

It may be of some interest to compare Nehru's autobiography with the autobiographies of some other nationalist leaders of his time. Gandhi's autobiography, published in instalments in ·his weekly journal, was in a class by itself: it was more a revelation of his moral and spiritual evolution than a political chronicle. Surendranath Banerjea, one of the founding fathers of the Indian National Congress, entitled his life-story *Nation in Making*. It was published in 1925, but by that time the 'Surrender-Not-Banerjea' of the Partition of Bengal days, had faded out of politics. His complacent and egotistic narrative of the pre-Gandhian phase of nationalist politics is interesting so far as it goes, but it barely scratches the surface of events and reveals a curious incapacity for introspection. Subhas Bose's autobiography, *The Indian Struggle*, was published in the same year as Nehru's, and covered the same period, 1920–34; as a record of the Gandhian struggle, it has a compactness and breathes a spirit of aggressive certitude missing in Nehru's book. Bose's account also bristles with strictures on Gandhi, Nehru, and indeed the entire Congress leadership. Another book which invites comparison with Nehru's book is Abul Kalam Azad's *India Wins Freedom*. Written—or rather dictated—during the last weeks of his life when Azad's health and memory were evidently failing, the book is replete with factual errors so gross that Rajmohan Gandhi has written a book[21] simply to list them. However, what jars most on the discriminating reader is the bland self-assurance with which the Maulana passes summary judgements in reviewing events in which he was at once a witness and a participant. The reader is given the impression that Azad's view was invariably right, and the judgement of his colleagues, such as Gandhi, Nehru, and Patel, wrong. In contrast with Azad's book, Nehru's autobiography is redeemed by continual introspection. Time and again Nehru thinks aloud and even psychoanalyses himself:

My real conflict lay within me, a conflict of ideas, desires and loyalties, of sub-conscious depths struggling with outer circumstances, of an inner hunger unsatisfied. I became a battle-ground where various forces struggled for mastery. . . .

Why am I writing all this sitting here in prison? The question is still the same in prison or outside, and I write down my past feelings and experiences in the hope that this may bring me some peace and psychic satisfaction.[22]

It has been said about the nineteenth-century biographies that they are monuments of rectitude and mausoleums of humbug. Since then the development of psychology—whether formally studied, or merely absorbed as part of the intellectual climate of our time—has changed the fashion in biography. Psychological insight is now regarded an essential ingredient in good biographies and autobiographies. In the account of his life, Nehru had not been afraid to turn the searchlight inward, but after the publication of the book, he simply disarmed his critics by saying that his book was not a record of all the important events of the period, but a record of his own thoughts and moods, and how they were affected by external happenings. The important thing, he argued, was not what happened, but what impression it had produced on him:

I write as an individual about an individual, but I may claim to have represented the mental conflicts of large numbers of others who worked in our freedom movement. Thorough understanding between friends as well as opponents comes through this psychological insight.

It was the psychological insight of the author, combined with his literary skill, which lifted this long chronicle of India's freedom struggle in the 1920s and 1930s to the level of literature. The style attains its high standard not through fine writing but through its author's sensitivity. He succeeds in transmuting his inner conflicts and anguish artistically so as to appeal to the reader's head and heart. 'The book was written', Nehru says in the preface, 'during a particularly distressful period of my existence.' It was indeed a very trying period for him. His mother had a serious accident and his wife was very ill. On 12 January 1934, soon after he heard that his mother had had a fall in Bombay, he noted in his diary:

I have grown lonelier than ever. The home that father built so lovingly goes to pieces. Kamala lies ill in Bhowali—a long, long illness with no cure in prospect, mother lying unconscious in Bombay, I in Almora jail.

A few days later, he wrote, 'There is nothing to be done for the present except to sit in this long prison barrack all alone, and think what a dreadful thing life is'. If the domestic scene filled him with anguish, the political scene, so far as he could determine from the newspapers, was also dismal. The compromises accepted by the Indian delegates at the Round Table Conference elicited some choice epithets in Nehru's prison diary: 'The chicken-hearted animal called the Indian Moderate[23] . . . the scandalous and shameful way the Liberals and others have agreed to the monstrous abortions which are the outcome of the RTC [Round Table Conference].'[24] However, when it came to the actual comment in the book on the Liberal leaders' performance, it was couched in elegant prose; the author did not lose his poise and good humour.

## IV

The autobiography was published in London in April 1935, and was an instant success. The success was expected neither by the author nor by the publishers. Indeed, until almost the last moment, fears were entertained that the book would be banned.

On 18 March 1936, M.K. Rahman of Kitabistan, publishers and booksellers of Allahabad, who had published Nehru's *Glimpses of World History* the previous year, addressed a letter to the Secretary, Home Department, Government of India, stating that he had received from John Lane, The Bodley Head, London, an announcement of the publication of Jawaharlal Nehru's autobiography. 'Before we place our indent with the publishers'. Rahman wrote, 'we would like to be sure that the book is not objectionable and will not be proscribed.'

Curiously, the Home Department of the Government of India had little information about the book until it received from the CID of United Provinces, a copy of an intercepted letter dated 22 March 1936 addressed to Jawaharlal Nehru by Ellen Wilkinson, a Labour M.P. 'Your publishers are worried', she wrote,

whether it will be banned. That, as you know, no one except V. Bigwigs can say. I suppose it will depend on the situation at the moment on publication . . . There is no accounting for the official mind of my countrymen. Something seems to happen even to the sensible ones when your country gets them.

On 6 May, the *Hindustan Times* informed its readers, on the authority of the Lucknow correspondent of the *Amrita Bazar*

*Patrika*, that Nehru's autobiography might be proscribed by the Government of India, as evidenced by the non-delivery of an advance copy sent to Nehru by airmail and the detention of a dozen parcels containing the book at Bombay under the Sea Customs Act.

The news of the proscription of the book was premature. Messrs John Lane had the book in print only in early April, sent advance copies to reviewers around 10 April, and despatched parcels to India by sea mail on 28 April. So, when the matter came up before the Home Department there was still enough time to ban the import of the book into India under the Sea Customs Act. The intelligence officers of the Home Department and of the C.I.D. in the provinces were not slow to smell sedition when it came to nationalist writings. Gandhi's *Hind Swaraj* had been banned as long ago as 1910. In February 1936, a proposal for proscribing Pattabhi Sitaramayya's innocuous *History of the Congress* was seriously considered, though not pursued.

The imposition of a ban on Nehru's autobiography was within the jurisdiction of the Home Department, which was headed at the time by M.G. Hallett, the Home Secretary, who was responsible to the Home Member, Sir Henry Craik. Because of the political standing of Jawaharlal Nehru, the ban required the approval of the Viceroy, Lord Linlithgow, and perhaps (because of the possible political fallout in England) of the Secretary of State for India. Hallett had been Secretary of the Home Department since 1932, and a key figure in the sternest repression under the Willingdon regime that the Indian National Congress had undergone in its history. Hallett was thus no friend of Indian nationalism. So it might well have been expected that he would jump at the idea of banning Nehru's autobiography. He did nothing of the kind. Deep down, perhaps, in this seasoned bureaucrat there was an intellectual, almost a liberal streak, which surfaced and enabled him to overcome his ingrained prejudice. He had received a copy of the book by airmail. His 2000-word review, partly typed and partly handwritten, was an extraordinary piece, coming as it did, from a senior British civilian who had until recently been conducting total war against the Indian National Congress.

'Nehru', Hallett wrote on 10 May, 'is a clean and honest fighter . . . and one point which struck me about the book is that it is written without any bitterness.' Hallett quoted from the book several incidents, including the tragedy of Jallianwala Bagh, to show how Nehru's description was consciously objective and free from exaggeration. He was particularly impressed by Nehru's 'honest' comments on Government methods: 'If we [Congressmen] choose to adopt revolutionary direct action methods, however non-violent they might be, we must expect every resistance. We cannot play at revolution in a drawing room, but many people want to have advantages of both.'

Hallett deliberately picked out passages from the book which could possibly be considered objectionable from the official point of view, and then pointed out that almost always there was a qualifying comment in these passages. In any case, such passages formed a very small portion of a book running to more than 600 pages. He was tickled by Nehru's ridicule of the Indian Liberals for their pro-government stance, and felt that it had 'a substratum of truth, or possibly even more than a substratum'.

Hallett quoted 'a most interesting passage' from Chapter 52:

I do not find any anger against England or the English people. I dislike British imperialism and I resent its imposition in India . . . I dislike exceedingly and resent the way in which India is exploited by the ruling classes of Britain. But I do not hold England or the English people as a whole responsible . . . They are as much the victims of circumstances as we are.

In the end Hallett expressed the view that there was no question of taking action against the book. He had expressed his views with remarkable clarity and courage in a file which he knew would go not only to his immediate superior, Sir Henry Craik, but to the Viceroy, on whom his future preferment depended.[25]

Sir Henry Craik endorsed Hallett's recommendation against the ban, but was evasive in his own comments on the book: 'I have kept the book to read, but, it will, I fear be sometime before I finish it.' Lord Linlithgow, while ruling out a ban on the book, wrote: 'I have read an advance copy through from cover to cover, and found it very dull.'

Lord Linlithgow had good reasons for fighting shy of a ban. He had recently taken over as Viceroy, and one of his principal problems was how to create favourable conditions for the working of the Reforms Act of 1935. A ban on Nehru's autobiography could create a furore not only in India, but also back home in England, and this did not fit in with the new Viceroy's immediate plans.

## V

It is not quite clear why Nehru decided to get the book published in England. 'I was not writing deliberately for an audience,' he wrote in the preface to the book, 'but if I thought of an audience, it was one of my own countrymen and countrywomen.' His earlier books, *Letters From A Father to His Daughter, Soviet Russia,* and the *Glimpses of World History* had all been published in India. The last book had in fact been released in the summer of 1935 when he was still in jail. He had not been able to see the proofs, and was shocked to find it 'chockful of errors and misprints'. 'What is one to do', he wrote in his jail diary, 'with sheer, unadulterated ignorance? I feel ashamed that such a product should be associated with my name.'[26] It is not surprising therefore that he should have wished to spare his new book (which he tentatively entitled 'In and Out of Prison') the fate of *Glimpses*. So he decided to take the manuscript with him when he left for Europe in September 1935 to join his ailing wife. It is also possible that he wanted to forestall the possibility of the book being banned in India: the writ of the Home Department of the Government of India did not run in England.

During the winter months of 1935–6, when his wife was critically ill in Germany, Nehru entrusted the task of finding a suitable publisher to V.K. Krishna Menon, who thus became Nehru's honorary literary agent in London. It soon became clear that British publishers were not going to queue up for a book which was avowedly anti-imperialist in tone. Allen & Unwin, who had published some books on India, showed interest, but their terms did not sound attractive enough. The book then went to John Lane, The Bodley Head, who did a remarkably quick job of publication, even though as late as 24 February 1936 Nehru was asking Krishna Menon; 'What about the title of my book? If you or Lane cannot think of a better one, I suppose "In and Out of Prison" will remain.'[27] In March the book was in page proofs; by the middle of April review copies had been dispatched; at the beginning of May the *Autobiography* was in the bookstores in London. It was reprinted thrice in May; a fifth impression was under print in June, and before the year was out, it had had ten impressions. Evidently, Lord Linlithgow's countrymen did not agree with him about the book being 'dull'.

The response in England was amazing. There was always a small group of 'friends of India' in and outside the British Parliament, such as Horace Alexander, who wrote in the *Friend*: 'If thousands of Englishmen and women read this book (as I trust they will) they will see Anglo–Indian relations in a new and truer light than they have ever done.'[28] However, what was astonishing was the reaction of newspapers and journals in Britain which had never been sympathetic to the nationalist, especially the Congress, cause. 'A book to read,' wrote *The Times*, 'however much one may disagree with the outlook of the author.' The *Spectator* noted the absence of bitterness and rancour. 'He is not anti-British,' wrote *The Economist*. 'He himself is in many ways a product of British education—but he is opposed to the rule of nation by nation or class by class. . . . It [the book] gains immensely from the enforced leisure [in jail] which made it possible for Mr Nehru to think deeply and write clearly of the fundamental problems not only of India, but of the world.'[29]

Not all the reviews were laudatory. The *Sunday Times* wrote that Mr Nehru was 'a good hater and seems to enjoy the procedure of verbal flagellation'.[30] But most of the British commentators were so impressed by the book's literary flavour and the human interest that they were able, at least momentarily, to overcome their political prejudices. Unlike Gandhi and even Tagore, Nehru wrote in an idiom which the West could easily understand.[31] 'Here is a man', wrote H.N. Brailsford in the *New Statesman*, 'who is one of us, by his culture, his humanity and his scientific vision.'

Apart from the merits of the book, there were other reasons why Nehru's autobiography should have evoked such intense interest in England in the summer of 1936. The original title, 'In and Out of Prison', was in some ways more apt, as the autobiographical element in the book was slight. Nehru's real theme was the fifteen-year-long struggle under Gandhi's leadership against the British Raj. The British public as a rule tended to be apathetic to Indian questions. But what with the civil disobedience movement, the Round Table Conferences in England, and the interminable debate over the passage of the Act of 1935, India had been much in the news in Britain for six years. There had been sharp clashes of opinion between and within British political parties. In the spring of 1936, the memories of fierce debates in the British Parliament and press had not yet quite faded. If the book had been published a year earlier, when the Reforms Act was still on the Parliamentary anvil, it might have suffered from the partisan reaction of a large segment of Tory opinion which was bitterly hostile to any political advance in India. A year later, the book might have proved a damp squib, because by then public interest in the Indian question would have evaporated. Indeed, this is exactly what happened. In 1937 when Allen & Unwin tried to cash in on the popularity of the *Autobiography*, and published a volume of Nehru's essays, entitled *India and the West*, they were disappointed with the response.[32]

The *Autobiography* was not Nehru's first book, but it was the first book which really brought him the pleasures and pains of authorship. He had completed the book on 14 February 1935. The entry in his diary for that day reads: ' "In & Out of Prison" has absorbed my attention . . . today I finished it! 976 pages of MSS in all. I feel as if a weight was off me.' The protracted negotiations with the publishers were an eye-opener for Nehru. In December 1935, he wrote to a correspondent in India:

One of my recent trials has been an attempt to come to terms with a publisher in London. I realized for the first time the differences in the mentality and outlook of publisher and author, and how the two clash . . . I saw no reason why the publisher should profit handsomely by my efforts and I should remain in the outer darkness. Not being a satyagrahi, pledged to living on Rs 12 a month, I decided to get the best terms I could get. But all this business was so utterly distasteful to me that I almost felt like hurling the manuscript into the fire. As an alternative I changed the publisher and accepted a much better offer. So to some extent I have peace now on this point.[33]

Nehru's satisfaction was short-lived. Even as his autobiography hit the bookstalls and became a best seller in England, the firm of Messrs John Lane, The Bodley Head, who had published the book, collapsed and became insolvent; its assets were taken over from the official receiver by Allen & Unwin and a few other firms, and the authors, including Nehru, were fobbed off with a small fraction of the royalties due to them. Krishna Menon, who had negotiated the contract, felt mortified and enraged, and proposed that Nehru should fight it out with Allen & Unwin and the firms which had purchased the old concern. 'I want to tell you', Nehru wrote to Krishna Menon, 'that I have no grievance against John Lane because the business collapsed. That was his misfortune as well as mine, and others' and, so far as I am concerned, I want to forget the affair and go ahead.' He turned down Menon's advice to go to law. 'The more I think of it,' he wrote,

the clearer I get in my own mind that I must not take the initiative in any litigation. The very thought of it has upset me sufficiently, the actuality will be far worse, and the wrong kind of publicity that this will give me in India and England will be a torture. I would sooner lose money any day than lose my peace of mind.[34]

## VI

For a book running to more than 600 pages and priced at 15 shillings, Nehru's autobiography sold well in India: 3690 copies were sold in 1937, and 234 in 1938, after which the sales tapered off. The book was predictably praised by the nationalist press, but even some of the British-owned papers acknowledged its literary merit and its commendable lack of bitterness. However, the book did not—to Nehru's dismay—provoke a serious debate on the issues raised by him. He had instructed his publishers in London to send complimentary copies to a number of his colleagues and friends in India. One of them was the nationalist Muslim leader Syed Mahmud, Nehru's Cambridge contemporary, to whom he wrote on 17 June 1936:

I presume you received my Autobiography . . . I wonder if you have had time or have cared to read it. You often ask me questions and love to talk at length . . . I was sorry when you told me that you had not read, as a whole my *Glimpses of World History* . . . But I find in India there is no habit or desire to read or think. We live superficially, on the surface, or rather in the ruts. It is an astounding country.[35]

Not that there was no interest in the book. A retired professor of English literature sent the author a closely written four-page letter pointing out 'breaches of idiomatic propriety'! And some of the Liberal leaders, whom Nehru had chastized in the book, wrote long and bitter rejoinders. 'Bad politics and worse history', was how

C.Y. Chintamani, the veteran journalist who belonged to the 'Responsivist' school of politics, headlined his review in the *Leader*.[36] N.C. Kelkar, of the Hindu Mahasabha, once the right-hand man of Tilak and B.S. Moonje, vented their spleen on the author. Nehru begged his critics 'to rise to a high plane and consider and criticize principles and not individuals'. He took both praise and criticism in his stride. 'It is pleasing to be told', he wrote, 'that one's book has been welcomed and has influenced in some degree other people.' He did not claim that his account of the course of Indian politics was wholly objective or definitive. The primary test of his book was, he said, psychological. It pleased him that English critics, who were opposed wholly to his politics, had gained 'a certain psychological insight into the mind and soul of our national movement'.

Strangely, one of the finest critiques of Nehru's autobiography came not from a historian or a literary critic but from Gandhi. Nehru had sent him a copy of the manuscript before publication. Gandhi was not very well at that time, but he read the manuscript; his reactions conveyed through his private secretary, Mahadev Desai, to Nehru were characteristic of the Mahatma:

It is needless to say that it is a brilliantly written book and a great literary production. There are parts, where I have my fundamental differences with you, and which I would like to criticize, but I will not do so, as it is scarcely necessary or useful. For when all is said and done, it is a highly introspective narrative, containing an expression of your innermost thoughts and convictions. Even if you could be persuaded to moderate or soften that expression, I should not attempt it, as it would result in taking away from it its naturalness, if not also its truthfulness. After all, we are helpless actors in the mighty flow of events, we have to act according to our lights, allowing or accepting the events to correct us where we err.[37]

Nehru is reported to have remarked many years later that the *Autobiography* was 'dated'. He had written in 1934 about India's freedom struggle under Gandhi's leadership. Much was to happen during the next thirty-three years both to India and to Nehru. But there is hardly any other book which gives us such penetrating insights into the struggle—its idealism, its leadership, its methods, its inner tensions and contradictions, its triumphs and its travails. Nehru was in his mid-forties when he wrote the book; his intellectual powers were at their peak. All his major works were written in jail, but the lack of access to libraries, which must have irked and handicapped him while writing the *Glimpses of World History* and the *Discovery of India*, was no limitation in writing the *Autobiography*. And the discursive style of writing, with its delightful digressions, which came so naturally to him, was perfectly permissible, and indeed an asset, in an autobiography.

It was the intellectual and emotional appeal of the book which etched itself on the minds not only of the young intellectuals in India in the late 1930s and 1940s, but on some of the up-and-coming men (such as Kenneth Kaunda) who were to lead the anti-colonial struggle in Asia and Africa in the post-war era.

## REFERENCES

1. *SWJN*, vol. 5, p. 494.
2. J. Nehru to Girdharilal, 20 March 1933 (NP).
3. Quoted by Arthur Melville Clark, *Autobiography: Its Genesis and Phases* (London, 1935), p. 14.
4. J. Nehru, *An Autobiography* (London, 1958 edn), p. 20.
5. Ibid.
6. Ibid., p. 26.
7. Ibid., pp. 448–9.
8. Ibid., p. 58.
9. Ibid., p. 219.
10. Ibid., p. 179–80.
11. Ibid., p. 194.
12. Ibid., p. 169.
13. Ibid., p. 117.
14. Ibid., p. 158.
15. Ibid., p. 66.
16. Ibid., p. 150.
17. Ibid., p. 148.
18. Ibid., p. 151.
19. Ibid., p. 129.
20. J. Nehru, Prison Diary entry, 4 June 1933, *SWJN*, vol. 5, p. 478.
21. Rajmohan Gandhi, *India Wins Errors* (New Delhi, 1989).
22. J. Nehru, *An Autobiography*, pp. 207–8.
23. Prison Diary, 29 March 1932, *SWJN*, vol. 5, p. 372.
24. Ibid., 5 Feb. 1932.
25. Home Dept, Pol. Confdl File, 121/36.

26. *SWJN*, vol. 6, p. 372.
27. NP.
28. *The Friend*, 2 July 1936.
29. *Economist*, 11 July 1936.
30. *Sunday Times*, 10 May 1936.
31. C.F. Andrews to J. Nehru, 6 Nov. 1935 (NP).
32. Horace Alexander to J. Nehru, 27 Jan. 1937 (NP).
33. J. Nehru to Goshiben Captain, 28 Dec. 1935 (NP).
34. J. Nehru to Krishna Menon, 5 April 1937 (NP).
35. J. Nehru to Syed Mahmud, 17 June 1936 (NP).
36. *Leader*, 10 June 1936.
37. Mahadev Desai to J. Nehru, 19 Dec. 1935 (NP).

# 16

## *An Overview*

### I

No political leader, with the exception of Gandhi, stirred the minds and hearts of the people of India so long and so deeply as Jawaharlal Nehru did. He became the quintessential embodiment of patriotism and self-sacrifice, and till the end remained the darling of the Indian masses—their prince charming. It was not only the unthinking multitude who adored him. He received encomiums from some of the most outstanding men and women of his time. Gandhi described him as being 'pure as crystal . . . truthful beyond suspicion . . . a knight *sans peur et sans reproché*'. Rabindranath Tagore hailed him as the Rituraj, 'representing the season of youth and triumphant joy of invincible spirit', who brought to his countrymen two priceless gifts: the right to live bravely and the right to think intelligently. Albert Einstein described Nehru as 'the Prime Minister of tomorrow', and Winston Churchill, in the evening of his life, complimented him as a man 'without fear and without hate'. To Pearl Buck, the eminent American novelist, Nehru was not only the greatest figure of modern India, but 'one of the very few truly great men in all the world'. André Malraux, the French writer who, as Minister of Culture in the De Gaulle government, visited India and met Nehru, has left a charming vignette of him in his memoirs. Alva Myrdal, the Swedish Ambassador in New Delhi, testified to Nehru's 'enormous charisma which surrounded him like a radiation'.[1] Then there were the globe-trotting journalists John Gunther, Edgar Snow, and Vincent Shean, alert to the foibles and peccadilloes of the famous and powerful, who could not resist Nehru's charm and have left flattering portraits of him.

In the newly liberated countries of Asia and Africa, Nehru's name was also something to conjure with: U Nu of Burma, Sukarno of Indonesia, Nkrumah of Ghana, Nasser of Egypt, and Kenneth Kaunda of Zambia held him in high esteem. In May 1964 when the news of Nehru's death reached Nairobi, the whole Kenyan Cabinet, headed by Jomo Kenyatta marched on foot to the Indian Embassy to convey their condolences.

Nehru had his detractors too: to the Conservatives he was an extremist, to the Marxists a renegade, to the Gandhians a non-Gandhian, and to Big Business a dangerous radical. Notwithstanding these critics, the contemporary view was overwhelmingly one of admiration for Nehru both in his days of struggle and power. When he passed away, Albert Moravio, the Italian writer, wrote that with Nehru's death India had entered a prosaic epoch, and Adlai Stevenson, the American representative to the United Nations, described Nehru 'as one of God's great creations in our time. His monument is his nation and his dream of freedom and of ever-expanding well-being for all men.'

Thirty years later, there seems to be a possibility of the pendulum swinging to the other extreme. To some extent such a reaction was only to be expected. Not only Lenin and Mao, but Churchill and Roosevelt have been pulled off the high pedestals they so long occupied in the hall of fame. Each generation is entitled to make its own assessment of the heroes of the past, their personalities, their achievements, and their limitations. A reappraisal of Nehru's role both in the freedom struggle and the years of power is thus justified, but it is important that it is made in the context of his life and times and is not unduly influenced by current events, such as the collapse of the Soviet Union, the eclipse of socialist ideologies, and the rise of religious fundamentalism. The chapters of this book have dealt with different facets of his life, but a brief resumé may be useful in placing in perspective his record both as rebel and ruler.

## II

Jawaharlal Nehru's total identification with the cause of Indian freedom came only in 1919 with Gandhi's impact on Indian politics, even though a patriotic streak can be discerned in the letters he wrote to his father from England when he was in his teens. He threw himself wholeheartedly into Gandhi's satyagraha struggle.

From the first he occupied a privileged position in the Congress party. Being the son of Motilal Nehru and a favourite disciple of Gandhi were definite advantages, but young Nehru had other assets too. He did not have to work for a living and could pay undivided attention to public work. With his western education, his extraordinary physical and intellectual stamina, his unremitting industry, his unquestioned integrity, his remarkable capacity for empathy with people from all walks of life and all parts of India, and his willingness to perform the tedious but necessary chores of running the office of the All India Congress Committee, he had already in the 1920s made himself almost indispensable to the Congress organization.

While the nationalist movement transformed Jawaharlal Nehru from a Cambridge-trained scientist and reluctant barrister into a national leader, he also transformed it. He brought to it an intellectual awareness of itself, a clearer socio-economic orientation and an insight into the currents of world politics. Above all, he brought to the nationalist movement an aura of romance; a boundless faith in the future of India and irrepressible optimism. 'There was a time not long ago', he wrote in 1931, 'when an Indian had to hang his head in shame; today it is a proud privilege to be an Indian.' To this national self-confidence during some of the most trying periods of the struggle Nehru's own contribution was significant. He turned to history to seek sustenance from India's great and creative past. He probed the causes of her stagnation and disunity. He drew his lessons for the future: India could never attain her place in the modern world unless she cast off the shackles of caste and creed, religion and language, superstition and fatalism. Almost alone among his contemporaries in Indian politics, he emphasized the roles of science and technology and industrialization as instruments of economic development.

After his return from Europe in the late twenties, Jawaharlal sought to give a new orientation to the policies of the Congress. He described the Indian struggle as part of the revolt of Afro–Asia against Western imperialism. He stressed the connection between colonial rule and vested interests within the subject countries; he assailed landlordism, capitalism, and the princely states as collaborators of the imperial power. He raised basic issues of social and economic reforms and of foreign policy to be followed by independent India. Most of his colleagues in the Congress hierarchy were amused, when not irritated, at his raising issues which seemed to them not only divisive but premature, when the fight against foreign rule was unfinished. The truth is that any politician who thinks in terms of decades instead of weeks and months, runs the risk of being dubbed an impractical idealist. Nehru was not deterred by these criticisms. He became the most eloquent ideologue of, what may be called 'left nationalism' in which political freedom was viewed primarily as a prelude to a new socialist order of society. He also denounced the rise of Fascism and Nazism in Europe, and called for the liberation not only of India but of all subject countries of Asia and Africa.

Throughout the 1930s Nehru had an uneasy relationship with the majority of his colleagues in the Congress Working Committee. Some of his admirers, such as Yusuf Meherally even feared that he would meet the fate of Trotsky. These fears were groundless. Nehru's position was secure, not only because he was the favourite disciple of Gandhi (who catapulted him into the Congress presidency at critical junctures in 1930, 1936, and 1946), but because his appeal to the youth, the peasantry, the industrial workers and even the intelligentsia was far too valuable an asset for the Congress party to throw away. Even in 1936, when Jawaharlal's tension with the older leaders was at its height, the object of the latter was not to oust him but to pull him back from postures which, in their view, were likely to weaken the Congress party.

Nehru's greatest service to the Congress was to act as a gadfly, to radicalize its policies and to move it away from its traditional path. Had it not been for the pressures he generated in the country and at the Calcutta Congress in 1928, it is doubtful whether the Congress would have deviated from the goal of Dominion Status, which almost all its leaders, including Dadabhai Naoroji, Gokhale, Tilak, C.R. Das, Motilal Nehru, and even Gandhi had taken for granted. The same may be said of Nehru's vigorous advocacy of fundamental rights of citizens at the Karachi Congress in 1931 and the demand for a Constituent Assembly for which Nehru was dubbed a visionary, but he lived to see his visions realized.

### III

Neither Nehru nor his critics could have foreseen the exact timing of the British withdrawal from India. Fortunately for Nehru—and here was an accident of history—he was fifty-eight and still at the peak of his intellectual and physical powers in 1947 when Independence came. If it had come ten years later, the burden may have been too heavy for him. It is rarely in history that a leader of revolutionary struggles gets the opportunity to handle tasks of reconstruction, but it came to Nehru, as it had come to George Washington and Lenin.

Nehru realized that India could not be governed from New Delhi, and so gave a lot of freedom to the state governments within the wide field left to them under the Constitution. Unlike his successors, he gave strong and able men, such as B.C. Roy, Govind Ballabh Pant, Morarji Desai, and Y.B. Chavan, the opportunity of becoming chief ministers of the States and to function without interference. It was only in the economic sphere that he made the Planning Commission an instrument of centralized planning; but here too he introduced methods of consultation and coordination through the National Development Council which included chief ministers of the States.

Though Nehru had never been a member of a legislative body he quickly developed into an outstanding parliamentarian. He respected the dignity, the procedures, and the practices of the Indian Parliament. He regarded it as the most important institution in the country; as a forum where discussion preceded decisions on lawmaking, and the executive government—the Council of Ministers—was accountable to the elected representatives of the people. He made it a point to spend a lot of time in the Parliament, and to be present during the debates. By example and by precept he tried to engrave on the national consciousness the attributes as well as the responsibilities of the parliamentary system of government. Parliamentary democracy, he said, meant 'tolerance not only of those who agree with us, but of those who do not agree with us'; it called for discipline and restraint, and above all for 'peaceful methods of action, peaceful acceptance of decisions taken and attempts to change them through peaceful ways again'. He dismissed the notion of a 'partyless democracy'. Five hundred men of ability and integrity, he said, could be useful, but in a Parliament they might pull in five hundred different directions and bring things to a grinding halt. Notwithstanding the overwhelming majority of his party in the Indian Parliament throughout his seventeen years of office, Nehru never ceased to be attentive and even responsive to the criticism of the opposition parties.

If the record of parliamentary democracy in India has been unbroken (barring the two years of the 'emergency', 1975–7) it was because he nurtured it during the first two decades of independence. It is sometimes argued that the credit for this goes to the British, who had done spadework for the parliamentary system in India by establishing legislatures under the Acts of 1909, 1919, and 1935. But they had done this in several other countries of Asia and Africa too, and yet when independence came most of these countries could not maintain the democratic system and fell under authoritarian regimes, whether military or civilian.

Unlike many of his contemporaries of Afro–Asian countries, who headed nationalist revolutions and came to power, Nehru freely allowed criticism of his government in the press and parliament, and submitted himself to the verdict of three successive general elections, the fairness of which was universally acknowledged. He was also concerned about nurturing institutions and traditions indispensable for the growth of parliamentary democracy, such as a free press, an independent judiciary, and the supremacy of the civil government over the armed forces.

Important as Nehru's contribution to the processes of nation-building was, his role in the formulation and execution of Indian foreign policy was decisive. His entire term as Prime Minister was coterminous with the acutest phase of the cold war between the two ideological-cum-military blocs led by the United States and the USSR. We have already seen the evolution of Nehru's policy, which came to be known as 'non-alignment', in this power struggle.[2] In the 1990s, after the collapse of the Soviet Union and the end of the cold war, there is an understandable temptation to dismiss non-alignment as an outmoded concept. For Nehru non-alignment was not a principle of foreign policy, but the application of a principle which he had early enunciated, that independent India had the right to consider each international issue as it arose on its merits instead of committing itself in advance to the policies of a particular power bloc. This principle Nehru would have followed even if the Soviet Union and the United States had not fallen out after the Second World War nor formed two rival armed camps.

Nehru's long-term objective was to seek points of convergence between the interests of India and the interests of world peace. In 1949 despite his past denunciation of the British Empire, he brought India into the Commonwealth and thus helped to transform what had been a 'white man's club' into a multinational and multiracial body. He blazed a trail which most of the Asian and African countries under British rule followed after attaining independence. As we have seen, Nehru's advocacy of non-alignment with the power blocs initially brought him brickbats from both the superpowers, but he persevered. His view that Communism was not a monolithic force, and in any case could not be combated by military means alone, was angrily rejected by the West in the 1950s. But this view later became the orthodoxy of international relations. He had the prescience to foresee the changes in the Soviet Union, the potentialities for Indo–Soviet friendship, and the likelihood of a Sino–Soviet rift long before they became realities. The argument that the end of the cold war has invalidated Nehru's policy of non-alignment is fallacious; this policy was articulated to meet a particular situation when the world trembled on the edge of a nuclear holocaust. Nehru had too great a sense of history to imagine that non-alignment was a self-sufficient or eternal concept of international relations for India or for other countries for all times. No one would have been happier than Nehru if the end of the cold war had come in his lifetime. Indeed, he worked for it and predicted a détente between the two power blocs. He knew his country was neither militarily nor economically a great power, but in the first two dangerous decades after the Second World War he tried to make India a link, a bridge, and a buffer between warring ideologies, races, and nations. In his later years he exercised a sobering influence on the leaders of Afro–Asia, urging them not merely to repeat anti-imperialist rhetoric, but to turn their minds from the past to the present and especially to the tasks of economic cooperation.

In the India–China war of 1962, there were doubtless lamentable lapses both in diplomacy and defence preparedness on the Indian side for which Nehru must take the blame, but in so far as the Chinese aggression was a fallout of the Sino–Soviet rift and of the intra-party tussles in Peking, the Himalayan war would have been difficult to avoid or predict. Further, with hindsight it would seem that India's policy of non-alignment was not an unmixed disadvantage in 1962; neither the USA nor the Soviet Union could afford to see India overrun by the Chinese juggernaut; this would immediately have been obvious had the Chinese not astutely timed their aggression to coincide with the Cuban crisis, the effect of which was to temporarily immobilize both the Superpowers.

Neville Maxwell, a sharp critic of India's conduct of international relations, has written that Nehru's foreign policy lay in ruins at the time of his death.[3] The history of the post-Nehru period does not seem to justify this verdict. It is true that in the initial shock of the Chinese aggression, Nehru sought and received some military aid from the Western powers, but within the few months which were left to him, he steered India back to a neutral position, and the broad framework of the Nehruvian foreign policy continued to serve the strategic and economic interests of India for the following three decades.

The Indian reverses in 1962 were certainly a great blow to Nehru. He had foreseen early the possibility of aberrations stemming from the Communist Revolution in China, but it is possible to argue even today that Nehru was right in the decision that India should pursue a friendly policy towards China in the 1950s rather than arm itself to the teeth and join the Western crusade against 'World Communism'. Not only was India thus spared the possible fate of Vietnam and Afghanistan; the militarization of India in the 1950s would not only have diverted attention from economic development, but jeopardized prospects of establishing a democratic polity in India. As it was, almost all the Afro–Asian countries which joined one armed camp or the other, fell under military or civilian dictatorship.

## IV

The task which Nehru undertook was a formidable one: the simultaneous pursuit of national integration, political democracy, economic development, and social justice. A few western countries have been able to achieve this synthesis, but they did so through a long process of historical evolution. Nehru sought to telescope this ambitious agenda into a few years, without abridging individual freedom and the rule of law. He himself made substantial contributions to the creation and durability of the political and economic infrastructure of the newly established Indian State, the parliamentary system of government, an independent judiciary, a free press, a 'mixed' economy with a socialist slant of a pluralistic and secular polity, and a humane approach to the problems of the rural poor, the scheduled castes, the tribals, the women, the children and other vulnerable sections of society. But there were doubtless deficiencies and failures which have been indicated earlier in this book: the failure to foresee the population explosion, to enforce land reforms, to accelerate universal elementary education, and to stem the slide in the standards of administration. These deficiencies and failures are attributable partly to Nehru's own limitations and partly to the actual working of his party and the political system. He once described politics as a field 'where every noble word or sentiment man has ever intended or thought of becomes base coin.' It was in this field that the lot of this man, whom a British journalist once aptly described 'as that most intellectual and moral of politicians', was cast.

Curiously, even his towering intellect could be a handicap. His ability to see several facets of a problem at once was not an unmixed advantage. Not easily satisfied with the work of others, he tended to take on things which he could easily have delegated to others. His tendency to persuade rather then overrule dissenting colleagues sometimes delayed the processes of decision-making. Unlike some of the democratic leaders of the twentieth century, he was not a good 'butcher', capable of 'slaughtering' ministers and advisers who failed to produce results; it was with the greatest reluctance that he sacked incompetent ministers.

Unlike Gandhi, Nehru lacked the gift of identifying and harnessing political talent, and failed to build up a second line of leadership. However, the charge that he sought to set up a political dynasty has no basis in fact. He stubbornly refused to nominate a successor. His profoundly democratic instincts apart, he was confident that India's democratic political system was capable of ensuring an orderly succession. A week before his death he said: 'If I nominated somebody, that is the surest way of his not becoming Prime Minister. People would be jealous of him, dislike him.' However, in his last illness, when he recalled Lal Bahadur Shastri to rejoin his Cabinet, it was taken as a hint that he favoured Shastri as a successor. As for Indira Gandhi, her opportunity was to come seventeen months later, after Shastri's death, when she was elected the leader of the Congress party in an open contest.

In fairness to Nehru, it must be said that he did not blame his tools; he rather blamed himself, but the fact is that both his instruments, the civil service, and the party did not measure up to his expectations. Soon after taking up office in 1946, he described the existing administrative structure as 'a ship of state, old, battered, slow-moving and unsuited to the swift changes that were taking place, and which would have to be scrapped'. No drastic change was, however, made. Sardar Patel, who as Home Minister was directly in charge of administration, was of the view that the machine was good enough; all that was needed was adequate masters to utilize it effectively. But even after Patel's death, Nehru, despite his overwhelming passion to get things done, effected hardly any changes. So much so, that the 'Rules of Business' framed for the civil service by the British were retained in toto, the only change being the substitution of the word 'Minister' for 'Executive Councillor' and Prime Minister for Governor-General. Unfortunately, even the utility of this administrative machine was progressively eroded by the erratic meddling of politicians.

The Congress party which could have helped Nehru in prodding the administration into effective action, was itself in the process of decline. In May 1948, less than a year after independence, Nehru was expressing his anguish to Govind Ballabh Pant at the 'progressive collapse of the moral and idealistic structure that we had built up'.[4] He publicly acknowledged the 'malaise' which had begun to afflict his party. One wonders whether he realized that he himself was partly responsible for it. In the days of the freedom struggle, there had been a healthy rivalry and tension in the Congress between the provincial Congress committees and the All India Congress Committee, and between the organizational and the legislative wings. When Nehru as Prime Minister also assumed the mantle of Congress President or made lightweight politicians Congress presidents there was little check on the ministerial wings of the party. Nehru himself had little aptitude for organizational work; even when he held the office of Party President, he functioned more as an inspired individual than as a party leader. In any case, so onerous were the burdens he carried as Prime Minister that he could give little time to party work. In 1958 he toyed with the idea of resigning to devote more time to the party, but was persuaded to desist from taking such a step. Five years later, he again thought of revitalizing the party through the Kamaraj Plan. It was a bold move to induct some of the seniormost leaders and ministers into organizational work, but it came too late. Nehru was already a dying man, and many people suspected that the Kamaraj Plan was only a stratagem to ease out certain ministers whom he did not like.

Some of the difficulties which Nehru and his successors faced in the tasks of governance and development arose from the operation of the democratic system itself. With adult franchise and the large constituencies this entailed, the politicians could not resist the temptation of exploiting caste, religion and language to build and preserve their 'vote banks'. The ruling parties, whether at the Centre or in the States of the Union, adopted populist programmes. The result was the emergence of a political and administrative system which Gunnar Myrdal, in his book *Asian Drama*, has described as a 'Soft State', implying unwillingness on the part of the government to enforce and on the part of the people to obey the rules laid down by the democratic processes. The tendency of the government, Myrdal wrote, was to use the carrot and not the stick. There was inevitably a fall in social discipline which affected both the administration and the economy. These trends were undoubtedly accentuated after Nehru's death. Indira Gandhi proved to be a brilliant politician, but she never felt as secure in office as her father had done, and tended to adopt radical postures and populist slogans, and to subordinate economic policies to political calculations. The result was that the Indian economy failed to make timely adjustments to the changing trends of global technology and trade in the 1970s and 1980s.

As one of the principal architects of India's freedom, as a nation-builder, and as a champion of world peace, Nehru was among the tallest figures of the twentieth century. He had too great a sense of history to imagine that he had found final solutions to all the complex problems which beset his country. He himself claimed neither omniscience nor infallibility. 'All of us', he once said, 'are likely to err and I rebel against the notion that an organization, an idea or a country can be infallible.' Eager to set India on the path of modernization he tried to speed up industrialization and to raise the living standards of the people. He did not spare himself. H.V.R. Iyengar, his private secretary in the early years, who watched him at work, was unable to find 'a purely physical or psychological explanation' for the amount of work Nehru was able to put in day after day. 'It was a case', Iyengar wrote, 'of the utter triumph of the spirit over the body, of a consuming passion for public work overcoming the normal mechanism of the human frame.' The jibe, 'the last Viceroy of India' is unjust if it suggests a conscious authoritarian streak in Jawaharlal Nehru. It is, however, true that for thirty years as a nationalist leader, and seventeen years as the head of the Indian government, Nehru took on himself political and administrative burdens which would have broken a lesser man in a few months.

Historians may differ in assessing particular policies of Nehru. They are, however, unlikely to question the soundness of his basic premises: his rejection of irrationality, social obscurantism, and fanaticism of all brands, whether racial, religious, or political; his respect for the freedom and dignity of human personality; his belief in the democratic processes; his aversion to regimentation and violence; his insistence that even good ends do not justify bad means and, finally, his conviction that in the atomic age the alternative to world cooperation is world disaster.

## NOTES

1. Interview with the author, Oral History Transcript (NMML).
2. *Supra*, ch. 12, 'Nehru and Non-Alignment.'
3. Neville Maxwell, *India's China War* (London, 1970), pp. 158–62.
4. J. Nehru to G.B. Pant, 6 May 1948 (NP).

# Index